After the Gunfire

Moral Injury in the Wake of a Mass Shooting

G. C. Smith

RESOURCE *Publications* • Eugene, Oregon

AFTER THE GUNFIRE
Moral Injury in the Wake of a Mass Shooting

Resource Publications
An Imprint of Wipf and Stock Publishers
199 W. 8th Ave., Suite 3
Eugene, OR 97401

www.wipfandstock.com

PAPERBACK ISBN: 979-8-3852-8799-4
HARDCOVER ISBN: 979-8-3852-8800-7
EBOOK ISBN: 979-8-3852-8801-4

VERSION NUMBER 06/24/26

The stories, experiences, and reflections contained in this book emerge from years of work in disaster response, ministry, and spiritual care. Some names, identifying details, and circumstances have been changed to protect privacy and confidentiality. Certain composite characters and scenes have been created from multiple experiences in order to preserve anonymity while remaining faithful to the emotional and moral realities described.

This book addresses themes including trauma, violence, grief, moral injury, institutional failure, and mass casualty events. Reader discretion is advised.

After the Gunfire

For those who carry what should not have been
theirs to carry.

For the ones who remember when
others have moved on.

For those who ask questions that do not have answers
—and refuse to stop asking them.

For the survivors who live with what remains.

For the families who speak the names that
must not be forgotten.

For the children who are learning the world is not what
they were told—and still learning how to live in it.

For the responders who continue to show up,
even when the weight does not leave.

For all who have been changed by what should
never have happened.

This book is for you.

May what is named here honor what you carry.

May what is spoken here make space for what remains.

And may you know, even in the silence—

you are not alone.

Contents

Introduction: **When Harm Has a Human Face**

There are disasters that arrive without intention.

The river rises.
The wind turns.
The ground gives way.

We search for meaning in these events, but we do not search for blame in the same way. Nature does not choose. It does not decide. It does not wake in the morning and act with purpose toward harm. Even in devastation, there is a kind of terrible neutrality.

A mass shooting is different.

It does not emerge from pressure systems or fault lines. It is not the result of shifting weather or unstable terrain. It is an act carried out by a person—someone who chose, prepared, and acted. The violence is not only physical. It is moral. It enters not just the body, but the shared understanding of what it means to live among other human beings.

This is where the wound begins to deepen.

After the gunfire ends, after the sirens fade, after the names are read and the cameras leave, something remains that does not fit easily into the language of trauma alone. People struggle, not only with what they experienced, but with what it means—what it says about others, about systems, about the world, and sometimes, about themselves.

This is what we call moral injury.

Moral injury is not simply fear. It is not only grief. It is not reducible to stress or even to trauma, though it often travels alongside both. Moral injury emerges when a person is confronted with, participates in, witnesses, or fails to prevent acts that violate their deeply held moral beliefs.

It asks different questions.

Not just:

- Am I safe?

But:

- How could this happen?
- Who is responsible?
- What did I do—or fail to do?
- What does this say about the world?

And sometimes, most painfully:

- What does this say about me?

In the wake of a mass shooting, moral injury does not belong to one group alone.

It moves through a community in layers.

Survivors carry it—those who ran, hid, waited, or lived when others did not. Their questions often circle around chance and choice: Why them? Why not me? What did I do in that moment?

Children carry it differently. They do not always have the language for what has happened. They absorb it through silence, through changed behavior, through questions that arrive sideways. They may come to believe, quietly and incorrectly, that something about them caused what occurred.

Responders carry it as well. Police officers, paramedics, firefighters, spiritual care providers—those who arrive after the first rupture and must act within it. They make decisions quickly, often with incomplete information, often within systems that constrain what is possible. They are trained for crisis. Still, there are moments that remain—choices made, lives reached or not reached, seconds that refuse to settle.

And then there are those who love them—partners, spouses, families—who were not present at the event but feel its impact in the changed presence of someone they know. They live with a different kind of question: You survived—so why does it feel like I am losing you anyway?

Moral injury is not contained within the moment of violence. It extends outward. It becomes relational.

This book is about what happens after.

Not the chronology of the event itself, though we will begin there. Not an investigation into motives or policy, though those questions matter. This is not a book that attempts to explain why a mass shooting occurs or how to prevent the next one.

It is a book about what remains in the people who must live in its wake.

It is about the teacher who made a decision that cannot be undone.

The child who cannot explain what they now feel.

The responder who followed protocol and still cannot rest.

The officer who wonders if hesitation cost something.

The spouse who sits across from someone they love and senses a distance that words cannot cross.

The caregiver who arrives to listen and discovers that some questions cannot be answered—only witnessed.

You will notice what this book does not do.

It does not rush toward resolution.
It does not offer easy language of healing or closure.
It does not insist that everything happens for a reason.

There are forms of suffering that resist explanation. Attempts to resolve them too quickly can deepen the injury rather than relieve it. Moral injury, in particular, demands honesty. It asks to be named clearly, even when clarity is uncomfortable.

There are moments in these pages where silence will carry as much weight as speech. Where what is unresolved will remain unresolved.

This is intentional.

There is, however, a direction.

Not toward fixing. Not toward returning to what was before—because that is not possible. But toward something quieter and more difficult:

- telling the truth about what happened
- learning how to listen without trying to repair too quickly
- recognizing the different ways moral injury appears across ages and roles
- creating spaces where people can remain human without pretending the wound is gone

If there is any hope here, it is not found in erasing what has occurred. It is found in refusing to lie about it—and in choosing, again and again, to remain present to one another in its aftermath.

There is a line that echoes through the ancient lament of Psalm 22:

"My God, my God, why have you forsaken me?"

It is not an answer. It is a question that refuses to be silenced.

And in Lamentations, the grief is communal, uncontained, and unresolved. The text does not hurry toward restoration. It lingers in the devastation, naming it with precision.

These voices endure because they tell the truth without rushing past it.

This book stands in that same space.

What follows is not a single story, but a set of lives moving through the same rupture from different directions. Their experiences will overlap, diverge, and sometimes contradict one another. That is part of the truth. Moral injury is not uniform. It does not resolve on a shared timeline.

But there is something they hold in common:

They are all living in a world where harm had a human face.

And they must decide, in ways large and small, how to go on living in that world.

After the gunfire, the silence is not empty.

It is filled with questions.

This book begins there.

Part I—**The Sound**

Chapter 1—The First Shot

Part I—The Ordinary Before

The bell does not ring so much as release. It is a sound everyone in the building has learned to anticipate—not consciously, not with attention, but with the kind of bodily awareness that settles over routine. A shift in weight. A glance toward the clock. The soft closing of a notebook before the sound even arrives. Marcus Hale is mid-sentence when it happens. " . . . and what we see again and again," he says, turning slightly toward the whiteboard, "is that history doesn't repeat itself exactly, but it—" The bell cuts him cleanly in half. There is movement immediately. Chairs scrape. Backpacks unzip. A low swell of voices rises, not chaotic, but layered—students speaking over one another, asking questions, making plans, laughing at something that will not matter in an hour. Marcus steps back from the board, marker still in his hand. "Homework is posted," he says, louder now, practiced. "Don't forget—read the primary source, not just the summary." A few nod. A few don't hear him at all. This is how it always is.

He watches them the way he always does—not as individuals in this moment, but as a collective pattern. Who lingers. Who rushes. Who waits for someone else before moving. He notices Lila Nguyen without meaning to. She is already packed. She always is. Her movements are efficient, quiet. She does not join the first wave to the door, nor the last. She exists somewhere in between, slipping through space rather than claiming it. She pauses at the threshold, as if orienting herself. Marcus has seen that before too. Not uncertainty. Not exactly. More like . . . calibration. "Lila," he says, not loudly. She turns her head, just enough. "You good?" A small nod. Not dismissive. Not warm. Simply sufficient. Then she is gone into the hallway.

The room empties in increments. Noise recedes, though it never fully disappears. There is always another class moving somewhere, another door opening, another voice carrying. Marcus caps the marker and sets it down. There is a brief, suspended moment he has come to recognize over the years—the few seconds between one group leaving and the next arriving. It is the closest the day comes to stillness. He exhales. In the hallway, lockers open and close in uneven rhythm. Metal against metal. A familiar percussion. He moves toward his desk, glancing at the next lesson, though he already knows it. He always knows it. Preparation is less about information now and more about steadiness. Outside, somewhere farther down the hall, someone laughs—loud, uncontained. It echoes.

Then—a sound.

Not loud. Not, at first, distinct. Marcus does not turn immediately. The brain does a small, efficient sorting: locker? dropped book? something falling? The hallway noise shifts slightly, but not enough to signal alarm. He reaches for a stack of papers. The second sound comes sharper. Not a slam. Not metal on metal. Something else. There is a pause in the hallway—not silence, but a thinning. Marcus looks up. He steps toward the door, not quickly, not yet. The body resists urgency when it does not understand the cause. At the far end of the corridor, beyond what he can see clearly, there is movement. Not organized. Not patterned.

A third sound.

This time it lands differently. It is not just heard. It is recognized—not fully, not consciously, but enough. Marcus stops. The ordinary does not shatter all at once. It fractures.

Lila does not hear the first sound as anything important. She is at her locker, turning the dial without looking. She has memorized the numbers through repetition, not intention. The combination exists in her hands more than in her mind. Around her, voices overlap. Someone is talking about a test. Someone else is complaining about lunch. A phone screen flashes briefly in her peripheral vision. The second sound interrupts the rhythm. She pauses—not because she is afraid, but because something doesn't fit. Her fingers rest on the metal. "What was that?" someone says nearby, but without urgency. Lila does not answer. She is not being asked. The hallway continues, but not quite the same. There is a space now, a small gap between sounds.

The third sound is louder. Not louder in volume, exactly—but closer, sharper, less able to be explained away. A locker door slams somewhere behind her, too hard, too fast. Someone laughs again, but it is different this time—shorter, thinner. Lila closes her locker. She does not move right away. There is a feeling she cannot name—not fear, not yet. Something like standing at the edge of a change you cannot see but can feel approaching. An adult voice carries from down the hall. Words, but not clear ones. The hallway shifts. People begin to move—not running, not yet—but faster than before. Less coordinated. Lila turns her head. She cannot see what is happening. Only that something is.

A fourth sound.

Now unmistakable.

The world does not explain it to her. It simply stops making sense.

Keisha Turner is in her patrol car when the call comes through. At first, it is routine. Dispatch voices carry a particular tone—measured, controlled, even when urgency rises beneath it. She has learned to listen not just to the words, but to the pace, the spacing, the way information is delivered. "Unit—stand by for possible—" Static. Then clearer. "Reports of shots fired." Keisha straightens slightly in her seat. Location follows. A school. There is a brief, internal recalibration. Training aligns with instinct. She reaches for the radio, acknowledges, turns the vehicle. The siren comes on almost automatically. Traffic parts in uneven lines. Some drivers move immediately. Others hesitate, unsure where to go. Keisha adjusts, weaves, accelerates. "Multiple callers," dispatch adds. "Unconfirmed number of victims." Unconfirmed. That word matters. It means everything and nothing at the same time.

Her grip tightens on the wheel—not from fear, but from focus. The body narrows its attention. Peripheral details drop away. Another unit responds over the radio. Then another. The channel fills. Keisha's mind moves through procedure—approach, entry, coordination. She has trained for this. Repeated scenarios. Timed exercises. Controlled environments. But training does not include the sound of uncertainty in real time. "Shots still being reported," dispatch says. Still. The word lands. Keisha presses the accelerator. The distance between where she is and where she is going feels both measurable and impossible. Ahead, the road curves slightly. She takes it faster than she normally would. In the space between one breath and the next, the day has changed. She does not yet know how much.

Back in the school, Marcus takes one step toward the hallway. Then stops. The instinct to move forward collides with something else—something slower, heavier. Another sound echoes down the corridor. Closer. A voice—shouting now. Not words he can make out. Only tone. Students begin to move past his doorway, faster now. One of them looks in, eyes wide, but does not stop. Marcus feels the shift fully now. This is no longer confusion. This is something happening. Something deliberate.

He turns, just slightly, back into the classroom—the empty desks, the half-erased board, the ordinary that still exists inside these walls. Then back toward the door. Time does not stop. But it no longer moves the way it did before. It fractures—into decisions, into seconds that will not hold still. The first shot is not just a sound. It is a dividing line. Everything on one side. Everything that follows on the other.

Part II—The Recognition

The hallway does not empty all at once. It thins. Students who had been moving without urgency begin to move with direction, though no one has given them any. A current forms where there was none before—bodies angling away from something not yet fully seen. Marcus stands at the threshold of his classroom, the door still open, his hand resting lightly against its edge. He is listening now. Not casually. Not passively. Listening with intent. Another sound. Closer than before. There is no mistaking it this time. The mind resists the conclusion even as it arrives. It searches for alternatives—something mechanical, something accidental, something that can be explained without consequence. There is nothing.

A student runs past his door. Not walking quickly. Running. "Go," the student says to someone behind him. "Just go." Marcus steps back into the room. The shift is immediate. Inside, everything is still where it was. Desks aligned. Chairs pushed in unevenly. The board still holding the unfinished sentence from earlier: Moral responsibility requires—The words look different now. Incomplete in a way that feels exposed. He moves to the door and closes it. The sound of the latch clicking into place is small, but final. He reaches for the lock and turns it.

Another sound in the hallway. Louder. Then something heavier—a body hitting something, or something hitting a body. The distinction is no longer clear. Marcus steps away from the door. "Okay," he says to the empty room, as if speaking to students who are no longer there. The word is reflexive, a habit searching for context. He exhales. Then he moves. He crosses the room in four strides and pulls the blinds down over the narrow window in the door. The plastic snaps slightly as it settles into place. Visibility narrows. The world outside reduces to sound. Marcus turns, scanning the room, not for students—there are none—but for space. For structure. For something that can be controlled.

Another set of footsteps passes outside. Fast. Then slower. Then gone. He moves to the light switch. Hesitates. Leaves it on. Darkness feels like a choice he is not yet ready to make.

Down the hall, Lila is no longer standing. She does not remember deciding to move, only that she is now near the wall, her shoulder pressed against the cool surface, her body angled slightly away from the center of the corridor. Around her, other students are doing the same thing—flattening themselves, compressing into space as if smaller is safer. "What is it?" someone whispers. No one answers. An adult voice rises again, louder now, but still not forming clear words. Urgency has replaced structure. The cadence is wrong. A door opens somewhere behind her. Another closes too hard. The hallway begins to break. Not physically, but in its rhythm. Movement loses its predictability. People move in directions that do not align. Some toward classrooms. Some away. Some standing, uncertain, caught between impulses.

Lila's breathing changes. Not faster. Shallower. She feels it in her chest, a tightening that does not expand fully when she inhales. Another sound. Close enough now that it does not travel—it arrives. The air reacts. So does she. Her hands lift slightly, not in defense, not in any practiced gesture, but in response to something her body does not understand but recognizes as wrong. A teacher appears at the end of the hallway, waving students toward a room. "Inside," the teacher says. "Now. Go." Lila does not move. Not immediately. The instruction reaches her, but something else holds her in place—a moment of misalignment between what she is told and what she feels. Then another sound. Closer. The decision is made for her. She turns and moves with the others, not leading, not following, simply carried by the current that has formed.

The music room door is open. Students press inside. The space fills quickly. "Sit down," the teacher says. "Quietly. Stay low." Lila moves to the back without thinking. The closet door is ajar. She notices it the way she notices everything—quietly, completely. A place. A boundary. A smaller space within a larger one. The room hums with breath and suppressed movement. No one is speaking now. Even the whispers have faded. The teacher steps into the hallway. "I'll be right back," she says. The door remains open. Lila watches it. The line between inside and outside feels too thin.

Another sound. Not distant. Not abstract. Real. The teacher does not return.

Keisha's car cuts through the last intersection before the school. The building comes into view all at once—brick, windows, flag at half-mast for something unrelated, something that no longer matters. There are already cars in the lot. Too many. Some parked. Some angled. One with the driver's door open. Keisha pulls in hard, tires catching slightly on loose gravel at the edge of the pavement. She does not wait for full stop. The radio is still active. "Units on scene—reports of shots fired inside—unknown location within the building—" Unknown. That word again.

She opens the door and steps out. The air feels different. Not quieter. Sharper. Sound carries differently here—fragmented, bouncing off surfaces, difficult to place. Another unit arrives behind her. Doors open. Voices overlap. Keisha moves toward the entrance. Her training speaks in clear, ordered steps: assess, locate, engage. But the environment resists clarity. A figure runs out of the building—student, young, eyes wide, not stopping. "Where?" Keisha calls. The student shakes his head, keeps moving. "I don't know—I don't know—" Keisha continues forward.

The front doors are open. No barrier. No threshold that signals entry into something different. Just a continuation of space. Inside, the hallway stretches ahead. Lockers. Fluorescent lights. Posters on the walls. Ordinary. Except for the absence of ordinary movement. There is no flow of students now. No casual noise. Only pockets of sound—distant, uneven.

Another crack echoes from somewhere deeper in the building. Keisha feels it register—not as surprise, but as confirmation. This is real. She steps inside. Behind her, another officer follows. They do not speak. There is no need. The moment has already divided itself. Before. And now.

Marcus stands in his classroom and listens. The sounds are closer now. Not constant. Intermittent. Which is worse. Each pause stretches, filled with anticipation of the next. He moves to the back of the room. Instinct. Distance from the door. He looks at the desks again. At the empty chairs. At the space where students had been minutes ago. He sees them now—not physically, but as possibility. If they had stayed. If the timing had been different. The thought arrives uninvited. He pushes it aside. Not now. There is only now.

Another sound. Very close. Right outside the room. Marcus freezes. Footsteps. Fast. Then stopping. A hand hits the door. Once. Hard. Marcus does not move. The handle rattles. Not turning. Shaking. A voice. "M—"

Cut off. Another sound. So close it erases distance entirely. The voice disappears. The hallway falls silent again.

Marcus remains where he is. Not because he has decided to stay. Because his body has already chosen. The lock holds. The door remains closed. The room is intact. Inside. Outside. The line has been drawn. And for the first time, clearly, fully, without resistance—Marcus understands what is happening. And that understanding changes everything.

Part III—The Division

The silence that follows is not empty. It is full. Full of what has just happened. Full of what might happen next. Full of everything Marcus does not yet know but now understands enough to fear. He stands at the back of the classroom, his hand resting lightly on the edge of a desk. He is aware of his breathing—not because it is loud, but because it is controlled. Too controlled. The room feels smaller. Not physically. Structurally, nothing has changed. The same desks. The same walls. The same unfinished sentence on the board. But the space has tightened around a new center. The door. Everything leads to it now. Every sound. Every thought.

Another noise in the hallway—not a crack this time, but movement. Dragging. Something being pulled, or someone trying to move something heavy. Marcus closes his eyes for a fraction of a second. Not to escape. To focus. When he opens them again, his gaze moves immediately to the board. Moral responsibility requires choice. The words are still there. Unfinished. Unprotected from what they now mean. He takes one step forward. Then stops. Because the next part of the sentence is no longer theoretical. It is not a discussion. It is not a question for students to answer. It is here. In the room. At the door.

Another sound. Closer. A shadow crosses the narrow gap beneath the door. Marcus's body reacts before his mind forms language. He steps back. Slowly. Carefully. As if movement itself could be heard. The shadow pauses. Then moves on. The hallway breathes again. Marcus exhales, but only slightly. The restraint remains. Choice. The word presses against him now—not as an idea, but as weight. He looks at the door. Then at the desks. Then back at the door. There is no instruction manual for this moment. No training. No precedent that feels sufficient. Only competing truths: someone outside might need help. Someone outside might bring danger. Both can be true at the same time. He feels the pull of both. It is not equal. But it is simultaneous.

Another sound. Further away now. But still within reach of imagination. Marcus does not move. Not because he does not care. Because he has already chosen. And the choice holds.

In the music room, the air has changed. It is not just quieter. It is heavier. The kind of quiet that presses inward, that makes every small movement feel too large. Lila is inside the closet now. She does not remember closing the door completely, only that the light is thinner than before. A narrow line along the edge. Enough to see shapes, not enough to see clearly. Her knees are pulled in tight. Her hands rest against them, fingers curled slightly, not gripping, not relaxed. Around her, the room exists in fragments. Breath. Shifting fabric. A small sound someone tries to suppress.

Then— a noise in the hallway. Close. Very close. Lila stops breathing. Not intentionally. It simply . . . stops. The sound is different from the others. Not just sharp. Directed. Followed by something else—movement, fast, then abrupt. A voice. Not clear. But louder than before. The kind of voice that does not belong in school.

Another sound. Right outside. Someone in the room gasps. Too loud. A whisper follows—"shhh"—urgent, strained. The door to the music room is still open. Lila knows this without seeing it. She feels it. The space is not sealed. The outside is still connected to the inside. That thought lands differently now. Not as information. As danger. Her body shifts slightly deeper into the closet, pressing against the back wall. There is nowhere else to go.

Another sound. So close it feels inside the room. Then— nothing. No footsteps. No voices. Just the absence of sound where sound should be. Lila's thoughts begin to form again, slowly, unevenly. Something bad is happening. That much is clear now. But the shape of it is still unclear. Her mind tries to fill it in. Fails. Tries again. Fails differently. The earlier thought returns, stronger now. Something went wrong. It expands.

Something went very wrong. And then, quietly, without logic but with certainty: Someone did something. The idea sits there. Heavy. Unmovable. She does not know who. She does not know why. But she knows this: this is not an accident. The world has changed. And it changed because someone made it change. Her fingers press into her knees. Not hard enough to hurt. Just enough to feel something certain. She waits.

Keisha moves down the hallway with measured steps. Not slow. Not rushed. Controlled. Her senses are narrowed now, focused on specific details: sound, movement, line of sight. The building feels wrong. Too still in some places. Too active in others. A locker door hangs open halfway down the corridor. A backpack lies on the floor beside it. No one nearby. The absence registers as much as any presence would.

Another crack echoes from deeper in the building. Keisha turns toward it. Direction. That matters. She moves. Another officer appears at the intersection ahead. They exchange a glance. No words. The coordination is immediate, unspoken. They advance together. The hallway turns. The angle shifts. Visibility changes. Keisha's mind tracks it all, mapping space in real time. Where are the exits? Where are the classrooms? Where could someone hide? Where could someone be?

Another sound. Closer. They stop. Not fully. Just enough to reorient. The air holds. Then— movement. A figure at the far end of the hall. Too far to see clearly. Too close to ignore. The figure moves. Not toward them. Across. Then disappears behind a corner. Keisha feels the moment sharpen. This is it. Or close to it. Her training aligns again, more tightly now. Assess. Locate. Engage. But beneath that, something else moves. Not doubt. Not hesitation. Awareness. That whatever happens next will not stay contained in this hallway. It will extend. Into reports. Into memory. Into something she will carry long after this building is empty again.

Another sound. Right side. A classroom door, slightly ajar. Keisha shifts her position, adjusting her angle, covering the space. The officer beside her mirrors the movement. They are inside the moment now. Fully. There is no before. There is only this.

Back in his classroom, Marcus has not moved. Time has stretched into something unrecognizable. Seconds feel longer. But also thinner. As if they might break if too much is placed on them. He listens. The sounds are further away now. Or different. It is hard to tell. The absence of immediate threat does not bring relief. It brings uncertainty. Which is worse.

He takes a step toward the center of the room. Stops. Listens again. Nothing. Then— distant movement. Voices. Not clear. But present. Marcus feels something shift inside him. Not resolution. Not safety. Possibility. He looks at the door again. At the lock. At the thin line where it meets the frame. The boundary. Inside. Outside.

He thinks of the hallway. Of the voice that had been cut off. Of the impact against the door. Of the students who had been there minutes ago. Choice. The word returns again. Louder now. Not spoken. Felt. He moves toward the door. Slowly. Each step deliberate. He reaches it. Places his hand on the handle. Does not turn it. Not yet.

He stands there, feeling the weight of it. The possibility of opening. The risk. The responsibility. Everything balanced in a single point of contact. He closes his eyes. Just for a moment. Then opens them again. The room behind him is silent. The hallway beyond is unknown. The line between them is his to hold. Or to break.

Marcus does not move. Not yet.

The moment stretches. Holds.

And in that space—the world, as it was, is gone.

What remains has not yet decided what it will become.

Chapter 2—**Confusion**

Part I—When Nothing Makes Sense

The morning after does not begin cleanly. It begins in fragments. A phone alarm that rings too long before being silenced. Light slipping through blinds that were never fully closed. The low, persistent hum of something left on overnight—television, refrigerator, thought. Marcus Hale wakes before he is ready. Not abruptly. Not from a dream he can recall. Just awake—eyes open, body still, awareness arriving faster than he would have chosen. For a moment, there is a gap. A narrow, fragile space where the day has not yet attached itself to memory. Then it does. Not all at once. In pieces. A sound. A hallway. A door. Marcus closes his eyes again. Not to sleep. To delay. It does not work.

The room around him is familiar—bedside table, lamp, the faint outline of a chair in the corner—but it feels slightly misaligned, as if something fundamental has shifted just enough to make everything else uncertain. Beside him, Sarah is awake. He can tell without looking. The way her breathing holds, just slightly, between inhale and exhale. "You up?" she asks quietly. Marcus nods, then realizes she cannot see it. "Yeah," he says. A pause. Neither of them moves. There are things they could say. There are things they should say. Neither reaches for them.

After a moment, Sarah sits up, swinging her legs over the side of the bed. The movement is careful, as if she is navigating a space that might not hold her weight the way it used to. "I'm going to make coffee," she says. Marcus nods again. "Okay." She stands. Leaves the room. The absence she creates is immediate. Marcus sits up slowly, placing his feet on the floor.

The wood is cool beneath them. Solid. Reliable. A small confirmation that something, at least, remains unchanged. He stays there for a moment, hands resting on his knees, eyes unfocused.

The mind begins its work. Not intentionally. Automatically. Reconstructing. The sequence is not linear. It moves in loops. The sound. The door. The decision. Marcus stands abruptly. Too fast. The room tilts, then steadies. He moves toward the window and pulls the curtain back slightly. Outside, the street is quiet. A car passes. A neighbor walks a dog. Ordinary movement. Unaware, or pretending to be. Marcus lets the curtain fall back into place. The normalcy does not comfort him. It confuses him.

Across town, Lila Nguyen wakes into a different kind of morning. She does not open her eyes right away. She lies still, listening. Not for anything specific. For absence. No hallway. No sudden sound. No voice cutting through space. The quiet is intact. That matters. She opens her eyes slowly. The ceiling is the same. The small crack near the corner she has noticed before is still there. Unchanged. She sits up. The room feels larger than it did yesterday. Or maybe she feels smaller inside it. Her backpack sits near the door. Untouched. Her shoes beside it. Placed the way she left them. Waiting. For a day that did not finish.

She swings her legs over the side of the bed and stands. The floor is warm. Different from Marcus's. She notices that. Does not know why. In the hallway, her mother is moving. Cabinets opening. Closing. The sound is louder than it should be. Or maybe Lila hears it differently now. She steps into the doorway. Her mother turns immediately. As if she has been waiting. "Hey," she says, too quickly. "You're up." Lila nods. "Yeah." A pause. "Do you want breakfast?" her mother asks. The question feels misplaced. Not wrong. Just . . . out of order. Lila shrugs. "I'm not hungry." Her mother nods. "Okay," she says. "That's okay." Another pause. Longer this time. "School's closed today," her mother adds. Lila nods again. "I know." She does. She knew before being told. It had settled somewhere in her overnight. A fact that required no confirmation.

She steps into the kitchen. Sits at the table. Her hands rest in front of her. Still. Her mother moves around the room, performing tasks that do not seem connected to anything. Pouring coffee. Setting it down. Picking it up again. Lila watches her. Not the actions. The pattern. The way movement replaces language. "Are we going somewhere?" Lila asks. Her mother stops. Just for a second. Then resumes. “I don’t know,” she says. “Do you want to?” Lila considers that. What does “somewhere” mean now? A store? A friend’s house? A place where nothing happened? “I don’t know,” she says. The words feel heavier than they should. Her mother nods. “Okay,” she repeats. Neither of them moves. The morning stretches. Unstructured. Uncertain.

Daniel Reyes wakes in his truck. Not because he intended to sleep there. Because he did. The seat is reclined slightly. His jacket is folded under his head. The angle is wrong for rest, but his body took it anyway. He sits up slowly. The stiffness arrives immediately. Neck. Shoulders. Lower back. A reminder of where he is. Of how he got there. He looks around. The parking lot is nearly empty now. A few vehicles remain. Marked. Unmarked. Residual presence. The tape is still up. Bright against the morning light. A boundary that has outlived the moment it was meant to contain.

Daniel reaches for the ignition. Stops. Lets his hand rest there. The silence in the cab is thick. Not oppressive. Dense. Filled with what has not been said. His phone sits in the cup holder. Dark. Still. He picks it up. The screen lights. Notifications. Messages. Missed calls. He does not open them. Not yet. He knows what they will contain. Questions. Information. Fragments of a larger picture assembling itself without him. He sets the phone back down. Looks out at the building. It is the same. Structure unchanged. Windows intact. Doors closed. From the outside, nothing suggests what occurred inside. Daniel exhales slowly. The disconnect is sharp. Between appearance and reality. Between what is seen and what is known.

He opens the door. Steps out. The air is cooler than he expects. He inhales. Deep. Holds it. Releases. A simple act. Grounding. He begins to walk. Not toward anything specific. Just moving. Because standing still feels like staying. And staying feels like something he is not ready to do.

At the station, Keisha Turner sits alone in the locker room. The bench beneath her is hard. Unforgiving. She prefers it that way. Her uniform is folded beside her. Neatly. Deliberately. As if order here might translate elsewhere. It does not. She stares at the locker in front of her. Door open. Contents visible. Nothing out of place. Everything exactly where it should be. She reaches out. Touches the edge of the metal. Cool. Solid. Predictable. Unlike the moment that continues to replay in her mind. Not the whole thing. Not a continuous memory. Fragments. The turn. The movement. The pause. Always the pause.

She closes her eyes. Sees it again. Not as it was. As it might have been. Variations. Alternatives. Small shifts that lead to different outcomes. None of them real. All of them present. Keisha opens her eyes. The locker remains unchanged. The room is quiet. Too quiet. She stands. Closes the locker door. The sound echoes. Louder than expected. She flinches. Just slightly. Then steadies.

In his office, Elijah Freeman writes. Not sentences. Words. Single words. Spaced across the page. Confusion. Silence. Fragment. After. He studies them. Not for definition. For relationship. How they connect. Where they overlap. What they leave out. The television in the corner is off. Intentionally. He has seen enough of what others are showing. Now he is listening for what is not being said. He leans back in his chair. Closes his eyes. Not to rest. To attend. To the quiet. To the questions forming beneath it.

Outside, a car door closes. Footsteps pass. The day is beginning. Again. Elijah opens his eyes. Looks at the words on the page. Adds one more. Disorientation. He underlines it once. Lightly. Because that is what this is. Not just shock. Not just grief. But the loss of orientation. The inability to place oneself in a world that has shifted without warning. He sets the pen down. The page remains. Incomplete. Like everything else.

By midmorning, the town is awake. Fully. Functionally. But not coherently. People move. Speak. Respond. But beneath every action is a question that has not found its place. What happened? The answers exist. In reports. In footage. In fragments. But the understanding does not. Not yet. And in that gap—between information and meaning—confusion settles in. Not as absence. As presence. A steady, disorienting force that reshapes everything it touches. The day continues. But it does not proceed. It drifts. And no one is entirely sure where they are within it.

Part II—Misreading the Moment

By midday, the town has begun to speak again. Not clearly. Not consistently. But enough that silence no longer holds. Words return first in small, careful ways—questions asked too gently, answers given too quickly, phrases repeated because they sound like something that should help. People reach for language the way they reach for familiar objects in the dark: not because they are certain it will work, but because not reaching feels worse. The problem is not the lack of words. It is that the words do not fit.

Marcus sits at the kitchen table with a notebook open in front of him. It is the same one he uses for lesson planning, though today there is no lesson to prepare. The pages are lined, structured, designed for clarity. He has written nothing on them. Across from him, Sarah scrolls through her phone, stopping occasionally, reading something more closely, then setting it down as if proximity itself might be too much. "They're saying it happened in three different places," she says. "At first." Marcus nods. "That's how it felt," he replies. Sarah looks up. "Felt?" she asks. Marcus leans back slightly. "Like it was everywhere," he says. "Like the building didn't have edges anymore." Sarah considers that. "But it didn't," she says. "Have edges, I mean. It was contained." Marcus shakes his head. "That's not how it works," he says. "Not when you're inside it."

He looks down at the blank page again. Tries to write. Stops. The pen hovers just above the paper. "What do you remember?" Sarah asks. The question is simple. Direct. Too direct. Marcus exhales. "Not in order," he says. "That's okay." "It's not," he replies, more sharply than he intends. Sarah doesn't respond. Marcus softens slightly. "It matters," he says. "Order matters. Cause and effect. What led to what." He taps the pen lightly against the page. "But it doesn't line up," he adds. "Not the way it should." Sarah watches him. "What do you mean?" Marcus closes his eyes briefly. "Things that happened at the same time feel like they happened hours apart," he says. "And things that happened minutes apart feel like they're on top of each other." He opens his eyes. "It's like trying to tell a story where the sequence keeps changing." Sarah nods slowly. "That sounds . . . hard," she says. Marcus lets out a short breath. "That's one word for it." He finally lowers the pen to the page. Writes a single word: Door. Then stops. Because everything that comes after it depends on where it goes next. And he does not know.

At the Nguyen house, the television is off, but the conversation has begun. Not fully. Not comfortably. But enough. Lila sits at the table now, a bowl of cereal in front of her. The milk has gone slightly warm. She has not taken a bite. Her mother sits across from her, hands folded, as if waiting for something specific to happen. "What did it sound like?" her mother asks. Lila looks up. The question lands differently than the others. Not abstract. Specific. "It was loud," she says. Her mother nods. "I figured." Lila shakes her head. "No," she says. "Not just loud." She searches for the right word. Does not find it. "It was . . . wrong," she finishes. Her mother leans forward slightly. "What do you mean?" Lila shrugs. "It didn't belong," she says. "Like when something breaks, but you didn't touch it." Her mother's face tightens, just slightly. "That makes sense," she says.

Lila looks down at the cereal. Moves the spoon once. Twice. Does not lift it. "Everyone said to be quiet," she adds. Her mother nods again. "That was good," she says. "That's what you're supposed to do." Lila looks up. "Why?" she asks. The question is immediate. Unfiltered. Her mother blinks. "Why what?" "Why be quiet?" Her mother hesitates. "So you can stay safe," she says. Lila considers that. "But it didn't stop anything," she says. Her mother opens her mouth. Closes it. Because there is no answer that resolves the question. Not honestly. Not now.

Daniel sits at a diner counter two miles from the site. He does not remember deciding to come here. Only that he is here now. A cup of coffee sits in front of him, untouched. The waitress moves past, refilling other cups, speaking in a tone that suggests normalcy is still possible. At the far end of the counter, a television plays the same footage from the night before. Muted. Subtitles scrolling. " . . . conflicting reports continue to emerge . . . " Daniel watches the words. Not the images. Conflicting. The word stands out. Feels accurate. Feels insufficient. A man two stools down shakes his head. "They don't even know what happened," he says to no one in particular. Another man responds. "They know. They're just not saying it." Daniel keeps his eyes on the counter. The conversation continues around him. Fragments of certainty built on incomplete information. "I heard—" "They said—" "Someone told me—" Each statement begins with distance. Ends with conviction.

Daniel wraps his hand around the coffee cup. It is warm. Grounding. He lifts it. Takes a sip. The taste is familiar. Bitter. Predictable. Unlike everything else. The man two stools down glances at him. "You were out there, right?" he asks. Daniel looks up. Holds his gaze for a moment. "Yeah," he says. The man leans in slightly. "So what really happened?" The question hangs. Heavy. Loaded. Daniel considers it. What really happened? He could answer. Describe. Detail. Offer a version. But he knows, already, that whatever he says will become something else in the telling. Simplified. Reshaped. Used. "I don't know," he says finally. The man frowns. "You were there." Daniel nods. "I was," he says. He takes another sip of coffee. Does not elaborate. Because the truth is not a single line. It is a field. And he is still standing inside it.

At the station, Keisha sits in a small office with the door closed. A report form is open on the desk in front of her. Blank. Structured. Boxes to fill. Lines to follow. Time stamps. Locations. Actions. She reads the headings. Knows what they require. Knows how to complete them. She has done it before. But this time—the structure feels too rigid. Too certain. As if the act of writing it down will fix the sequence in a way that does not match her experience of it. She picks up the pen. Writes the time of arrival. Stops. Because even that feels unstable. Was it 11:17? 11:18? The difference is small. It is not small. She taps the pen against the paper. Once. Twice. The sound echoes in the small room. She closes her eyes. Sees the hallway again. Not as a line. As a series of moments overlapping. The turn. The sound. The movement. The pause. Always the pause.

She opens her eyes. Looks at the form. At the expectation of order. Sequence. Clarity. She writes the time. 11:17. Underlines it once. As if that will make it certain. It does not.

Elijah sits across from a couple in the church office. They are not members. He does not know their names yet. It does not matter. They sit close together, but not touching. Their bodies angled slightly toward him, as if he might hold something they cannot access on their own. "We just want to understand," the woman says. Elijah nods. "I know," he replies. The man leans forward. "What actually happened?" he asks. Elijah takes a breath. Not to prepare an answer. To choose how to respond. "There are a lot of pieces," he says. "Some of them don't line up yet." The man frowns. "But there has to be a sequence," he says. "Something that explains it." Elijah tilts his head slightly. "Explains what?" he asks. The man hesitates. "All of it," he says. Elijah nods slowly. "That's what people want," he says. "A version that makes sense of everything." He pauses. "Sometimes that comes later," he adds. "Sometimes it doesn't come the way we expect."

The woman looks down at her hands. "So what do we do in the meantime?" she asks. Elijah considers the question. Then: "We listen carefully," he says. "And we don't rush to make it fit." The man exhales. "That's hard." Elijah nods. "Yes," he says. "It is."

By afternoon, the town is full of explanations. None of them complete. All of them certain. People begin to settle into versions. Not because they are accurate. Because they are bearable. Marcus writes one word and stops. Lila asks a question no one can answer. Daniel refuses to simplify what he knows. Keisha forces a sequence onto something that resists it. Elijah holds space for what does not yet make sense. The confusion does not lift. It deepens. Not as chaos. As structure forming too quickly around incomplete truth. And in that space—between what is known and what is said—misunderstanding begins to take root.

Part III—What Gets Filled In

By late afternoon, the gaps begin to close. Not because the truth has fully emerged. Because people cannot live inside open space for long. Where there are missing pieces, something moves to fill them. Memory stretches. Assumption settles. Fragments connect themselves, whether they belong together or not. The mind prefers a flawed story to an unfinished one. The town begins to choose. Not consciously. Not all at once. But steadily.

Marcus sits in the same chair, the notebook still open, the single word—Door—now surrounded by others that have appeared in uneven spacing across the page. Sound. Voice. Impact. Silence. He has written them in no particular order. Or rather, in the only order available to him. He studies the page. Attempts to connect them. Draws a line between Sound and Voice. Stops. Erases it. Draws a line between Door and Impact. Stops again. Nothing holds. He leans back, pressing his hands against his eyes. The memory shifts even as he tries to stabilize it. Details become sharper, then blur. He hears the voice again—the one in the hallway. Tries to isolate the words. Fails. Replaces them with something that sounds close enough to stand in their place. That is when he realizes it. He is not remembering. He is reconstructing. The distinction is subtle. It is not small.

He lowers his hands and looks at the page again. What he is writing is not a record. It is an attempt to make coherence out of fragments. To give shape to something that did not arrive in order. He circles Silence. Presses the pen harder than necessary. Because that part is clear. What came after. What held. What stayed. Everything else moves. He closes the notebook. Not because he is finished. Because he is not.

At the Nguyen house, the conversation has expanded. Not deeper. Wider. More voices, more input, more interpretations entering the space. Lila's mother stands near the counter, phone pressed between shoulder and ear, speaking in a tone that tries to balance concern with control. "Yes, she's okay," she says. "She was in one of the rooms . . . no, she didn't see anything directly . . . yes, I know, it's just—" She stops. Listens. Her eyes move briefly toward Lila, then away. "No," she says more firmly. "That's not what she said." Lila watches her. Not the words. The correction. The way something is being adjusted in real time. Replaced. Clarified. Or maybe changed.

Her mother hangs up. Exhales. "That was Mrs. Carter," she says. "She heard that—" She stops herself. Shakes her head. "It doesn't matter." Lila tilts her head slightly. "What did she hear?" she asks. Her mother hesitates. "That someone . . . opened a door," she says. "At the wrong time." The words settle into the room. Heavy. Directional. Lila feels them land. Not as information. As implication. "Which door?" she asks. Her mother shakes her head quickly. "I don't know," she says. "And we don't need to figure that out right now." But the question has already taken shape. It does not leave. Because now there is a version. Not confirmed. Not complete. But present.

Lila looks down at her hands. Imagines doors. Open. Closed. The space between. She remembers the closet. The way the door felt in her hand. The way it closed. Quietly. Correctly. She did it right. She knows she did. And yet—something still happened. Something that did not stop. The version she has been given does not match the version she lived. The mismatch remains. Unresolved.

Daniel returns to his truck as the light begins to fade. The diner had filled, then emptied. Conversations started, shifted, ended, resumed. He had remained. Listening. Not participating. Now, back in the cab, he sits with the engine off again. The quiet returns. His phone buzzes. He picks it up this time. Opens the message. A link. He taps it. A timeline appears. Clean. Structured. A sequence of events laid out in precise increments.

11:16—First report. 11:17—Dispatch initiated. 11:19—Units en route. 11:23—First arrival. Daniel reads it once. Then again. The numbers are exact. Confident. Final.

He feels something tighten in his chest. Not disagreement. Recognition. And dissonance. Because the timeline is correct. And it is incomplete. What it does not show is what exists between the numbers. The seconds that stretch. The moments that compress. The decisions that do not fit neatly into a line. He scrolls. Sees commentary beneath it. "Too slow." "Could have been faster." "Why the delay?" Each statement builds on the one before it. Certainty stacking on partial truth. Daniel closes the link. Sets the phone down. The timeline remains. Not on the screen. In the air. Because now it exists. And it will be used.

At the station, Keisha sits at the desk again, the report now partially filled. Times entered. Locations noted. Actions described. It looks right. It reads clearly. It does not feel accurate. She reads the line she has written: Entered hallway. Advanced toward sound. It is true. It is not complete. She adds another line. Paused to assess. The word sits there. Neutral. Clinical. Acceptable. It does not capture what the pause held. The uncertainty. The calculation. The impossibility of knowing what waited beyond the turn. She stares at the word. Paused. She could leave it. She should leave it. It fits the structure.

She writes another word beside it. Smaller. Less visible. Hesitated. She looks at it. Then crosses it out. Not because it is wrong. Because it will be read differently than it was lived. She leans back. Closes her eyes. The hallway returns. Always the same. Always different. She opens her eyes again. Leaves the report as it is. Because the form requires completion. Even if the experience does not.

In the church office, Elijah sits with a small group now. More people have come. Drawn by the need to speak. To hear. To place themselves somewhere within what has happened. "I heard they waited," one man says. "They didn't wait," another replies. "They couldn't get in." "That's not what I was told." Elijah listens. The conversation moves quickly. Versions emerging, colliding, reinforcing. Each one grounded in something. None of them whole. "What matters," Elijah says gently, "is not just what happened, but how we're understanding what happened." The group quiets. Not entirely. But enough. A woman speaks. "But understanding is all we have right now." Elijah nods. "I know," he says. "That's why we have to be careful with it."

He looks around the room. Meets each person's eyes, briefly. "Because once we settle on a version," he adds, "it becomes harder to see what doesn't fit." The words hang. Not as correction. As invitation. To hold the space open. A little longer.

As evening approaches, the town continues to fill in the gaps. Stories solidify. Details harden. What was uncertain becomes stated. What was stated becomes believed. Not because it is verified. Because it answers something. Marcus closes his notebook. Lila carries a question that has been shaped by someone else's answer. Daniel rejects the timeline even as he understands it. Keisha edits her own experience to fit a form. Elijah resists the closure others are reaching for. The confusion has not disappeared. It has changed. From not knowing—to believing something that may not be true. And in that shift—something new takes hold. Not clarity. Not yet. But the beginning of conviction. Built on incomplete ground. And spreading.

Chapter 3—**Run**

Part I—The Body Decides

There is no moment when it becomes clear. No clean signal that says: now you must choose. It happens before that. In the body. Marcus Hale stands in the classroom and listens. The sounds that had been close are no longer close. They have moved. Or stopped. Or changed in a way that no longer reaches him the same way. He cannot tell which. The room holds. Desks. Chairs. The board with the unfinished sentence. Moral responsibility requires— He does not look at it again. The silence stretches. Not empty. Held. Too complete.

He moves toward the door. Not quickly. Not slowly. The distance is the same as it was before. It does not feel the same. His hand lifts. Stops just short of the handle. The metal is there. Solid. Waiting. He listens again. Nothing. Then—something. Not a sharp sound. Not the crack that had come before. Something else. A movement. A shift. A presence in the hallway that is not loud enough to name. His body leans toward it before his mind catches up.

Someone could be out there. Not gone. Not safe. Just—out there.

The thought does not arrive as decision. It arrives as pressure, expanding, filling the space the silence has left behind. It does not leave when he moves. It stays just beneath the next breath.

He looks back into the room. Empty. But not neutral. He sees it as it had been minutes ago. Filled. Occupied. Dependent on him in ways that were structured. Clear. Now—nothing in the room asks anything of him. Everything outside might. His hand closes around the handle. He does not turn it. Not yet. The weight of the door is different now. Not physical. Meaning. Inside. Outside. Holding. Leaving. Both feel like action. Both feel like risk.

Another sound. Closer this time. Not loud. But unmistakable. A voice. Cut short. Marcus flinches. The hesitation breaks. Not resolved. Interrupted. He turns the lock. The click is small but final, louder than it should be. He waits half a breath, as if the sound itself might change what follows. It does not.

He opens the door just enough at first. A narrow space. A line of sight into the hallway. Light spills through the gap, brighter than the room behind him. The hallway is not empty. It is not full. It is moving. A student runs past, fast, not looking in. Another follows, slower, looking back over their shoulder—not at Marcus, but at something further down the hall. Marcus opens the door wider and steps into the threshold, then stops, because the hallway does not offer clarity—only motion and fragments.

To his left—a classroom door open, students inside pressed low, a teacher holding a hand up, stillness as instruction. To his right—movement, faster, less contained, bodies moving away from something he still cannot see. The building no longer behaves like a building. It behaves like a series of choices, none of them complete.

Marcus steps out. The door behind him remains open. He does not turn back to close it. He does not notice that he doesn't. The hallway takes him in—not gently, not forcefully, simply completely. The air is different now. Too thick. Too thin. He cannot tell. Another sound echoes from somewhere down the corridor, closer than before. His body reacts—a flinch, a tightening in his chest. He turns, not fully, just enough to orient.

And in that turning, he sees them. Three students. One pressed against the wall, hands over their ears. One running, backpack swinging loose, unzipped. One frozen in the middle of the hallway, eyes fixed on something Marcus cannot see. Three different responses. All at once. Hide. Run. Freeze. Marcus registers it not as theory but as reality. The body decides before the mind can name it.

"Go!" The word comes from somewhere—behind him or in front of him. He cannot place it. It does not matter. It lands. Marcus moves down the hallway, away from the sound, toward something he does not fully understand—an exit, maybe, or just distance. His steps are uneven at first, catching slightly as if the floor itself has shifted beneath him. Then they find rhythm—not steady, not controlled, but continuous. Movement becomes its own logic. Run.

The doors along the hallway are open—some, closed—others. The difference feels important. He does not know why. A classroom to his left—students huddled in the corner, a teacher crouched in front of them, finger pressed to lips. Another to his right—empty, chairs overturned, a backpack lying in the doorway as if dropped mid-motion. Each room holds a different version of the same moment. Each one asks a different question. Marcus does not stop. He cannot. Stopping feels like choosing something he does not have enough information to choose.

Another sound, louder, closer. The hallway shifts again. Someone ahead of him turns sharply, disappearing through a side door. Marcus hesitates for a fraction of a second—enough to feel the pull of that option. Hide. The door is there. Open. Available. A place to disappear, to become still, to wait. His body leans slightly in that direction. Then—another sound behind him. The decision collapses. Run.

He pushes forward, past the door, past the possibility of stopping. Someone could be out there. The thought flickers—out of place now, but not gone. His breath comes faster, not controlled, not even—sharp inhales, short exhales. His chest tightens with each one. The hallway stretches longer than it should. Distances distort. The end never seems closer. And yet—he is moving. That matters. Movement is survival. Or feels like it.

And somewhere, beneath the motion, beneath the urgency, beneath the survival, the thought remains. Someone could be out there. Not a question yet. But it will be.

Part II—The Split Second

There is no time to weigh it. Only time to move. Or not. The moment does not arrive with options neatly arranged. It fractures into impulses—each one urgent, each one incomplete. The body does not debate them. It selects.

Marcus does not remember turning into the stairwell. He remembers the hallway narrowing. The crowd thickening. The sound behind him closing distance in a way that made direction feel less like choice and more like necessity. But before the stairs—there was a second. Small. Almost invisible. Where everything slowed.

A student grabbed his sleeve. Hard enough to stop him. "Wait—" the student said. Marcus turned. Not fully. Just enough to see. A face. Young. Eyes wide in a way that did not ask for permission. "Where do we go?" the student asked. The question landed. Too large. Too immediate. Marcus opened his mouth. Nothing came out. Because there was no answer that could be given in time. Because the answer depended on something neither of them could see. Another sound. Closer. The student flinched. So did Marcus. The moment collapsed. Run.

Marcus pulled free. Not roughly. But completely. The contact broke. The question remained. Unanswered. He moved. Into the stairwell. Down. Away. The student—he does not know what the student did. Followed. Stayed. Turned back. That piece does not settle. It shifts every time he tries to hold it.

In another part of the building, a different decision is made. Or not made. A teacher stands in a doorway, hand on the frame, eyes scanning the hallway that no longer behaves like a hallway. Students move past her. Some entering the room. Some continuing forward. She feels the pull of both. Bring them in. Send them away. Contain. Release. She raises her hand. "Inside," she says to one group. Then to another: "Keep going—don't stop." The contradiction is immediate. Necessary. There is no single instruction that holds. Each moment requires its own answer. Each answer excludes another. She knows this. And still—the weight lands. Because every direction given is also a direction denied.

Down the hall, a boy crouches behind a locker. Hands over his head. Body folded in on itself. He does not move. Cannot. The sound reaches him. Not as something to run from. As something that removes the possibility of movement altogether. Freeze. His breath becomes shallow. Almost silent. His body makes him small. Smaller. As if reducing space might reduce presence. As if presence might invite danger. He does not think this. He becomes it.

Outside the building, Marcus reaches the edge of the parking lot. Slows. Stops. Turns back. Not all the way. Just enough. The doors are still open. People still moving. Still coming out. Still running. He watches. Counts without meaning to. One. Two. Three. A gap. Then more. Each person emerging becomes a measure. Of what? He does not know. Who is out. Who is not. Who might still be inside. The numbers do not settle. They shift with every new figure. The counting does not help. He does not stop.

Sirens cut through the air. Louder now. Closer. The sound splits the space again. Some people move toward it. Drawn by authority. By the promise of structure. Others move further away. Seeking distance. Silence. Marcus stands between. Not moving toward. Not moving away. Suspended. His body has already done what it needed to do. Now—it does not know what comes next.

Inside, the teacher in the doorway makes another decision. Closes it. The sound of the latch is definitive. Inside. Outside. A line drawn. Students huddle. Press together. Some crying. Some silent. Some watching the door as if it might open on its own. The teacher leans against it. Not heavily. Just enough to feel the boundary. To hold it. To become part of it. Her breathing is uneven. She tries to steady it. Because they are watching her. Because her body will tell them what this moment is. Even if she does not know herself.

Marcus steps backward. Further from the building. The space around him widens. Voices blur into one another. Information arrives. Fragments. "Did you see—" "Someone said—" "I think—" Nothing lands. Nothing holds. He looks down at his hands. They are shaking. He had not noticed. He notices now. Because the running has stopped. Because the body, no longer moving forward, begins to process what it has carried through. The shaking is not fear. Not exactly. It is release. Of motion. Of tension. Of something that has not yet found language.

The student who grabbed his sleeve—Marcus sees him now. Across the lot. Standing alone. Looking back at the building. Marcus recognizes him immediately. Not by name. By the moment. Their eyes meet. Just for a second. Neither moves. Neither speaks. The question passes between them again. Unanswered. Unanswerable. Then someone calls the student's name. From behind. He turns. Moves toward the voice. The connection breaks. Again.

The split second does not end when the moment passes. It stretches. Extends. Lives on in what follows. In what was done. In what was not. Marcus ran. The teacher closed the door. The boy stayed still. Each action complete. Each one partial. Each one carrying something forward. Not just survival. Something else. Something that will not settle. Not yet. Not here. But coming. As the body slows. As the mind catches up. As the question returns—not about what happened—but about what was done in the space where there was no time to decide.

Part III—After the Motion

The body cannot run forever. Even when the moment feels like it never ends. At some point, movement stops. Not because the danger is fully gone. Because the body reaches its limit.

Marcus stands at the far edge of the parking lot, the building now distant enough to feel unreal. Not safe. Just farther. His breath is still uneven, pulling in too fast, releasing too sharp. His chest aches—not from injury, but from exertion that has not yet found its way out of him. Around him, people continue to move, but the urgency has shifted. The running has broken into smaller motions—pacing, turning, gathering in uncertain clusters. The body slows. The mind begins.

"What happened?" The question comes from somewhere to his left. A woman he does not know. Her voice is steady in a way that suggests she is trying to make it so. Marcus turns his head slightly. Opens his mouth. Closes it. Because the answer is not there. Not in a form that can be given. "I don't know," he says. The words feel insufficient. They are the only ones available. The woman nods. As if she understands. As if she does not. She turns away. Asks someone else. The question continues. Moving outward. Looking for a place to land.

Marcus looks down at his hands again. Still shaking. Less than before. Enough to notice. He flexes his fingers once. Twice. As if testing whether they belong to him again. They do. But not in the same way.

The sirens arrive fully now. Vehicles pulling into the lot. Doors opening. Commands shouted. Clear. Directed. Structured. The opposite of what came before. People begin to respond. To move toward instruction. To follow lines that have been drawn for them. Marcus does not move immediately. He watches. As if observing something separate from himself. As if the scene has shifted into a version he is no longer part of.

Inside the building, the teacher remains pressed against the door. The room behind her is quieter now. Not silent. Contained. Breathing. Whispers. The small sounds of people trying to stay present without drawing attention. She has counted them. Three times. The same number each time. She holds onto that. As if consistency might anchor something that feels like it is drifting. A student near the back begins to cry. Soft at first. Then harder. The sound spreads. Not loudly. But enough. The teacher moves away from the door. Just slightly. Enough to cross the room. She kneels beside the student. Places a hand on their shoulder. Does not speak. Because words feel too large. Too likely to break. The student leans into her. The contact is immediate. Necessary. Around them, others shift closer. Not all. Some remain where they are. Arms wrapped around themselves. Eyes fixed on the door. Waiting.

In the hallway, the boy behind the locker has not moved. Time has changed shape for him. Collapsed. Expanded. He cannot tell. The sounds have become distant now. Or maybe his hearing has narrowed. Focused inward. On breath. On the space his body occupies. He knows he should move. Somewhere. Anywhere. The thought arrives. Does not translate. His legs do not respond. Freeze. Not a decision. A state. He presses himself further into the corner. As if merging with the structure might make him invisible. As if stillness might be protection. He waits. For what, he does not know.

Outside, Marcus takes a step backward. Then another. Distance increases. The building recedes. But the connection does not. He can still see the doors. Still see people emerging. Still see the gaps between them. Each gap a question. Each delay a possibility he cannot resolve. He turns away. Finally. Not because he wants to. Because looking has become something he cannot sustain.

A hand touches his arm. He flinches. Pulls back instinctively. The person steps away immediately. "Sorry," they say. Marcus nods. The reaction lingers longer than the contact. His body still primed. Still expecting. He exhales slowly. Tries to bring himself back into the moment that is now. Not the one that just passed.

"Over here," a voice calls. An officer. Directing people toward a specific area. A point of gathering. Of containment. Marcus moves this time. Not quickly. Not slowly. Following. Because following is easier than choosing. Because the body, having made so many decisions without thought, now seeks something external to guide it. He steps into the designated space. Joins a group. Stands among them. Not speaking. Not asking. Just present.

The questions begin again. "Did you see—" "Were you—" "Do you know—" Marcus hears them. Does not answer. Not because he refuses. Because he cannot. Not yet. The answers require sequence. Clarity. Meaning. None of which have settled.

Across the lot, the student who grabbed his sleeve stands with a group now. Surrounded. Held. Marcus watches from a distance. Feels something shift. Not relief. Not regret. Something more complex. Because he left. Because the student asked. Because the question remains. He looks away.

Inside the building, the teacher hears the sound of footsteps in the hallway. Different this time. Measured. Intentional. A voice follows. "Police! If you can hear me—" The word lands. Different from all the others. Authority. Structure. End. Or the beginning of something else. The teacher stands. Moves back toward the door. Her hand hovers over the handle. The decision returns. Open. Or wait. The room behind her holds its breath. She closes her eyes. Just for a second. Then opens them. Turns the handle.

Outside, Marcus hears the shift. Not the specific words. The change in tone. In movement. In the way the crowd responds. Something is happening. Different from before. He feels it in his body before he understands it. The transition. From immediate danger—to aftermath. He does not feel safe. Not yet. But something has changed. The running is over. The body knows this. Even if the mind has not caught up.

He stands there. Among others. Alone in a way that has nothing to do with proximity. The motion has ended. The moment has not. It lingers. In his muscles. In his breath. In the questions that now begin to take shape.

Not about what he did. Not yet. But about what remains. Who is here. Who is not. What comes next. The body decided. The body moved. The body stopped. Now—the mind begins its work. And what it finds will not be simple. Will not be clean. Will not be finished anytime soon.

Chapter 4—**Stay Quiet**

Part I—The Smallest Sound

The first thing is the breathing. Not hers. Everyone's. Too loud. Too fast. Too close. Lila Nguyen presses her lips together, trying to make her own disappear inside her. The air pushes against her mouth, wanting out, wanting to be heard. She swallows it back, holds it for a second, then another—but not too long. Too long becomes panic. Panic becomes sound. In through the nose. Out through—no, too much. Too loud. She stops.

The closet is darker than it should be. Not completely dark. There is a thin line of light at the bottom of the door, a narrow strip cutting across the floor like something placed there on purpose. It does not move. It does not flicker. It is the only thing that feels steady. She watches it, not because she wants to, but because it is the only thing that does not change.

Around her, bodies press close without touching exactly, close enough that every shift becomes shared. Someone's knee rests against her leg. Someone's shoulder hovers near her arm. The space is full without being crowded, tight without anyone speaking about it. Someone shifts. Fabric brushes fabric. Too loud. Everything is too loud.

A whisper begins somewhere behind her. "Don't—" It cuts off before finishing. It doesn't need to.

Stay quiet.

The words are not spoken again, but they don't have to be. They are already everywhere—in the way bodies hold still, in the way breath is swallowed, in the way even thinking feels like it might make a sound if it gets too big.

Lila presses her hand flat against her chest, not to calm herself but to feel where the noise is coming from. Her heart. Too fast. Too strong. It feels like it is hitting the inside of her ribs hard enough to be heard outside of her, through her shirt, through the walls, through the door. She presses harder, as if pressure will make it quieter, as if she can push it back into herself. It doesn't change. It keeps going.

A sound comes from the hallway. Not like before. Not sharp. Not sudden. Something else. A movement, or the memory of one. She cannot tell if it is real or if she is making it real by listening too hard.

Her eyes stay fixed on the line of light. If she looks away, something might change. If she keeps watching, maybe it won't.

The light shifts. Just slightly. A shadow crosses it, then disappears, then returns. Her breath catches. She doesn't mean for it to. It just stops. Her chest tightens. The air does not move. She does not move. She does not try to fix it, because fixing it would be sound.

Someone is crying. Very quietly. The sound is broken into pieces, pulled in and pushed out, held back before it can become anything larger. It sits in the room like something fragile, something everyone can hear but no one can acknowledge. Lila does not turn toward it. Turning would mean moving. Moving would mean sound. Sound is not allowed.

Her foot starts to tingle. She notices it all at once—pins and needles, sharp and distant at the same time. It feels wrong, like it doesn't belong to her anymore. She wants to move it just a little, just enough to make it stop. She doesn't. Because movement is sound. Even if it isn't, it feels like it is.

Time does not move the way it usually does. It stretches, then stops, then stretches again. There is no before, no after, only this—the closet, the breathing, the light, the not moving.

A memory tries to come in—her classroom, the sound of someone laughing, a pencil tapping on a desk. It doesn't stay. It doesn't fit here. It slides away, like it cannot exist in the same space as this.

Her throat is dry. She wants water. The thought appears quickly, then disappears just as fast, because wanting something is too close to needing something, and needing something might make her move.

Another sound. Closer. Definitely closer. Footsteps, or something like them. She is sure of it—no, not sure. Nothing is sure. The steps stop right outside the door. Or not. The space between her and the hallway collapses. Everything is at the door now, even if it isn't.

Her breath is still caught, still halfway, still not moving. Her chest aches. She ignores it.

The line of light disappears. Completely. Covered. Blocked. Her eyes widen. No one else moves. No one makes a sound. The entire room becomes one thing: stillness—not breathing, not shifting, not existing beyond what is absolutely necessary.

Seconds pass, or maybe longer, or shorter. Time does not hold its shape.

Then the light returns. The shadow gone, or moved, or—she doesn't know. She doesn't know anything.

Her breath comes back all at once, too fast, too loud. She clamps down again, forces it smaller, quieter, less.

Stay quiet.

The words return again, not spoken but felt, pressed into everything.

She starts counting again—not numbers, but moments, breaths, spaces between sound. If she can make them even, if she can make them small enough, if she can disappear into them.

Her hand slips slightly against her chest. Sweat. Cold. She wipes it against her jeans, slow, careful, controlled. Her eyes never leave the light.

Someone shifts again. A shoe against the floor. A tiny scrape. Lila flinches, not outwardly but inside. Everything tightens, as if the sound has weight, as if it has direction, as if it could travel under the door and into the hallway.

Nothing happens. No response. No new sound. The hallway remains—whatever it is.

Her mind tries to ask a question. Are we safe? It doesn't finish, because finishing it would mean needing an answer, and there isn't one.

Instead: stay quiet.

That is the only instruction, the only rule, the only thing that makes sense.

Her legs ache now, a slow, deep pain from holding still too long, from not moving, from staying exactly where she is. She lets it stay. Pain is allowed. Sound is not.

Another breath. Another. Another. Each one smaller than the last, each one controlled, each one effort.

The light remains. Unchanged. For now.

And Lila stays exactly where she is—not because she chooses to, but because everything inside her has already decided.

Stay quiet.

Part II—The Sound Inside

The next thing is the inside noise. Not the hallway, not the footsteps, not the almost-sounds that come and go. The noise inside her is louder, harder to control, harder to understand.

Lila tries to make her breathing smaller. It won't stay small. It keeps slipping, coming back too fast, too uneven, like it doesn't belong to her, like it has its own reason for being here. She presses her lips tighter, feels the air build behind them, push, wait, hold—one second, two—no, too long. Her body takes over. Air rushes in, too sharp, too loud.

She freezes. Listens. Did anyone hear that? No one moves. No one reacts. But that doesn't mean anything.

Her ears feel open, too open, like everything is getting in—every shift, every breath, every almost-sound, even the ones that might not be real. A sleeve brushing fabric. A knee adjusting. Someone swallowing too hard. All of it too clear, too close.

Her heartbeat rises, not just fast now but loud. She can feel it everywhere—in her throat, in her wrists, in her face. It feels like knocking, like something trying to get out.

Stop.

The thought comes as pressure, not words, not language, just a push inward. She presses her arm harder against her chest, trying to hold it still, trying to quiet it, trying to make it less. It doesn't work, but she keeps doing it.

Someone beside her inhales too quickly—a sharp sound—then gone, pulled back, hidden. Everything is always pulled back.

Stay quiet.

The words feel different now, not just instruction but expectation, like something is waiting for them to fail.

Her mind starts moving faster, faster than her body. Thoughts begin but don't finish. They can't.

What if—
No.
What if someone—
No.

The thoughts stop themselves, cut off before they become too much. Thinking feels dangerous, like it could turn into something else, something louder.

Her mouth is dry. Her tongue sticks to the roof of it. She swallows. The sound is too big. She feels it in her throat, in her ears, in the space around her. She winces, waits. Nothing happens. Still, she doesn't do it again.

The floor presses into her legs, hard, unmoving. Her foot is gone now—not really gone, but not there the way it should be. Numb, but also sharp, a quiet kind of pain. She wants to move, just a little, just enough to feel it again. She doesn't. Because movement is sound. Even if it isn't, it could be. That's enough.

Another sound outside, closer, different. Not footsteps. Something else—a bump, a brush, something against the wall or the door. Her body locks tighter, if that's possible. Everything pulls inward.

The light under the door flickers once, then still, then again. Her eyes stay fixed. She doesn't blink. Blinking feels like losing something, like missing something important.

Her breathing starts to shake, not loud but not steady—small tremors. In. Out. In—no, too fast.

She tries to match someone else, the person next to her, slower, quieter. But their breath changes too. Everyone's does. Nothing stays the same.

A sound escapes someone—small, broken, not quite a sob, not quite a breath, something in between. Lila feels it in her chest, like it might happen to her next, like it is already starting. She clamps down harder on everything—on breath, on movement, on thought.

Stay quiet.

The rule tightens, becomes something else, not just about sound but about control, about holding everything inside.

Her mind tries again. Are we—
No.

It doesn't finish. It can't. Because the answer would be too big, too loud.

Another bump, closer, or the same one again, repeating, echoing. She cannot tell.

Her body starts to shake, not from cold but from holding too still, from stopping too much, from not letting anything move. She presses her hands into her legs, hard, trying to stop it, trying to keep it inside, trying to keep it from becoming visible. Even though no one can see, it still matters.

The closet feels smaller, or she does, or both. The air feels thinner, harder to take in, harder to keep quiet.

She takes a breath too fast. It catches halfway, stops. Her chest tightens. Pain, sharp, immediate. She stops breathing again, not on purpose but because she doesn't know how to fix it without making it worse.

Seconds pass, or longer, or shorter. Time does not help.

Then air comes back all at once, too much. She forces it down, swallows it, makes it smaller, quieter.

Nothing happens. No reaction. No consequence.

But the fear stays, because the next one might be different.

Her eyes stay on the light. Always the light. It hasn't changed. That means something, or nothing.

Stay quiet.

The words are everything now, the only thing.

And inside that rule, inside the effort to follow it, Lila understands something without saying it: the hardest sound to control is the one her own body keeps making.

Part III—When Stillness Breaks

The breaking does not begin loud. It begins small, so small it almost doesn't count.

A shift—fabric against fabric, a knee slipping, a hand catching itself too late against the floor. The sound is soft, barely there, but in the closet it feels enormous, like it fills every inch of space at once.

Everything reacts. Not outwardly. No one gasps. No one speaks. But inside, everything tightens.

Lila feels it before she understands it—the way the air changes, the way the silence stops being still and becomes something else, something listening.

Stay quiet.

The words return, but now they carry something heavier, not just instruction, not just survival, but expectation, like something is waiting for them to fail.

The person who moved freezes completely, as if stillness can undo what just happened, as if it can pull the sound back into their body and erase it. Their breathing disappears. Their shape becomes rigid, fixed.

It doesn't undo anything. Nothing can.

Nothing happens at first.

The hallway remains—whatever it is—distant and close at the same time, everywhere and nowhere. The absence of response becomes its own kind of pressure, its own kind of sound.

Lila holds her breath halfway again, not fully in, not fully out. Her chest tightens, the air caught where it shouldn't be, but she does not move to fix it, because fixing it would be sound.

Seconds stretch longer than they should, long enough that they begin to lose shape.

Then someone exhales too quickly—a small break, a small failure, another piece of sound added to the room.

It spreads, not loudly, not all at once, but in pieces—breaths that can't be held anymore, tiny adjustments of bodies that have been still too long, the body pushing back against control in ways that cannot be fully stopped.

Lila feels it in herself—the urge to move, to shift her weight, to release the tension in her legs, in her chest, in her throat. She does none of it, but the urge does not leave. It grows.

Stay quiet.

The rule tightens, becomes harder to hold, not because it changed, but because everything inside her is starting to push against it.

Another sound outside, different this time, clearer, closer—a voice, not sharp, not shouting, but not soft either. It cuts through the hallway in a way that feels controlled, deliberate, but the words do not reach her clearly. They blur against the door, against the distance, against the fear that fills in the parts she cannot hear.

Lila leans toward it without meaning to, just a fraction, just enough. Her shoulder brushes the wall—a tiny scrape. The sound is barely there, but it feels like everything.

She freezes immediately.

Her body locks so fast it almost hurts. Her heart slams harder, faster, as if trying to make up for all the silence everywhere else. She presses her lips together tighter, presses her arm harder against her chest, tries to contain everything at once.

The voice outside again, closer now, different. A word forms—or almost forms. She cannot make it out. She tries harder. Listening feels like control, like doing something, like not just waiting.

The light under the door shifts, not a flicker this time, not a passing shadow. Something stays there—a shape, a presence, blocking the light.

Lila's body goes completely still, more still than before, if that is possible. No one moves. No one breathes fully. Even the quiet crying has stopped. Everything is held.

The shadow remains long enough to matter, long enough to become something real.

A sound at the door, not loud but definite—a contact, a weight.

The handle—

Her attention locks onto it, even though she cannot see it directly, only feel where it should be, just above the line of light, just beyond the edge of what she can know.

It doesn't turn. Or maybe it does, just slightly, enough that she thinks it might, enough that her body reacts as if it has.

Her breath disappears again, gone completely.

The room becomes something else—not people, not bodies, just stillness, each person reduced to the smallest possible version of themselves, the smallest sound, the smallest movement, the smallest presence.

Then the shadow shifts, pulls back, moves away.

The light returns, full, unbroken.

For a moment, no one exhales, as if even that is too dangerous, too soon.

Then it happens slowly—one breath, then another, then more, each one careful, each one controlled. The room fills again, not with noise, but with presence.

Lila feels something in her body release, not fully, not safely, just enough to keep going. Her chest loosens slightly. Her breath finds a rhythm again, not steady, but possible.

Stay quiet.

The words return again, but they feel different now, not just a rule, not just something to follow, but something they held, something that held them, something that worked, for now.

The closet is still the same—dark, close, unmoving.

But it does not feel the same.

Something has shifted.

Not outside.

Inside.

Inside the space.

Inside the people.

Inside her.

Lila does not try to name it, does not try to understand it, because understanding would require more than she has, more than she can risk.

But she knows something anyway, without words, without thinking it through:

Stillness does not mean safe. It only means nothing has happened yet.

Chapter 5—The Call Comes In

Part I—Before It Has a Name

It starts like any other call. A tone. A voice. A location. Nothing about it announces what it is, not yet.

The dispatch room is steady. Fluorescent lights hum overhead. Screens glow in rows. Chairs roll slightly as people shift, adjust, settle into long hours built on repetition. Call. Response. Clear. Repeat.

"911, what's your emergency?" The words come automatically—measured, neutral, trained to hold whatever comes next without becoming part of it.

The voice on the other end is not neutral. It is breath first, then sound, then words that do not come in order. "I—there's—something—" The dispatcher leans forward slightly, not visibly, internally, a shift that happens before conscious thought.

"Okay," she says. "Take a breath for me. Tell me what's happening."

"I heard—there was—at the school—" The word school lands, not differently, not yet. It is just a location, a place among many.

"Which school?" the dispatcher asks, fingers already moving across the keyboard.

The name comes through, clear enough, enough to enter, enough to place. Typing. Clicking. Pulling up the address. The system responds as it always does—coordinates, mapping, units nearby.

"What's happening there?" she asks.

"I don't know—there were sounds—like—like—" The caller stops. Breath again. Then: "Like gunshots."

The word enters the room. Not physically, but it arrives.

The dispatcher does not react outwardly. Her voice remains even. "Okay. Stay with me. Are you inside the building?"

"No—I'm outside—I was—I heard it—people are running—"

The cadence changes, not dramatically, just enough. The rhythm of the call shifts from uncertain to directional.

"Are you safe where you are?"

"I think so—I don't know—people are—"

More voices in the background, layered, overlapping, not clear, but not controlled.

The dispatcher types faster. The initial call becomes an entry. The entry becomes a signal.

Across the room, another tone sounds. Another dispatcher answers. "911, what's your emergency?"

"Something's happening at—" The same school.

The second call overlaps the first, not identical, but close enough.

A third tone. Another line opens.

"—there's someone—"
"—I heard—"
"—people are—"

The room shifts—still seated, still controlled, but different.

The supervisor looks up, not at one call, but at the pattern.

"Confirm location," he says, not loud, not urgent, but direct.

The first dispatcher nods, gives the name, the address, already entered, already active.

"Units en route?" he asks.

"Dispatching now."

Keys move. Radios click.

"Unit 12, respond to—" The address is read, calm, measured, routine.

"Copy," a voice responds.

The system moves forward, because it always does.

Another call comes in. Then another.

"—my daughter—"
"—they said lockdown—"
"—I can't reach—"

The words begin to stack, not in sequence, in weight.

The dispatcher listens, filters, separates what can be used from what cannot—location, status, immediate threat. Everything else waits.

"Stay on the line with me," she says.

"I hear more—"

"How many?"

"I don't know—I can't—"

The caller's voice breaks, not into silence, into something less structured.

The dispatcher does not follow it there. She holds the line where it needs to be.

"Listen to me," she says. "You're doing fine. Stay where you are. Do not go inside."

The instruction lands, not because it is complete, but because it is something.

Across the room, radios increase. More units. More acknowledgments.

"Unit 7 responding."
"Unit 14 en route."
"Supervisor en route."

The map updates. Icons move. Converging.

The supervisor stands now, not quickly, but with purpose.

"What do we have?" he asks.

The answer is not singular. It comes in pieces.

"Multiple calls."
"Reports of shots fired."
"Unknown suspect."
"Unknown injuries."

The words are standard, familiar, structured.

But something beneath them is not.

The dispatcher feels it—not as fear, not yet, but as a shift in density.

Calls continue.

"—he's still—"
"—I think someone's—"
"—we're hiding—"

The word hiding enters. Different from the others. It stays longer.

"Where are you?" she asks.

"In a room—we locked—"

"Stay there," she says immediately. "Do not open the door for anyone unless law enforcement tells you to."

Her voice is steady, but the instruction carries more weight now.

The system continues, because it must.

Call. Response. Dispatch. Repeat.

But the repetition no longer feels routine. It feels accelerated, compressed.

Time narrows.

The first units arrive.

"Dispatch, Unit 12 on scene."

The room listens, even those not assigned.

"Go ahead," the dispatcher replies.

There is a pause—short, but present.

"Multiple victims," the voice says. "Shots fired inside."

The words land heavier than before, more defined.

The supervisor exhales once, not visibly, but it happens.

"Upgrade response," he says.

The instruction moves outward, immediate.

"Active shooter protocol."

Now it has a name.

The room changes, not in movement, in understanding.

What was forming becomes fixed. What was uncertain becomes declared.

The dispatcher's screen updates—new fields, new codes.

She does not look away, does not pause.

"Stay with me," she says to the caller.

"I'm still here," the voice answers.

In the background—breathing, silence, something held.

The dispatcher listens, holds the line.

Because this is the moment, the one where routine ends, not abruptly, but completely.

The call came in like any other.

Now it is something else, and everything that follows will move because of it.

Part II—En Route

Keisha Turner hears the first version of it through static. Not the whole call, not the full shape, just fragments moving through the radio, clipped at the edges by signal and urgency.

"Unit 12 . . . respond . . . " A location, then the name of the school, then: "Reports of shots fired."

Her hand tightens on the steering wheel before she realizes it has moved.

The day had been ordinary until then—patrol, traffic, a call about a minor collision that had already resolved itself before she arrived, a brief conversation with a store owner about vandalism that may or may not have been done by teenagers. Nothing that asked more of her than attention, patience, paperwork.

Now the air in the car changes.

The radio continues. "Multiple calls received. Unknown number of injuries. Unknown suspect location."

Unknown.

The word lands harder than the others.

Keisha reaches for the mic. "Unit 18 responding." Her voice is steady. Good. She hears it and takes comfort from that, though the comfort is brief.

The siren comes on. The vehicle responds immediately, as if it knows what the body is still trying to accept—lights, sound, acceleration. The routine mechanics of emergency turn the ordinary street into a corridor.

Cars ahead begin to move aside. Some quickly. Some too slowly. Keisha adjusts—left, right, forward. Her training rises, clean and sharp.

Approach. Assess. Enter. Stop the threat.

She has said the words, practiced them, walked hallways in training facilities where the walls were temporary and the danger controlled. She has moved toward paper targets and role players and simulated chaos while instructors watched with clipboards.

But the school ahead is not a training site.

It has children inside.

Teachers.

Classrooms.

Doors.

Her mind tries to map what she knows of the building—main entrance, east lot, service doors, gym corridor. She has been there before for traffic duty, basketball games, one career day where a student asked whether she had ever been scared. She had smiled then and said fear was part of paying attention.

The radio cracks again. "Additional callers reporting students running from the north entrance."

North entrance.

She changes lanes, calculates distance, traffic, time. The numbers form automatically, but they do not calm her.

Another unit comes on. "Unit 7 en route from Maple." Then another. "Unit 14, two minutes out."

Two minutes.

The phrase sounds small.

It is not small.

In two minutes, anything can happen.

In two minutes, everything can.

Keisha presses the accelerator.

The town moves past in flashes—gas station, pharmacy, church sign with letters announcing a youth fundraiser, a man standing near a crosswalk holding a grocery bag, staring as she passes.

Ordinary life witnessing emergency without yet knowing its name.

The radio gives more. "Caller states they are hiding in a classroom."

Keisha breathes in, keeps it controlled.

"Caller reports shots still being heard."

Still.

The word enters the car and stays there.

Her jaw tightens.

She hears the instructor's voice from training, clear and firm: You move toward the sound. You do not wait for perfect information.

Perfect information does not exist.

Not here.

Not now.

A truck ahead hesitates, uncertain where to pull over. Keisha taps the horn—not angrily, just enough. The truck shifts right. She passes.

The school is closer now.

Not visible yet.

But close enough that the route begins to narrow into inevitability.

She reaches down, checks her gear by touch—radio, weapon, tourniquet, keys—each object where it should be. Order in small places. That matters.

The dispatcher's voice comes through again, tighter now, though still controlled. "Units responding, be advised: active shooter protocol initiated."

There it is.

Named.

The words do not create the reality, but they fix it in place.

Active shooter.

Keisha feels the phrase move through her body like cold water. Not panic. Recognition.

This is the call everyone trains for and no one wants.

This is the call that changes the air in every room after it is spoken.

She turns onto the road leading to the school. Other sirens converge now, distant at first, then overlapping. The sound fills the street from more than one direction. She sees lights ahead, another patrol car taking the turn too fast, tires catching slightly before correcting.

They are moving toward the same point.

Different streets.

Same center.

The radio becomes crowded.

“Command staging—”
“Negative, shots still active—”
“Need units at—”
“Students exiting west side—”

Voices overlap, then separate, then overlap again.

Keisha filters what she can.

The rest becomes pressure.

Her breathing remains steady.

She checks it intentionally— in, out, not too fast, not too shallow.

Her hands are firm on the wheel but not locked.

She has trained her body for this.

Still, something beneath the training asks a question she does not want:

Will you move when it is time?

She pushes it away.

Not now.

The school comes into view—brick building, flagpole, buses lined along the far curb, a place built for morning routines, announcements, lunch periods, homework forgotten in lockers.

Now students are running from it.

That is the first image that breaks the training frame.

A boy with one shoe.

A girl clutching her backpack against her chest like a shield.

Two students pulling another between them, moving awkwardly, too fast and not fast enough.

Keisha pulls into the lot hard. The tires grind against the pavement. She stops behind another cruiser but leaves room for movement.

Door open.

Feet out.

The sound outside hits differently—sirens, shouting, distant pops that may be doors, may be something else, may be what she already knows they are.

She moves.

No dramatic thought.

No speech.

Her body follows the line training has drawn.

Toward the building.

A student runs past her, face streaked, eyes unfocused.

"Where?" Keisha calls.

The student shakes his head. "I don't know—I don't know—"

He keeps going.

Keisha does not chase the answer.

There is no time.

Another officer reaches her side.

They exchange a glance.

Enough.

No one needs to say what both already understand.

They move toward the entrance.

The front doors stand open.

That feels wrong.

A school entrance should ask something of you—sign in, wait, state your reason, be buzzed through. Today the doors are open as if the building itself has lost the ability to protect its boundaries.

Keisha steps inside.

The air changes—cooler, fluorescent, charged.

The hallway ahead is ordinary in the cruelest way—lockers, posters, a bulletin board announcing spring concert auditions, a water bottle rolling slowly against the wall.

Then another sound.

Deeper inside.

Sharp.

Unmistakable.

Keisha turns toward it.

Her body moves before the thought completes.

This is the shift.

From responding to arriving.

From arriving to entering.

From routine to something else entirely.

Behind her, another officer says, "Move."

She does.

Into the hallway.

Toward the sound.

Toward whatever is still happening.

Toward the moment that will not wait for her to be ready.

Part III—Something Else

Daniel Reyes knows the tone before the words finish. Not the dispatch tone—the other one, the one beneath it, the one that enters a voice when routine is still trying to hold but no longer can.

He is at the ambulance bay, one foot on the running board, restocking trauma supplies from a plastic bin—gauze, tape, gloves, tourniquets—the small inventory of things meant to make catastrophe manageable, at least in pieces.

The radio is on behind him. It always is. Most of the time it becomes background—medical assist, lift assist, chest pain, fall injury, difficulty breathing—address, unit, response—the shape of need repeated until repetition creates distance.

Then the dispatcher says the name of the school.

Daniel looks up, not sharply, just enough.

The next words come through clipped and controlled. "Reports of shots fired. Multiple calls. Unknown injuries."

The bay seems to narrow—not physically, but in function.

The bin of supplies in his hand is no longer inventory.

It is preparation.

Across the bay, his partner Malik stops mid-step. They look at each other. No speech. No need.

Daniel sets the bin down and moves. The body knows before the mind begins arranging thoughts—door open, gear checked, monitor secured, trauma bag, airway kit, extra gloves—more than usual, always more than usual.

Malik climbs into the driver's seat. Daniel takes the passenger side, pulling the door shut as the engine turns over. The ambulance backs out of the bay, then swings toward the street.

The siren rises.

The sound fills the cab.

Daniel reaches for the radio. "Medic 3 responding."

"Copy, Medic 3," dispatch answers. "Stage until cleared. Law enforcement en route."

Stage.

The word lands as instruction and restraint—do not enter, do not rush in, do not become another casualty.

Daniel knows the protocol.

He believes in it.

Mostly.

The ambulance accelerates. Malik drives with both hands steady on the wheel, face forward, jaw set.

"School," he says.

Not a question.

Daniel nods. "Yeah."

Nothing else.

There are conversations that happen on ordinary calls—quick assessments, dark humor, practical reminders, who takes lead, who gets the monitor, whether the last patient cleaned out the good blankets.

Not now.

Now silence does the first work.

The radio continues—more units, more voices, more confirmation.

"Active shooter protocol initiated."

Daniel closes his eyes for half a second, then opens them.

There is no room for reaction.

Not yet.

He begins running through possibilities—triage, hemorrhage control, airway, pediatric patients, adults, multiple victims, scene safety, staging location, transport priority, hospital notification. The list assembles itself, clinical and necessary—a structure to stand inside.

But beneath it is something else.

A school.

Children.

Teachers.

Hallways.

Daniel has been a paramedic long enough to distrust the word prepared. Prepared means you know what bag to grab. It does not mean you are ready.

The ambulance turns hard onto a main road. Cars pull aside unevenly. A delivery truck blocks half the lane before correcting too late. Malik mutters something under his breath—not anger exactly, more release than language.

Daniel watches the road ahead.

His phone buzzes in his pocket—once, then again.

He ignores it.

The world outside the call is already trying to enter.

He will not let it in yet.

Dispatch updates. "Reports of victims near east hallway. Unknown access."

Unknown access.

That matters.

Daniel writes it mentally—east hallway, unknown access.

Then another transmission. "Students exiting north side."

North side.

Movement.

Chaos.

Possible walking wounded.

Possible separated minors.

Possible families arriving.

He reaches back and checks the trauma bag again even though he already knows what is there. His hand rests briefly on the tourniquets—small bands of material, simple, brutal, necessary.

The ambulance approaches the outer edge of the school zone. Sirens overlap now—not just theirs—multiple directions, police, fire, EMS. The sound is familiar, but the convergence is not.

Not like this.

Malik slows before the final turn. "Where are they staging us?"

Daniel listens.

Dispatch answers almost as if hearing the question. "EMS stage at secondary lot until law enforcement clears corridor."

Malik turns.

The school appears through the windshield—brick, glass, flagpole, cars, people running.

The image arrives too fast.

Daniel feels his body narrow into function.

There will be time later for what the image means.

There is only time now for what must be done.

They pull into the designated lot— not close enough, too close—both feel true.

Other units arrive nearly at the same time, vehicles angling into place, doors opening before engines fully settle.

Daniel steps out.

Sound hits immediately—sirens, shouting, radio traffic, a distant noise from the building he refuses to identify until he has to.

A firefighter moves toward them. "Command's setting up here. We're holding until they call us forward."

Holding.

Again.

Daniel nods.

He understands.

He hates it.

The trauma bag hangs from his shoulder—heavy, ready, useless until it isn't.

He watches law enforcement move toward the entrance—fast, tight, directed.

He watches students come out in waves—some running, some walking too slowly, some looking behind them, some not looking at anything at all.

His instincts pull forward—assess, treat, move—but the line holds.

Scene not secure.

Do not enter.

Protocol is not cowardice.

He knows that.

He tells himself that.

More students emerge—a teacher with blood on one sleeve, a boy limping, a girl barefoot.

Daniel takes one step forward before realizing he has done it.

Malik's voice stops him. "Dan."

Not sharp.

Just enough.

Daniel stops.

The firefighter waves the limping boy toward them. "Walking wounded coming your way."

Now there is permission.

Now there is work.

Daniel moves.

The first student reaches him, breathing too fast, face pale, hands shaking. "No, no, I'm okay," the boy says before Daniel asks anything.

Daniel lowers his voice. "I know. I'm just going to check you."

He scans quickly—no obvious bleeding, breathing rapid but clear, shock, maybe sprain, maybe nothing visible.

That means nothing.

"Sit here," Daniel says, guiding him toward the curb. "Stay where I can see you."

Another arrives.

Then another.

The call becomes bodies.

Not numbers.

Not categories.

Bodies.

Faces.

Hands.

Breath.

The radio calls again. "Need EMS forward when cleared. Multiple down inside."

Multiple down.

Inside.

Daniel hears it.

Keeps working.

A girl clutches his sleeve. "My friend is still in there," she says.

Daniel's hand stills for less than a second.

Then resumes.

"What's your name?" he asks.

She does not answer.

"My friend is still in there."

The sentence repeats.

Not information now.

Prayer.

Daniel looks toward the building—law enforcement at the doors, students still coming, the corridor not yet cleared, the line still holding.

Stage until cleared.

He feels the first weight settle then—not guilt, not yet—something earlier, the awareness that need exists beyond reach, that help can be present and still delayed, that training can be right and still feel morally wrong.

He turns back to the girl.

"I hear you," he says.

It is not enough.

It is all he can honestly offer.

Behind him, Malik calls for more supplies.

Daniel moves again—gloves, gauze, assessment, direction—one person, then another.

The routine returns, but changed.

No longer routine.

Something else wearing its shape.

The call had come in as a tone, a voice, a location.

Now it has become a field of need expanding faster than anyone can name.

Daniel keeps working, because that is what he knows, because stopping would mean feeling the distance between where he stands and where he cannot yet go.

And somewhere beyond the doors, the call is still unfolding.

Chapter 6—**Arrival**

Part I—The First Decision

The door is already open. That is the first thing Keisha notices—not the sound, not the movement, the door, open in a way it should not be. A school door is supposed to slow you down, ask a question, require permission. Today it offers none.

She crosses the threshold without breaking stride. The air changes immediately—cooler, still, wrong.

Behind her, two officers move in formation, spacing instinctive, not spoken—one to her left, one slightly back. The geometry of entry forms without instruction. Forward. Scan. Listen.

The hallway stretches ahead—lockers, posters, a bulletin board announcing a fundraiser, normal objects holding their places in a space that is no longer normal.

Then—sound.

A sharp crack further down the corridor. Not imagined. Not mistaken.

Keisha turns toward it. Her body moves before the thought completes.

"Contact front," she says.

Her voice is steady. It needs to be.

They advance—not running, not walking, something between, controlled speed. The floor carries everything—footsteps, echo, the distant sound ahead.

A figure appears at the far end of the hallway, running toward them.

"Police!" Keisha calls. "Stop!"

The figure slows—a student, hands raised, eyes wide. "I don't know—I don't know—"

Keisha reaches him, quick scan—no weapon, no immediate injury.

"Keep moving," she says, guiding him past. "Exit behind us. Go."

He hesitates for half a second. "My friend—"

"Go."

The word is firmer now.

He goes.

Keisha turns back—forward, always forward.

Another sound. Closer.

The hallway branches. Left. Right.

Training speaks: Move toward the sound.

But another voice enters—not external, internal. What if someone is here?

She does not stop. She cannot.

"Left," she says.

They turn.

The corridor narrows. Classroom doors line both sides—some closed, some open.

An open door on the right. Inside—movement.

Keisha slows just enough to see—students pressed low, a teacher at the front, finger to lips. Stillness, held.

Their eyes meet hers for a second.

No words.

The teacher mouths something.

Please.

The request is not clear—stay, help, protect.

All of it.

Keisha feels it, the pull, immediate, strong, human.

But the sound comes again, further down, closer now.

Her body shifts—forward.

She keeps moving.

The teacher's eyes follow her. The door remains open. The room remains behind her.

The first decision has already been made.

Ahead—a body in the hallway.

Keisha stops, not fully, just enough.

A student on the ground, not moving.

Blood.

Not contained.

Her body leans toward them—instinct, immediate.

Help.

The word arrives without language.

But the sound comes again, from further ahead, active, present.

Training overrides.

"Hold," she says to the officer behind her.

She moves past the student.

The decision cuts—not physically, internally.

She feels it as she passes, as if stepping over something that should not be stepped over.

Forward.

The hallway turns again.

Another officer joins from a side entrance. Four now. Formation adjusts. No one speaks.

Another classroom, door closed, hands visible through the small window, pressed against the glass.

A muffled voice: "Please—"

Keisha does not stop.

The word follows her.

Another sound, closer, immediate.

A figure appears at the end of the hall—not running, not still.

Weapon.

Keisha raises hers. Everything narrows—sight, breath, time.

Commands—clear, loud. "Drop it!"

The figure moves, not compliant.

Everything that follows happens inside a space that does not measure in seconds.

Action.

Response.

Force.

Then—silence.

Not total, but different.

The immediate threat is gone, or seems to be.

Keisha holds position, weapon still raised, breath controlled.

"Clear," someone says.

The word moves through the team, not relief, not yet.

Keisha lowers her weapon slightly, just enough.

Then she turns back the way she came.

The hallway is the same and not.

The student on the floor—still there.

The open classroom—still there.

The closed doors—hands still visible.

Everything waiting.

Now the decisions change.

She moves to the student first, drops to a knee, hands already moving—pressure, assessment.

"Stay with me," she says, even if she does not know if they can.

Another officer moves to the classroom, opens the door. "Police."

The room exhales, not loudly, but completely.

More movement now, controlled, directed.

Keisha presses down on the wound. Blood slows—not enough, but some.

"Medic!" someone calls.

The word carries down the hallway, out the door, across the distance.

The line between inside and outside begins to shift.

Keisha does not look up, does not track it.

Her world is here—this student, this moment, this pressure.

But inside her, something has already started.

The first decision—to move past, to not stop, to leave help for later.

It does not feel like a decision now.

It feels like something that will return.

Later.

But not yet.

Now there is only this.

Arrival is not a single moment. It is a series of choices made too quickly, held too long.

And the first one has already been made.

Part II—The Hallway of Choices

The hallway does not settle after the first contact. It shifts—not calmer, rearranged.

Keisha feels it as she stands, not in the air, but in the way her body no longer tracks one direction. Forward is no longer the only answer.

"Clear left," an officer says. "Clear right."

Voices return—controlled, professional, but carrying something underneath.

Keisha moves back down the hallway, past the point where the first decision was made.

The student she stepped over is still there—still not moving, still bleeding.

She drops to her knees beside them. No hesitation now.

Hands move—pressure, locate the source. Too much blood. Too fast.

"Stay with me," she says again. The words come out the same. They do not mean the same.

The student's eyes flicker, barely, but enough.

"Good," she says, even if she does not know if it is true.

Behind her, another officer opens the classroom door she passed earlier. "Police. You're okay. Stay where you are."

The words are both true and not.

A sound comes from inside the room—not crying, not speaking, release.

Keisha presses harder. Her hands are slick now. Grip shifting. Adjust. Hold.

"Where's EMS?" someone calls.

"Staged," another voice answers. "Waiting for clearance."

The word again—waiting.

Keisha feels something tighten in her chest—not panic, not fear, friction.

The student's breathing changes—shallow, uneven.

"Stay with me," she says again. She keeps saying it, because saying something is better than silence.

Another officer appears at the far end of the hallway. "More down in the next corridor."

The words land—not new, but heavier.

Keisha does not look up, not immediately.

Her hands are here. This person is here.

"Go," she says to the officer behind her. "Check it."

The officer moves without question.

The hallway fills with movement now—not chaotic, but layered.

Doors opening. Voices calling. Students emerging—some walking, some carried.

A girl stands in the doorway of the classroom—the one Keisha passed.

She is holding onto the frame, not stepping out, not going back.

"Hey," Keisha says, her voice softer now, different.

The girl does not move. Her eyes are fixed.

"My teacher said stay," she says.

Keisha nods. "Stay is good. You're doing exactly right."

The girl looks down—at the student on the floor, at the blood.

Her grip tightens on the doorframe.

"Look at me," Keisha says.

The girl doesn't.

"Hey."

This time she does.

"Stay in the room. Okay?"

A pause. Then a small nod.

The girl steps back. The door remains open.

Keisha returns her focus to the student—pressure, still bleeding, less, but not enough.

Her training runs through options—tourniquet, bandage, stabilize—but she has only what she brought in, what she carries.

"Need a kit!" she calls.

An officer tosses something toward her—basic supplies, not enough, but something.

She works. Hands moving. Steps practiced.

Behind her, the hallway continues to change.

Another student passes, supported by two others.

"Sit them down there!" someone calls.

A makeshift triage begins to form without naming itself.

This one breathing. That one not. This one walking. That one still.

Categories form—not spoken, understood.

Keisha feels it—the shift again.

Now it is not just one person.

It is many.

Her mind begins to divide—time, attention, need.

She looks down at the student under her hands, then up at the hallway.

Three more, closer now, all needing something.

Her chest tightens, not from fear, from weight.

Who first?

The question arrives fully now, not theoretical, immediate.

She answers without thinking—the one in front of her.

Because she is already here.

Because leaving would cost something she cannot measure.

But the others—

The thought does not finish.

"Stay with me," she says again, to the student, to herself.

Another officer kneels beside a second victim further down.

The hallway becomes a line of moments, each one demanding, each one incomplete.

"EMS coming in!" someone calls.

The words move through the space like a release valve.

Footsteps behind, different, heavier, faster.

Keisha does not look up, not yet.

Her hands are still here.

The student's breathing shifts again—weaker.

"No," she says quietly, not to anyone else.

She adjusts pressure, changes angle, holds.

The world narrows again to this, to now.

But the question remains.

Who first.

Who next.

Who waits.

It will not leave.

Even when help arrives, even when hands multiply, even when the hallway fills with more skill, more supplies, more structure.

The question has already taken hold.

Keisha presses down harder.

"Stay with me," she says again.

Because it is the only answer she has right now.

And because every decision is already becoming something she will have to remember.

Part III—Who Waits

Daniel enters when the hallway has already become more than one scene. That is the first thing he understands—not consciously, professionally. There is no single center, no one place where the need gathers neatly enough to be handled in order. The need is everywhere.

"Medic coming through!" The call moves ahead of him, not loud enough to silence the hallway—nothing could—but enough to clear a narrow path.

Daniel moves with the trauma bag against his side, gloves already on, eyes scanning before his knees ever bend. Airway. Breathing. Bleeding. Movement. Stillness. He reads bodies the way he has been trained to read scenes, but training does not make it simple. It only gives him a way to begin.

Keisha is on the floor halfway down the corridor, both hands pressed hard against a student's wound. Her arms are locked. Her shoulders tense. Blood has darkened the cuffs of her sleeves.

Daniel recognizes the posture immediately—someone holding more than they can hold for long.

He drops beside her. "What do you have?"

Keisha does not look up. "Bleeding. Slowing, but not enough."

Daniel opens the bag—gauze, pressure dressing, tourniquet ready. He moves quickly, not roughly.

"Keep pressure," he says.

"I am."

There is no irritation in her voice, only strain. He hears it, does not answer it. There is no time.

The student's breathing is shallow, pulse fast, skin pale. Daniel's hands move—assess, pack, press, secure. The sequence gives the moment a shape, but only a small one.

Behind him, someone calls, "We've got another one over here!" Another voice: "This one's conscious!" Another: "Need help!"

The hallway pulls at him from three directions at once.

Daniel does not turn yet. He cannot treat everyone by looking at everyone. He stabilizes the person under his hands. That has to be enough for the next breath, then the next.

Keisha looks at him then, just briefly. Her eyes ask what her mouth does not—is this enough, will they live, did I do the right thing?

Daniel knows all three questions. He cannot answer any of them.

"Hold here," he says, guiding her hands to the dressing.

She nods.

He shifts his weight, preparing to move.

Her hand catches his sleeve, not hard, just enough.

“There are more,” she says.

“I know.”

The words come out quieter than he expects, because he does know, and knowing is not the same as reaching.

He stands.

The hallway tilts into layers—a student sitting against the lockers, rocking slightly; another lying near the intersection; a teacher on the floor with one hand raised, trying to direct attention away from herself; children gathered inside an open classroom, faces pale, bodies pressed together.

Daniel points. “You—keep pressure there.” An officer nods. “You—keep them seated.” Another nod. “Anyone walking, move them to the far wall unless they’re bleeding heavily.”

The instructions assemble a little order. Not enough, but some. Order is never enough. It is only the first mercy.

He reaches the student near the intersection. No movement. He kneels. Checks—airway, breathing, pulse. Nothing obvious at first. Then something faint, present, barely.

“Need transport priority here,” he calls.

His voice carries differently now—sharper, command shaped by urgency.

A firefighter appears beside him. “What do you need?”

“Backboard if we can get it. Bleeding control first. Then move.”

The firefighter nods and goes.

Daniel works. The student beneath him is small—not a child like Lila, but young enough that the difference does not help, young enough that Daniel’s mind refuses to complete certain thoughts. He keeps them clinical—pulse, pressure, airway, response—not name, not age, not someone’s child, not yet.

A voice from behind him breaks through. "My friend—please—she's over there—please—"

Daniel does not turn, not immediately, because turning costs attention, because attention is treatment, because treatment is time.

The voice continues. "She was right behind me—please—"

Daniel closes his eyes for half a second—not to escape, to stay precise.

Then he opens them. "Show another responder. Not me. I'm here."

The words are correct.

They feel cruel.

The voice breaks.

Daniel does not follow it.

He cannot.

Keisha hears it from where she kneels—the plea, the refusal, the correctness of it, the cruelty of it, all at once. She keeps her hands where Daniel placed them—pressure, hold, do not move.

The student beneath her makes a sound—small, human.

Keisha leans closer. "I'm here," she says.

It is true.

And not enough.

More responders enter. The hallway becomes crowded with skill—gloves, bags, radios, commands. Every person moving with purpose, and still the need exceeds them.

That is the part no training fully prepares for—not the blood, not the noise, the excess, the fact that even good response can be smaller than the harm.

Daniel moves again—from one body to another, from one assessment to the next.

This one can wait.

This one cannot.

This one is breathing.

This one needs pressure.

This one needs transport now.

The categories come quickly. They have to. But every category is a sentence someone will live inside—or not.

He reaches the teacher with her hand raised.

"I'm okay," she says before he asks.

Her face says otherwise.

"Let me check."

"No," she says, turning her head toward the classroom. "Them first."

Daniel follows her gaze—students, huddled, watching, waiting.

He looks back at her.

"You're bleeding."

"They're scared."

"So are you."

She gives the smallest laugh—not humor, recognition.

Daniel places gauze against her arm. "Hold this," he says.

She obeys, not because she is convinced, because being given a task is easier than needing help.

He knows that too.

The radio crackles from somewhere behind him. "Transport ready."

Good.

Not enough.

But good.

Daniel points to the student near the intersection. "That one first."

Then he looks toward Keisha. "And that one next."

Keisha's eyes lift. She hears the ranking—first, next—not because one matters more, because time forces sequence, because bodies cannot be carried all at once, because help, even when present, arrives one person at a time.

The student near the intersection is lifted—careful, fast.

The hallway adjusts around the movement. People step back. Doors close slightly. Voices lower as if volume might disturb the fragile thread between life and loss.

Daniel stays beside the stretcher until it turns the corner.

Then he returns.

Already scanning.

Already choosing.

Again.

Keisha is still kneeling. Her arms tremble now—not visibly to everyone, but Daniel sees it.

"Switch," he says.

She resists for half a second, then lets him take over.

Her hands lift away slowly—red, shaking.

She stares at them.

Daniel presses down where she had been holding.

"You did good," he says.

She looks at him.

The words do not land.

Not yet.

Maybe not ever.

"Did I?" she asks.

The question is quiet, too quiet for the hallway.

Daniel keeps pressure. "Yes," he says.

He does not know if she believes him.

He is not sure he believes any word that simple.

But he says it anyway.

Because sometimes care begins with a sentence that cannot carry everything but must carry something.

Outside, another siren arrives.

Inside, another voice calls for help.

The hallway keeps widening—not physically, morally.

Every choice opens another.

Every answer leaves something unanswered.

Who first.

Who next.

Who waits.

Daniel moves when called.

Keisha stands because someone tells her to stand.

A student is carried past.

Another remains.

The building holds all of it—the urgency, the skill, the limits.

And beneath the movement, beneath the commands, beneath the effort to save whoever can still be saved, something quieter begins to form.

Not blame.

Not yet.

A record.

A ledger written in seconds.

In hands.

In bodies passed and bodies reached.

Arrival is not the end of danger.

It is the beginning of choosing inside it.

And some of those choices will keep arriving long after the hallway is empty.

Chapter 7—The Last Sound

Part I—After It Stops

The last shot does not announce itself as the last. It sounds like the others—sharp, final, unmistakable. Then—nothing.

The hallway does not change immediately. Bodies still move. Hands still press. Voices still call, because the body does not trust silence, not yet.

Keisha hears it before she understands it—the absence, the space where the sound should be. Her head turns slightly, as if she might catch something she missed, another shot, another movement, something to confirm the pattern is over.

Nothing comes.

"Did you hear—"

The voice stops. No one finishes the question.

Daniel does not look up. His hands are still on the student—pressure, hold, check, again.

"Keep breathing," he says. The words sound louder now, not because his voice changed, but because the hallway has.

Silence is not quiet. It has weight. It presses.

The radios continue, but even they sound different—lower, more contained.

"Suspect down."

The words come through, not declared, not celebrated, reported.

Keisha hears it, does not react, not outwardly. Her hands are still moving, still working, still inside the moment that began before the silence.

"Confirm."

A pause, then: "Confirmed."

The word settles into the space, heavy, unmoving.

The threat is over.

The sentence forms. It does not land.

Because the hallway is still full—of bodies, of blood, of breath that is not steady, of voices that are not finished.

A student cries out, not loud, not continuous, a single sound, then nothing. It echoes more than it should.

Keisha looks down. The student beneath her is still there, still breathing, barely.

"Stay with me," she says again. The words do not change. They feel different.

The urgency has shifted. Not gone. Changed.

Before, it was forward—toward, into, find the sound.

Now it is here—stay, hold, do not lose what is still present.

Daniel feels it in his hands, the difference. The pressure he applies now is not against active harm. It is against what remains of it.

"EMS inside," someone calls.

Footsteps move through the hallway—different now, less urgent, more directed. Stretchers. Kits. Voices that know what to do next.

The structure begins to form.

But the silence stays.

It fills the spaces between words, between movements, between breaths.

A teacher steps into the hallway, slow, uncertain. "Is it—" She stops, does not finish.

An officer nods once.

The teacher exhales, but not fully.

Relief does not arrive.

Because relief requires certainty.

And certainty does not exist here.

Only absence.

The absence of gunfire.

Lila hears it from inside the closet—not the last shot, the lack of the next one. Her body notices before her mind does.

The waiting changes.

She listens harder.

Nothing.

The silence stretches, different from before.

Before, it held something—hidden, moving.

Now it holds everything that has already happened.

Stay quiet.

The rule remains, even without the sound that required it.

No one moves.

Because silence could break at any moment.

Lila's breath comes back slowly, carefully, as if the air itself might make noise.

A voice outside—different now.

"Police."

The word reaches the door, through it, around it.

No one responds.

Because the rule has not changed.

Stay quiet.

Another voice, closer. "You're safe."

The words stop at the door.

They do not enter.

Safety is not something that can be heard, not yet.

Lila does not move.

Her hand is still on her chest, her body still pressed into the space she has made for herself.

The light under the door remains, unbroken.

Time stretches again.

Then—a knock.

Not loud.

But enough.

Everything inside her tightens again.

The silence shifts.

Keisha hears the knock from down the hallway, turns her head.

"Clear the rooms," someone says.

The words begin to move outward through the building—doors opening, voices entering spaces that have been closed too long.

Daniel lifts his hands briefly, repositions, applies new pressure.

"Stay with me," he says again.

The words continue, even after the reason for them has changed.

The hallway fills with more people, more movement, more sound.

But underneath it, the silence remains.

Not empty.

Full.

Holding everything that just ended and everything that has not yet begun.

The last shot has already happened.

But the moment it created is still here.

And no one yet knows what to do with what comes after it stops.

Part II—Not Relief

The word spreads faster than understanding—"Confirmed," then "Threat down," then "Scene transitioning." Each phrase moves through the hallway, through radios, through bodies still crouched behind doors, beneath desks, inside closets, pressed into corners, held by fear long after the sound has stopped. The words are supposed to change something. They do, but not enough.

Keisha hears them and keeps her hands where they are. The student beneath her is still breathing, still losing color, still caught between staying and leaving. The silence does not make that less true. If anything, it makes it sharper.

Before, the gunfire had filled the hallway with direction—move toward, stop the threat, find the sound. Now that sound is gone, and everything left behind has become visible. Everything asks at once.

She looks up, for the first time, really looks. The hallway is no longer a line. It is a field—a body near the lockers, a teacher seated against the wall holding gauze to her own arm, a student standing barefoot in the middle of the corridor as if waiting for someone to tell her how to leave, another student sitting with knees drawn up, staring at nothing, open doors, closed doors, hands visible through narrow windows, faces behind glass, breathing, crying, silence.

Too much silence.

"Keisha," someone says.

She turns. An officer she knows is standing over her, one hand extended.

"I've got this. EMS is here."

She does not move immediately. Her hands remain pressed to the dressing.

"I've got it," he says again.

She nods, lets go slowly. Her fingers lift one at a time, reluctant, as if pressure has become the only thing keeping the world in place.

When she stands, her knees feel uncertain.

The officer drops beside the student.

Daniel appears behind him, already reaching in, already asking questions.

Keisha steps back. Only one step.

It feels like leaving.

Daniel does not experience the silence as silence. He experiences it as space—a dangerous kind of space. The hallway has opened now, not because the harm is over, but because everyone can hear what remains. The absence of gunfire makes room for sounds that had been covered before—a low moan, someone calling a name, a radio repeating instructions, a child whispering, "Can I go home now?"

Daniel hears all of it and cannot answer any of it.

He kneels beside the student Keisha had been holding. Pressure dressing. Pulse. Airway. Skin. Transport. The sequence returns.

Thank God for sequence.

"Ready to move?" someone asks.

"Not yet," Daniel says.

He adjusts the dressing, checks the bleeding, makes the call inside himself— not first, not yet, soon.

Every decision now has a shadow.

Who first.

Who next.

Who waits.

He has made those decisions before—accidents, fires, storms, multi-car pileups—but this is different. The injuries are not the only thing being sorted. So is the meaning of response.

He can feel eyes on him—students, teachers, officers, the living waiting for him to tell them, without saying it, who is in danger and who can wait.

He hates that part.

He does it anyway.

"You," he says to a firefighter, "stay with this one. If the bleeding picks up, call me immediately."

The firefighter nods.

Daniel stands and turns toward the next voice.

Inside the music room closet, Lila hears the words before she trusts them—"Police," then "You're safe." The words reach her like something from another room, another world, another language.

Safe.

The word does not fit inside the closet.

The closet has rules—stay quiet, stay small, do not move, do not make sound.

Safe belongs somewhere else—morning, home, the back seat of her mother's car, a blanket pulled under her chin, not here, not with her foot asleep and her chest tight and the light under the door still holding her attention like a command.

No one opens the door yet.

No one inside moves.

The rule still holds because no one has told them what replaces it.

A knock comes—soft, too soft.

"Police," the voice says again. "If you can hear me, stay where you are. We're coming in."

The classroom door opens first, not the closet. Sound changes outside—the room sound, larger than the closet sound, footsteps, a voice telling people to keep their hands visible, a teacher crying, someone saying, "It's okay," in a way that does not make it okay.

Then light widens.

The closet door opens slowly.

Too bright.

Lila turns her face away, not because she wants to hide, because the light is too much.

A person kneels in front of them, not close enough to touch, close enough to see.

“You’re okay,” the person says.

Lila looks at the badge, the uniform, the mouth moving.

She does not answer.

The person’s voice softens. “You can come out now.”

Can.

Not must.

The word matters.

But her body does not believe it yet.

The others begin to move first—knees unfolding, shoes scraping, small bodies becoming larger again. Someone sobs openly now, as if the permission to move has also become permission to make sound.

Lila stays where she is.

The officer does not rush her.

That matters too.

After a moment, her foot sends a sharp line of pain up her leg as feeling returns. She gasps.

The sound escapes before she can stop it.

Her eyes widen.

No one reacts.

Nothing happens.

The officer only says, “I know. Slow.”

Slow.

That word fits better than safe.

Lila moves one hand, then the other, then finally begins to come out.

Marcus stands outside the building when the sound stops. He does not know it is the last one, not at first. He only notices that the next one does not come.

People around him keep moving. Some cry into phones. Some call names. Some stare at the doors. A teacher nearby repeats a student’s name over and over, not loudly, as if volume might make the answer worse.

Marcus watches the entrance. Students continue to come out—some walking, some helped, some carried. Each emergence changes the shape of the waiting crowd. Each absence changes it too.

A man beside him says, “Is it over?”

No one answers.

The question feels dangerous, as if saying yes might summon sound back into the world.

Marcus looks at his hands. They are no longer shaking as much.

That feels wrong.

His body is calming before his mind has agreed to it.

He looks toward the building again.

A stretcher appears.

Then another.

The crowd shifts backward, not from instruction, from recognition.

Marcus tries not to look.

He looks.

He tries to identify faces.

He fails.

He is relieved.

He is ashamed of the relief.

The thought comes again, faint but present: someone could be out there.

Now the phrase is no longer about the hallway.

It is about every door he passed, every voice he did not answer, every person not yet accounted for.

Sarah is not there yet.

No one has reached him.

His phone is in his pocket.

He has not looked at it.

He cannot make himself.

Because the moment he checks it, the world will become specific—names, questions, messages, proof that time has continued outside what happened.

He keeps watching the doors instead.

The silence outside is not quiet either.

It is sirens without urgency, radios without clarity, parents arriving without answers, students speaking in fragments, a town gathering around an absence and calling it news.

Marcus hears someone say, "They got him."

Another voice: "Thank God."

Marcus understands the words.

He does not feel what they seem to require.

Thank God.

For what?

That it stopped?

That it happened?

That some are out?

That some are not?

The words do not settle.

They scatter.

Keisha stands in the hallway with her hands red and empty.

That is when the silence reaches her—not when the gunfire stops, not when the radio confirms, now, when no one needs her weapon raised, when no one needs her moving forward, when her hands are no longer doing something that explains them.

She looks down.

Blood in the creases of her fingers, under her nails, on the heel of her palm.

Someone passes her with equipment.

She steps aside, too slowly.

"Officer?" a voice says.

She looks up.

A girl stands in the classroom doorway, the same girl, the one whose teacher told her to stay.

"Can we go now?" the girl asks.

Keisha opens her mouth.

The answer should be simple.

But it isn't.

Not yet.

Not here.

"In a minute," Keisha says.

The girl nods, accepts it, because children accept temporary answers when adults sound certain enough.

Keisha watches her step back into the room.

Then she looks down the hallway—at Daniel kneeling, at stretchers moving, at doors opening, at the place where the sound had been.

The gunfire has stopped.

But nothing feels over.

Not in the hallway.

Not in her body.

Not in the choices already beginning to take root.

Relief does not arrive.

Something else does.

A silence large enough to hold everything that remains.

Part III—What Remains in the Silence

The building does not exhale all at once.

It releases in pieces.

A door opening here.
A voice rising there.
A stretcher rolling past.

Each one small. Each one incomplete.

Daniel feels it as interruption.

Not relief.

Never relief.

Interruption.

He is midway through an assessment when someone touches his shoulder.

"Another one in the next room."

He looks up.

Just long enough to register direction.

Then back down.

"This one first," he says.

The responder nods.

Moves on.

The hallway continues to divide itself.

Into before.

And after.

Before the silence—

everything moved toward stopping.

After the silence—

everything moves toward deciding.

Daniel presses down.

Checks again.

Pulse.

Still there.

"Okay," he says.

Not to anyone.

To the body beneath his hands.

He signals.

"Ready to move."

The stretcher comes in.

Metal against tile.

Sound sharper than it should be.

They lift.

Careful.

Fast.

The student's arm falls slightly to the side.

Daniel adjusts it.

Places it back.

The smallness of that action stays with him longer than it should.

They move past him.

Out of his space.

Into someone else's.

He stands.

Already turning.

Already choosing again.

The next room is worse.

Not in volume.

In stillness.

Two bodies.

One moving.

One not.

The moving one sees him.

Reaches.

Daniel goes to them first.

Not because he doesn't see the other.

Because he does.

"Hey," he says.

His voice is lower now.

Closer.

"I'm here."

The student's hand grips his sleeve.

Hard.

"Don't go," they say.

"I'm not going anywhere."

The sentence is true.

And not.

He works.

Quick.

Focused.

Bleeding.

Breathing.

Response.

Behind him, another responder kneels by the second body.

No words.

Daniel hears it anyway.

The absence.

He keeps working.

Because stopping would mean knowing too much too soon.

Keisha walks.

That is new.

Not running.

Not advancing.

Walking.

Her hands hang at her sides.

Empty.

She looks into rooms now.

One at a time.

Faces.

Bodies.

Movement.

Stillness.

Each room asks something different.

"Officer—"

A teacher reaches for her.

"They need help."

"I know," Keisha says.

The words feel insufficient the moment they leave her mouth.

Because knowing is not helping.

Because seeing is not fixing.

Because being here is not enough for what is here.

She steps inside.

The room smells different.

Metal.

Fabric.

Something else.

She moves to a student in the corner.

“You’re okay,” she says.

The words come automatically.

The student shakes their head.

“No.”

Keisha does not correct them.

Because she cannot.

She kneels.

Her body remembers what to do.

Even when her mind cannot hold it.

Hands steady.

Voice low.

Presence.

The student leans toward her.

Not fully.

Just enough.

Keisha feels it.

The transfer.

Of fear.

Of need.

Of something that has nowhere else to go.

“I’ve got you,” she says.

The sentence lands.

For now.

Outside, Marcus steps closer.

The line has moved.

Not officially.

Naturally.

People press forward.

Then stop.

Then press again.

No one knows where they are supposed to be.

A parent calls out a name.

Again.

Again.

No answer.

Marcus feels the silence differently now.

Before, it was waiting.

Now, it is counting.

Who comes out.

Who does not.

A stretcher passes.

He looks.

He cannot stop himself.

The face is covered.

He looks away.

Too late.

The image stays.

His phone vibrates again.

He pulls it out this time.

Messages.

So many.

Are you okay?
Where are you?
Call me.
Please call me.

One name stops him.

Sarah.

He opens it.

"Marcus where are you"

No punctuation.

That tells him everything.

His hands shake again.

He types.

Stops.

Deletes.

Types again.

"I'm outside"

He sends it.

The message goes.

Something shifts.

The world is becoming specific.

Names.

Connections.

Consequences.

He looks back at the building.

Someone could be out there.

Now the thought has weight.

Not abstract.

Personal.

Inside, the hallway continues.

Not quieter.

Not calmer.

More defined.

Every action now leaves a mark.

Daniel moves between them.

This one stabilized.

That one not.

This one waiting.

That one beyond waiting.

He does not say the last category out loud.

He cannot.

But it exists.

And it grows.

Not in number.

In recognition.

Keisha feels it too.

In the rooms she enters.

In the ones she leaves.

In the ones she avoids looking into for one second too long.

The silence holds all of it.

Not empty.

Full.

Full of decisions already made.

Full of ones still coming.

The last sound is gone.

But what it opened remains.

And every step they take now

is inside that opening.

A space where nothing is loud enough to guide them.

And everything is loud enough

to stay.

Part II—The Fracture

Chapter 8—**Someone Chose This**

Part I—The Shape of Intention

Marcus does not understand it at first, not fully. He understands that it happened. He understands the sound, the running, the doors, the waiting, the stretchers, the way people say names like they are trying to pull someone back into the world. But he does not yet understand this: someone chose it.

He stands near the edge of the parking lot now, far enough from the building to see it whole, close enough that every ambulance arrival still hits his chest like a second impact. The school looks the same. That is the problem. Brick. Windows. Flag. Nothing about it shows what is inside. Nothing about it marks what just happened.

A reporter's voice drifts somewhere nearby. " . . . still unfolding . . . " " . . . suspect believed to be . . . " " . . . community in shock . . . "

Shock. Marcus hears the word. It feels like something he has already left behind.

His phone buzzes again. Sarah. "Where are you exactly" He types faster this time. "by the south lot near the buses" He sends it, watches the message go, watches the screen as if something else might follow immediately. It doesn't.

A man nearby is pacing. "Who would do this?" he says, not to anyone, to the air, to the silence, to the absence of an answer.

Marcus feels something shift, not in his body, deeper.

Before, everything had been reaction—move, hide, wait, survive. Now there is space, and inside that space something begins to form.

Who would do this?

The question lands differently than the others. Not like Is it over? Not like Are they safe? This one points somewhere. Toward a person.

Marcus turns his head, looks back at the building. Someone was in there. Not hiding. Not waiting. Moving. Choosing.

The thought does not arrive all at once. It assembles, piece by piece.

They walked in. They brought something with them. They raised it. They aimed. They pulled. Again. Again. Again.

Marcus feels it in his chest—a tightening, different from fear, hotter.

A student stumbles past him, supported by two others. "He just—he just—" The sentence breaks.

Marcus watches them go. The image stays, not abstract, not distant.

Someone did that.

The thought becomes a sentence, clear, complete.

Someone chose this.

His hands curl slightly. He doesn't notice at first. His breath changes—not shallow, not panicked, sharper.

A voice behind him says, "They caught him, right?" Another answers, "I think so."

Marcus turns. "Where is he?" he asks.

The question surprises him.

The person shrugs. "I don't know."

Marcus nods, but the question does not leave.

Where is he?

Not what happened. Not who got hurt.

Where is the one who did it?

The direction of his thinking has shifted—from inward to outward, from survival to source.

Sarah appears at the edge of the lot. He sees her before she sees him. She is moving fast, not running, but close. Her eyes scan the crowd, searching.

Marcus lifts his hand. She sees him. Everything in her body changes at once—relief.

She reaches him. "Are you okay?"

The question lands.

Marcus nods. "I'm okay."

The words feel strange, incomplete.

Sarah steps closer, checks him without touching, eyes scanning for something she cannot name. "I couldn't—" she starts, then stops.

Marcus nods again. "I know."

They stand there, close, not touching, the space between them filled with everything that just happened.

Sarah exhales, finally. "They said it's over," she says.

Marcus looks at her. "Is it?" he asks.

She hesitates. "I mean—the shooting—"

Marcus shakes his head. "That's not what I mean."

Sarah studies him. "What do you mean?"

Marcus looks back at the building. “They chose it,” he says.

The words come out flat, not emotional, too clear.

Sarah follows his gaze. “Marcus—”

“They chose to do that,” he says again.

His voice shifts now, not louder, sharper. “They walked in and did that to people.”

The sentence hangs between them.

Sarah does not answer right away, because there is no answer, not one that fits.

“I know,” she says finally.

Marcus shakes his head again. “No—you don’t.”

The words are not cruel. They are not meant to be. They are precise.

“Knowing and—knowing are different,” he says.

He struggles for the second word, does not find it.

“Someone decided to do that,” he says instead.

Sarah watches him carefully now. Something has changed. The shock is thinning, and underneath it something else is taking its place.

Anger.

Not explosive. Not loud.

Focused.

Marcus feels it settle, not as a reaction, as a position.

“They didn’t have to,” he says.

The sentence lands harder than anything else he has said.

"They didn't have to."

Sarah steps closer. "I know," she says again, this time softer.

Marcus's hands tighten fully now. He feels it. Does not release it.

"They chose it," he says one more time.

The words are no longer discovery. They are declaration.

Around them, the scene continues—sirens, stretchers, voices—but for Marcus, the center has shifted. Not the building. Not the victims.

The decision.

The moment someone said yes to something that should never be yes.

And now that he sees it, he cannot unsee it.

Shock had protected him, blunted the edges, made everything feel unreal. But this—this is real.

Someone chose it.

And that truth does not fade.

It sharpens.

And it stays.

Part II—The Turn Toward Anger

Keisha does not feel it all at once. Anger does not arrive like the gunfire did. It builds—quiet, layered.

At first, there is only motion—room to room, door to door. "Police." "Anyone here?" "Hands where I can see them." The words come easily. They still belong. They still do something.

But underneath, something is shifting.

She enters another classroom—desks pushed aside, backpacks scattered, a chair overturned. A student sits in the corner, not crying, not moving.

Keisha approaches slowly. "Hey," she says.

The student does not look up.

"I'm Officer Turner," she says.

No response.

She kneels. "You're okay now."

The words land, but they do not settle.

The student finally looks at her—eyes wide, not empty, full, too full.

"He just—" the student says, then stops.

Keisha waits.

The student tries again. "He looked at us."

The sentence lands harder than anything Keisha has heard yet. Not he fired. Not he came in. He looked. At us.

Keisha feels it—a shift. Something in her chest tightens, then sharpens.

"What's your name?" she asks.

The question is instinct.

"Lena," the student says.

"Lena," Keisha repeats.

The name anchors the moment.

"He just looked at us," Lena says again, as if saying it might make it different.

Keisha nods. "I hear you."

She does not say anything else, because there is nothing else that fits.

She stands and moves into the hallway again.

The sounds are different now—less urgent, more broken, fragments of speech, pieces of story.

"He came in—"
"—I thought it was—"
"—we hid—"

Each one incomplete. Each one pointing in the same direction—toward a person.

Keisha feels it now, clearly. Not just what happened, but who did it.

She walks past the spot where the first body had been. It is empty now. Only a smear remains, evidence of something that had been there, of something she stepped over.

The memory hits differently now—not as a decision, as a consequence.

She had moved past because she had to, because that was the order of things.

But now there is space to feel it.

And in that space, the question changes.

Not Did I do the right thing?

But Who made this necessary?

Her jaw tightens.

Her pace slows.

For the first time since entering, she is not moving toward something.

She is standing inside it.

Daniel feels it differently—not in a moment, in accumulation.

Every patient. Every wound. Every face.

Each one adds something, not just to the work, to the understanding.

He moves to another student. "What's your name?"

"Carlos."

"Carlos, I'm Daniel. I'm going to help you."

The script holds, but beneath it a second layer forms.

Why Carlos?

Why this hallway?

Why today?

The questions do not belong to treatment, but they arrive anyway.

He pushes them aside. Focus—bleeding, breathing, stabilize.

But the thoughts do not leave.

They wait.

For space.

He finishes with Carlos, moves to the next.

A teacher this time.

"I'm fine," she says immediately.

She is not.

"I need you to sit," Daniel says.

She shakes her head. "My students—"

"I know," he says.

The words come faster now, more force behind them.

"Sit."

She does, not because she agrees, because she recognizes the tone.

Daniel kneels.

His hands are steady, but something inside him is not.

He looks at the wound, then at her face, then away, because something about this—this combination—is too much.

He returns to the work, but the thought is there now.

Someone did this.

Not an accident. Not a storm. Not a failure of structure.

A decision.

Repeated.

Marcus feels it settle fully, not as a flash, as a stance.

He watches the building, every person who comes out, every stretcher, every pause. Each one feeds the same realization.

They chose it.

Not once.

Again and again.

He imagines it now, not because he wants to, because he cannot stop—walking in, seeing people, knowing, continuing.

The anger sharpens—not explosive, directed.

He feels it in his hands, his jaw, his breath.

Sarah watches him. "Marcus," she says.

He doesn't look at her.

"They didn't have to," he says again.

The sentence has become fixed, a truth he cannot move past.

"They didn't have to."

Sarah steps closer. "I know," she says.

But this time Marcus hears something different—not agreement, distance.

Because she does not feel it the same way, not yet.

He turns to her.

"They chose it," he says.

The words are harder now.

"They chose to do that to people."

Sarah nods slowly. "I know."

Marcus shakes his head.

"No," he says. "Knowing and—knowing are different."

He cannot finish the thought, but he does not need to, because the anger is finishing it for him.

Inside, Keisha reaches the far end of the hallway, the place where it ended, the place where the last sound came from.

It is quieter here, not peaceful, contained.

An officer stands nearby. "Suspect is down," he says.

Keisha nods, does not move closer, does not need to see, because she already knows enough, because the details will not change the truth.

Someone stood here.

And chose.

Again.

And again.

She feels it fully now, not confusion, not shock, anger—cold, precise, not about what happened, about who made it happen.

Daniel feels it as he stands again between patients, between decisions, the moment where there is nothing immediate to do, just enough space for thought.

And the thought arrives.

Someone chose this.

He exhales, not release, recognition, then moves again, because the work is not done, because the anger has nowhere to go, not yet.

But it is there now.

In all of them.

Different shapes.

Different speeds.

Same center.

The shift from shock to anger is not loud. It does not announce itself.

It settles.

And once it settles, it does not leave.

Part III—The Weight of Knowing

The understanding does not stop where the anger begins. It deepens, spreads, settles into places that were still protected a moment ago.

Lila feels it differently than the others. She does not have the words for it, not yet, but she feels the change.

She is sitting against the wall now, outside the classroom, knees pulled close, arms wrapped around them. The hallway is louder than the closet had been, brighter, more open, but none of it feels safer.

A woman kneels in front of her. “Can you tell me your name?”

Lila hesitates. The question feels larger than it should.

“Lila,” she says.

The woman smiles gently. “Lila, I’m here to help you.”

Lila nods, but her eyes drift back to the classroom, back to the door, back to the place where the rule had been—stay quiet.

The rule had made sense. It had held everything together.

Now there is no rule.

Only voices. Movement. Hands reaching.

And something else.

“He looked at us.”

The words come back from somewhere else in the hallway, from someone else, but they land inside her.

He looked.

Lila does not know who he is, not exactly, but she understands something anyway.

This was not noise.

Not an accident.

Someone saw.

And still did it.

Her grip tightens around her knees.

The understanding does not become anger, not yet. It becomes something colder, a fracture.

Daniel feels it as accumulation. He has moved through enough patients now that the pattern is undeniable—not random, not scattered, directed.

The injuries tell a story.

He does not want to read it, but he cannot ignore it.

He stands for a moment at the edge of the hallway, between rooms, between needs, between one decision and the next, and the thought arrives fully formed.

This was intentional.

Not in the abstract.

In the physical.

Step by step.

Choice by choice.

He exhales, not deeply, just enough to keep moving, because if he stops, the thought will expand, and there is no space for that yet.

"Medic!"

The call pulls him back.

Good.

He moves, because movement is still protection, for now.

Marcus cannot stop seeing it, even without images, even without detail.

His mind fills in the space—the walking, the seeing, the choosing, over and over.

"They didn't have to," he says again.

Sarah stands beside him. She does not interrupt this time, because she hears something new in his voice—not just anger, certainty.

"They didn't have to," he repeats.

The sentence is no longer about understanding. It is about judgment, a line drawn, a refusal.

Sarah looks at the building, at the people still moving, at the ones who are not, and she feels it too, not as sharply, not as quickly, but it is there.

Someone chose this.

The thought is heavy. It does not move easily. It does not resolve.

It sits.

Keisha stands near the end of the hallway, close enough now, not to see, but to know.

The officer nearby does not speak again. There is nothing left to say about it.

The body is there.

Still.

Contained.

The source.

Keisha does not approach, because the distance is not physical.

It is something else.

A boundary.

Between action and aftermath.

She feels the anger settle fully now, not explosive, not overwhelming, anchored.

She looks back down the hallway, at the rooms, at the people, at the movement still happening, and then briefly toward where it ended.

Someone chose this.

The sentence lands in her differently than anything before, not as question, as fact, and inside that fact, a second realization begins.

Someone chose.

And everyone else is left to carry it.

Daniel feels that part next, not during treatment, between it, in the moment where he reaches for something and finds nothing to reach for, the pause.

He looks at his hands—gloves stained, movements automatic, and beneath it the awareness.

He did not choose this.

None of them did.

But they are inside it now.

And they will be after.

That is the part no training names, not triage, not protocol.

Inheritance.

Lila feels it as confusion. The adults are moving, talking, helping, but something is wrong in a way that does not go away.

"Are we going home?" she asks.

The woman in front of her hesitates. "Soon," she says.

Lila nods, but she does not believe it, not fully, because home belongs to before, and before is gone.

Marcus feels it as direction. His anger has somewhere to point now, not at the event, at the person who made it.

That clarity feels dangerous, but also necessary.

"They chose it," he says one last time, not to Sarah, to himself, because saying it keeps it real, because not saying it would let it drift into something else, something easier.

He will not let that happen.

Inside, the hallway continues to move, but underneath something has settled—not peace, not resolution, recognition.

Someone chose this.

And that truth changes everything that follows.

It changes how they remember, how they speak, how they carry it.

It does not fade.

It does not soften.

It stays.

And each of them, in their own way, has begun to feel what it means to live on the other side of that choice.

Chapter 9—**Did I Do Something Wrong?**

Part I—The Quiet Question

Lila does not ask it out loud, not at first.

The adults around her are speaking in careful voices now—soft, measured, shaped in a way that feels like they are trying not to break something fragile. "You're safe." "You did exactly right." "It's over now." The sentences come one after another, like they have been practiced somewhere else, somewhere before this.

Lila nods when they say them, because that seems like the correct response.

She is sitting in a different room now, not the classroom, not the closet, a space that feels temporary—chairs lined up, a table with water bottles, a box of tissues already half empty.

Someone had guided her here, a hand on her shoulder, a voice she does not remember.

She sits with her hands folded in her lap. They look normal, still, clean now. Someone had wiped them. She remembers that part, the way the cloth felt, too soft.

Around her, other children sit—some crying, some talking too fast, some not talking at all.

Lila is not crying.

A woman kneels in front of her, the same woman from before.

"Lila, can you tell me what you're feeling?"

The question floats in the space between them.

Lila does not answer, because she does not know how.

She feels something, but it does not have a word.

The woman nods, as if silence is an answer.

"That's okay," she says. "You don't have to talk yet."

Lila nods again.

The nod feels like a task she can complete.

Across the room, a boy is speaking.

"I ran," he says. "I didn't even think—I just ran—"

His voice breaks.

A teacher kneels beside him.

"You did exactly what you needed to do."

The words are firm, reassuring.

The boy nods, but he keeps talking.

"I didn't go back," he says. "I didn't—"

His voice disappears.

Lila watches him, watches the way the adults respond. They say things like, "You're here." "You're safe." "You did the right thing."

The same sentences, repeated.

Lila listens carefully, because somewhere in those sentences she thinks there must be a rule, a way to understand what happened.

She looks down at her hands again, tries to remember.

The closet.

The rule.

Stay quiet.

She stayed quiet.

She did that right.

But—

There had been a moment.

Small.

Quick.

She had moved.

Just a little.

Her foot had slipped.

It had made a sound.

Not loud.

But not silent.

Lila feels something tighten in her chest.

The memory sharpens.

What if—

The thought forms slowly.

What if that mattered?

The woman in front of her is still speaking.

" . . . your body did what it needed to do . . . " " . . . you listened . . . " " . . . you stayed safe . . . "

Lila nods again, but the words are not landing in the place where the question is forming, because the question is not about what she did right, it is about what she might have done wrong.

A man enters the room—uniform, but softer now.

He kneels beside another child.

"Hey," he says. "You did great."

The child does not respond.

The man nods anyway.

"You were really brave."

The word brave moves through the room.

It lands on different people in different ways.

For some, it lifts.

For Lila, it does something else.

Because brave sounds like a choice.

And she does not remember choosing.

She remembers freezing.

She remembers not knowing what to do.

She remembers the sound.

And the not-sound.

And the way her body decided things before she could.

"Lila," the woman says gently.

Lila looks up.

"Can you tell me where you were when it started?"

The question feels safer, concrete.

"In the music room," Lila says.

"Okay," the woman nods. "And what did you do?"

Lila hesitates.

"I hid," she says.

"That was exactly right," the woman says immediately.

Lila nods, but the hesitation remains, because that is not the whole answer.

"I made a noise," Lila says quietly.

The woman pauses.

"What kind of noise?"

"My foot," Lila says.

She looks down again.

"It slipped."

The room feels smaller suddenly.

The sounds around her fade.

The question becomes sharper.

What if—

The woman leans in slightly.

"That's okay," she says.

Her voice is gentle, but it is too quick, too ready.

Lila hears it, feels it, and something in her does not accept it, because the woman was not there, the woman does not know.

“What if he heard it?” Lila asks.

The words come out before she can stop them, small but clear.

The woman’s expression shifts, not dramatically, but enough, a flicker of something—concern, care, the weight of answering.

“He didn’t come in, right?” the woman says.

Lila shakes her head.

“No.”

“Then it didn’t matter,” the woman says.

The sentence is meant to close the question, to resolve it, but it does not, because didn’t matter is not the same as wasn’t wrong.

Lila feels the difference, even if she cannot name it.

Across the room, the boy who had been talking earlier is quiet now. A teacher has her arm around him.

“You’re okay,” she says.

He nods, but his eyes are somewhere else, not in the room.

Lila watches.

She notices something.

The quiet ones.

The ones not crying, not speaking.

The adults move past them more quickly, pause less, as if silence means something is fine, as if stillness is strength.

The woman in front of Lila smiles again.

"You're doing really well," she says.

Lila nods, because that is what she has learned to do, because nodding makes the moment move forward.

But inside, the question stays.

It does not grow louder.

It does not demand attention.

It settles.

Quiet.

Persistent.

Did I do something wrong?

No one hears it.

Because it is not spoken.

And the silence that holds it looks too much like strength.

Part II—Mistaken for Brave

By afternoon, Lila has been called brave three times. The first time, she had nodded. The second time, she had looked down. The third time, she had stopped hearing the rest of the sentence.

Brave is becoming one of those words adults use when they do not know what else to say. It is not a bad word. It is not wrong exactly. But it does not fit. Not on her. Not here. Not with the sound of her shoe still caught somewhere inside her memory.

She sits beside her mother now in a room that is too bright, too open, too full of people trying to be gentle. Her mother's hand rests on her shoulder, warm and steady. Every few minutes, it tightens slightly, as if checking that Lila is still there.

A counselor sits across from them with a clipboard in her lap, not writing much, mostly watching.

"You've been very quiet," the counselor says.

Lila looks at her.

The counselor smiles softly.

"That's okay. Some children need quiet after something frightening."

Lila nods.

Her mother exhales.

"She's always been quiet," her mother says, and then seems to hear how that sounds. "I mean—not always. She talks. At home she talks."

The counselor nods in a way that says she understands.

Lila watches the nod.

Adults nod a lot now. They nod when they do not know. They nod when they want something to be true. They nod when they are hoping the nod itself can hold the room together.

"She seems very composed," the counselor says.

Composed.

Lila does not know exactly what that means, but she knows it is supposed to be good.

Her mother's hand tightens again.

"She's strong," her mother says.

Lila looks down.

Strong. Brave. Quiet.

The words gather around her like coats handed to the wrong person.

She does not know how to refuse them.

So she wears them.

The counselor leans forward slightly.

“Lila, can you tell me one thing you remember?”

One thing.

There are too many things—the light under the door, the breathing, the shoulder against the wall, the scrape, the shadow, the foot, her foot.

“My shoe made a sound,” she says.

Her mother shifts beside her.

The counselor waits.

That helps, a little.

“It scraped,” Lila says. “On the floor.”

The counselor nods again, slower this time.

“That must have scared you.”

Lila does not answer, because scared is not the question.

The counselor continues.

“When we are frightened, our bodies sometimes move without us meaning to.”

Lila looks at her.

That sounds close.

Not right.

But close.

"I didn't mean to," Lila says.

"I know."

The words come too quickly.

Lila hears that.

Her mother hears something else.

"Sweetheart, nobody thinks you did anything wrong."

Lila's stomach tightens.

Nobody thinks.

That is not the same as knowing.

The counselor's face softens.

"Your job was to survive," she says.

Lila looks down at her hands.

Her job.

The word does something strange inside her.

A job is something you can do right.

Or wrong.

A job is something someone can check.

She had one job.

Stay quiet.

She had not done it perfectly.

Her mother bends closer.

"You were so brave," she says.

There it is again.

Lila nods.

The room relaxes slightly around her nod.

So she understands something new:

Nodding helps adults feel better.

Silence helps them decide she is okay.

Quiet looks like bravery from the outside.

Inside, it is something else.

Inside, the question is still sitting there.

Small.

Hard.

Did I do something wrong?

The counselor asks if she wants water.

Lila shakes her head.

Her mother says she should drink something.

Lila takes the bottle because taking it ends the exchange.

The plastic crackles in her hand.

Too loud.

She freezes.

No one else does.

The sound belongs here.

Apparently.

That is confusing too.

Some sounds matter.

Some sounds don't.

There is no way to know which is which until after.

She twists the cap.

It clicks.

Small.

Sharp.

Her hand stops.

Her mother watches her.

"Do you need help?"

Lila shakes her head.

She opens the bottle the rest of the way.

The room continues.

No one looks toward the door.

No one listens for footsteps.

The sound does not change anything.

She takes a sip.

The water is warm.

She swallows carefully.

The counselor says, "That's good."

Lila wants to ask why.

Why is drinking water good?

Why was hiding good?

Why was being quiet good if it did not stop anything?

Why was her noise okay if noise was not allowed?

But the questions feel too tangled, too likely to make everyone look at her differently.

So she holds them.

Her mother speaks to the counselor in a low voice now, as if Lila is not fully in the room.

"She hasn't cried," her mother says.

The counselor answers just as softly.

"That can be normal."

Normal.

Another word.

Lila does not feel normal.

She feels like the closet is still around her, even though there are no walls close enough to touch.

"She may process later," the counselor says.

Later.

Adults keep putting things there.

Later is where hard things go when no one knows what to do with them now.

Lila looks across the room.

The boy from earlier is crying again.

Two adults are with him.

One has a hand on his back.

One is handing him tissues.

He is not being called brave right now.

He is being helped.

Lila wonders if crying is the way to show the question.

But she cannot make herself do it.

Her body will not.

It has learned something else.

Stay quiet.

A volunteer walks by and smiles at her.

"You're doing so well," the volunteer says.

Lila nods automatically.

Her mother smiles back, tired and grateful.

The volunteer moves on.

The counselor looks at Lila's mother.

"We'll want to keep an eye on her," she says.

Lila hears it.

Keep an eye.

Like watching is care.

Like watching from the outside can see what is happening inside.

Her mother nods.

"I will."

Lila believes her.

That almost makes it worse.

Because her mother will watch for crying, for nightmares, for not eating, for being scared.

But Lila does not know if anyone will watch for the question.

The counselor says they can go home soon.

Home.

The word should feel good.

It does not.

Home means her room, her bed, her backpack by the door, her shoes, the same shoes, the ones that made the sound.

Her mother squeezes her shoulder.

"Almost done," she says.

Lila nods.

Again.

The counselor smiles.

"You really are very brave."

This time, Lila does not nod right away.

For one small second, she almost says it.

Not loudly.

Not dramatically.

Just enough.

I'm not brave. I'm quiet.

But her mother is watching with tired, hopeful eyes.

The counselor is waiting.

The room wants the easier answer.

So Lila gives it.

She nods.

Everyone accepts it.

And the quiet question stays with her, carried out of the room under the name of bravery.

Part III—The Wrong Kind of Quiet

By evening, everyone is relieved that Lila is quiet. Not in those exact words. No one says at least she isn't falling apart, no one says at least she isn't screaming, no one says at least she seems okay, but the feeling is there. It moves through the house in small ways.

Her mother speaks softly on the phone in the kitchen. "She's calm," she says. A pause. "Yes. Quiet. But calm."

Lila hears this from the hallway. She is standing near her bedroom door, still wearing the clothes from earlier. Her shoes are off now, placed neatly beside the wall. She can see them from where she stands. The right shoe has a scuff near the toe. She does not remember if it was there before.

Her mother keeps talking. "I think she's just tired." Another pause. "I know. We'll watch her."

Lila looks at the shoes. The scuff looks small, almost nothing, but she cannot stop seeing it.

Her room is exactly the same. That is part of the problem. The bed is made the way she left it. A book lies open on the floor beside the nightstand.

Her music folder rests on the desk, one corner bent slightly upward. Nothing has changed. Everything has changed.

She steps inside carefully, as if the room might react. It doesn't. She sits on the edge of the bed.

Her mother appears in the doorway a moment later. "You okay?"

Lila nods.

Her mother watches her. "You don't have to keep saying you're okay if you're not."

Lila looks down. The sentence sounds kind. It also sounds impossible, because if she says she is not okay, then something has to happen next. Someone has to ask why. And then she might have to say it—the shoe, the scrape, the sound, the question.

So she shrugs.

Her mother comes in and sits beside her, leaving a small space between them. "I'm so proud of you," she says.

Lila's throat tightens.

Proud is another word that does not fit.

"You did exactly what you were supposed to do."

Lila presses her hands between her knees, her fingers disappearing.

"What if I didn't?" she asks.

Her mother turns toward her. "What do you mean?"

Lila does not look up. "My shoe made a sound."

Her mother exhales, soft and quick. "Oh, sweetheart."

The words arrive before the answer.

Lila hears that too.

Her mother reaches for her hand. Lila lets her take it.

"That didn't do anything," her mother says. "You're here. You're safe."

Lila nods because her mother needs her to.

But the answer slides past the question.

It did not do anything.

Maybe.

But that is not the same as saying it was not wrong.

Her mother squeezes her hand. "You survived," she says.

Lila looks at the floor.

Survived sounds like something finished.

It does not feel finished.

At dinner, she eats three bites of macaroni and cheese. Her mother watches every one, not obviously, but Lila can feel it. Her father has come home early and sits across from her with his hands folded near his plate. He is trying not to stare. He is trying not to ask too much. She can see the effort in the way he keeps looking at his food and then back at her.

"You don't have to finish," he says.

Lila nods.

Her mother says, "She's doing really well."

Her father nods quickly. "Yeah. Really well."

Lila looks at both of them.

Doing well seems to mean sitting still, eating some, not crying, answering when asked. She can do those things. She has been doing those things all day. So maybe that is what they need from her. Maybe quiet is her job now too.

After dinner, her father asks if she wants to watch a movie. Her mother suggests a shower. Someone from school texts her mother with information about counseling. The phone keeps lighting up. Each glow makes Lila look. Each vibration makes her stomach tighten.

Her mother notices. "Too much?" she asks.

Lila nods.

Her mother turns the phone face down. "There," she says.

Lila wants to feel better. She does not, because the phone is still there. It can still make sound, even face down.

At bedtime, her mother sits on the edge of the mattress. The lamp is on. The room is soft, too soft.

"Do you want me to stay for a while?"

Lila nods. This nod is real.

Her mother smiles sadly and brushes hair away from Lila's forehead. "You were very brave today."

Lila closes her eyes.

The word follows her into the dark behind her eyelids—brave, quiet, good, safe. They move around each other, none of them landing where they are supposed to.

Her mother begins to hum, a small sound, gentle, familiar. Lila used to like it. Now she listens to whether it can be heard outside the room. She knows that does not make sense. She knows they are home. She knows there is no closet door, no hallway, no shadow.

Still, her body listens.

Her mother stops humming after a while. "Too much?" she whispers.

Lila opens her eyes. "I don't know."

It is the truest thing she has said all day.

Her mother nods. "That's okay."

There it is again.

Okay.

Lila almost asks it then, the whole question, not about the shoe, not just that, the bigger one—Did I do something wrong? But her mother looks so tired, so relieved that Lila is lying still, so grateful for the quiet.

So Lila swallows the question, quietly, carefully, the way she had swallowed her breath in the closet.

Her mother sits beside her until Lila pretends to sleep, then she leaves the door open a crack. A line of light falls across the floor, thin, unmoving.

Lila stares at it.

Her body remembers what to do.

Stay quiet.

Do not move.

Listen.

The house settles around her. A pipe clicks. A car passes outside. Her father murmurs something down the hall.

Normal sounds.

Safe sounds.

But Lila does not yet know how to tell the difference.

Her foot moves under the blanket, just slightly. The sheet whispers against her skin.

She freezes.

Nothing happens.

No footsteps. No shadow. No voice. No consequence.

Still, her heart begins to pound.

She waits for it to quiet.

It does not.

In the hallway, her mother speaks softly again. “She’s asleep.”

Her father says something Lila cannot hear.

Then her mother: “She’s handling it better than I thought.”

Lila keeps her eyes open.

The light at the door remains.

She is not asleep.

She is not handling it.

She is holding it.

And because holding looks quiet from the outside, everyone thinks it is strength.

Inside, the question curls tighter.

Did I do something wrong?

It does not need an answer to stay alive.

It only needs silence.

And silence is something Lila already knows how to keep.

Chapter 10—I Couldn't Get to Them

Part I—The Space Between

Daniel does not notice when the work slows, not at first. There is no clear moment where urgency ends, no signal, no voice that says you can stop now. It changes gradually—fewer calls for immediate help, more standing, more waiting, more looking. He finishes with one patient, moves to another, but the rhythm is different now, less frantic, more spaced. Between one action and the next there is time, and in that time something begins.

He stands near the end of the hallway, the same place he passed through again and again, but now he is not moving through it—he is in it. The stretchers have thinned. The voices have softened. Someone is collecting equipment. Someone is writing. Someone is speaking quietly into a radio. Daniel looks at his hands. The gloves are still on, streaked, creased, marked by the work. He flexes his fingers slightly. They feel stiff, used. He does not take the gloves off, not yet, because taking them off would mean something. An ending. And he is not sure it has ended.

"Good work."

Daniel turns. A medic stands a few feet away, gear hanging loose now, posture less rigid than it had been inside. Daniel nods. The words do not land. Good work. He tries to understand what that means here—who he treated, who he stabilized, who he sent out, who left breathing because hands had arrived in time. The sequence is clear enough. The actions can be traced. The decisions can be defended. But something interrupts the accounting before it becomes reassurance.

A gap. A hallway. A voice.

"My friend is still in there."

The memory arrives without warning, sharp, present, almost close enough to touch. Daniel closes his eyes briefly and sees her again, the girl with her hand on his sleeve, her face turned toward him, her voice breaking around a sentence that was not information, not exactly. It was direction. It was plea. It was a map he could not follow.

He had not gone. He had stayed because he had to, because someone else needed him, because the one in front of him could not wait, because scene control and triage and treatment all demanded that he remain where he was. All of it true. All of it necessary. All of it defensible. And still, the gap remains.

He opens his eyes. The hallway is quieter now, but the memory is not. He walks a few steps, stops, looks toward the rooms he passed earlier. Some doors are open now, empty. Some are closed, marked. He does not read the marks. He does not need to. He already knows enough to know they mean something he is not ready to take in.

"I couldn't get to them."

The sentence forms, not spoken, not yet. It does not arrive as accusation. That would almost be easier. It arrives as recognition, as if some part of him has begun recording the space between need and reach.

"You heading out, Reyes?"

Daniel turns slightly. Another responder watches him from beside the wall, one hand resting against a supply bag. Daniel shakes his head.

"Not yet."

The responder nods and moves on, accepting the answer because there are too many unfinished things in the hallway to question one more.

Daniel stays. He moves toward the intersection, the place where everything had split, where decisions had multiplied faster than anyone could name them. He remembers the student there, the one he marked first, the one he called for transport, the one whose pulse had been faint but present beneath his fingers. He got to that one. He knows that. He can trace it clearly.

But there are others he cannot trace, not clearly, not fully. The hallway holds them in pieces—a hand, a voice, a shoe near a doorway, a shape on the floor, someone calling from behind him while his hands were already committed elsewhere. He had moved through the space the way he was trained to move, reading bodies, sorting urgency, choosing where seconds belonged. Now the seconds come back without the structure that made them bearable.

He leans back against the wall, carefully, as if the wall might not hold or as if he might not.

"I couldn't get to them."

This time the sentence is real. Quiet. Contained. Spoken low enough that it could be missed, but he hears it fully.

A medic passes, pauses. "You good, Reyes?"

Daniel nods. "Yeah."

The medic holds his gaze a second longer, then nods once and moves on.

Daniel exhales. He had done what he was trained to do. He had followed the order of things. He had made the right calls, or at least the calls that could be made with the time and information he had. He knows this professionally, clearly, in the part of himself that can review a scene and understand why each action followed the last.

And still—the sentence does not change.

The hallway seems longer now than it had when he was moving through it. Before, it had been a sequence of tasks. Now it is a place. A place with corners he did not turn toward, rooms he entered too late or not at all, voices that became part of the background because another body needed him first. He hates that phrase—background. Nothing here should have been background. No one should have become part of the noise. But that is what happens when there is too much need. The mind sorts. The hands choose. The body moves. Later, the names return.

If there are names.

He realizes that too. Names came late. Names came after pressure, after breath, after pulse, after transport decisions. In the moment, there had been bodies. Wounds. Signs. Categories. Walking. Not walking. Breathing. Not breathing. Can wait. Cannot wait. Needs now. Needs next. He had used the categories because categories save time. But now each category begins to feel like a person standing behind a closed door.

He pushes off the wall and takes a few steps toward the exit, not quickly, not slowly. His body is tired in a way he does not yet feel fully. The exhaustion is there, waiting its turn. At the doorway, he pauses and looks back.

The hallway is almost empty now, but not empty. It holds something. Everything that happened. Everything that did not. Everything he reached. Everything he didn't.

"I couldn't get to them."

The sentence settles, not loud, not overwhelming, but fixed.

Daniel steps outside. The air feels lighter, too light, as if the world beyond the doors does not understand the weight he is bringing with him. The noise returns—sirens, voices, movement, radios, people calling names across distance—but inside him, the hallway stays. And in that hallway, the space between what he did and what he could not do begins to take shape.

He does not name it.

Not yet.

But it is there.

And it is not going away.

Part II—What Stays Behind

The work follows Daniel outside, not physically—the gear is set down, the gloves come off, the radio continues—but the work he feels now is not the same as the work he was trained to do. The parking lot is full—vehicles, lights, movement, command forming, tape rising—and order is returning, slowly, deliberately, as if structure itself can hold what just happened in place. Daniel steps into it because there is nowhere else to go.

Someone calls out, "Medic—over here." He turns automatically, moves toward the voice, because turning toward is still the rule. A responder sits on the back step of an ambulance, head down, hands resting on their knees, posture folded inward in a way that has nothing to do with injury.

"I'm fine," the responder says before Daniel asks.

Daniel nods. "Okay."

He stands there for a moment, neither of them moving, both of them holding something that does not require words. The responder looks up. "You were inside?" Daniel nods again. The responder exhales. "Yeah."

Recognition. Not explanation.

Daniel shifts his weight. The ground feels steady. Too steady.

"You good, Reyes?" the responder asks.

Daniel nods. "Yeah."

The word lands the same way it has every time—correct, practiced, incomplete. The responder watches him for a second longer, as if deciding whether to push further, then nods and looks away. The moment closes without closing anything.

Daniel moves toward the curb and sits because his body decides before he does. The concrete is solid beneath him, unchanging, indifferent. He looks at his hands—bare now, clean, the skin marked only by pressure lines that will fade. They do not show what they held, what they pressed, what they could not reach. He rubs them together as if something might come off.

It doesn't.

He looks up. The parking lot has shifted into something else—parents moving quickly, searching, calling names; students wrapped in blankets; responders guiding, redirecting, containing. Everything has a pattern again. Everything is moving toward something that resembles order.

He watches a mother reach a child.

The moment is immediate, uncontained. She pulls them in, arms tight, too tight, as if pressure alone can confirm reality. The child presses back, not resisting, not questioning, simply there.

Alive.

Reached.

Daniel feels it in his chest—not relief, not exactly, something sharper, more defined.

That one made it.

That one was reached.

The thought completes itself without permission.

Some weren't.

"I couldn't get to them."

The sentence returns, not new, not surprising, but settled now in a place that does not shift. It connects to what he sees, what he remembers, what he cannot undo.

He traces it without meaning to. The hallway. The intersection. The rooms. The moments where he turned, where he stayed, where he moved past. Each decision had a reason. Each one had a logic. Each one had been correct in the moment it was made.

And still—

they do not resolve.

A medic lowers himself onto the curb beside him. Not close enough to crowd. Not far enough to ignore.

"Hell of a scene," he says.

Daniel nods. "Yeah."

They sit in silence. Not empty silence, but the kind that holds space without asking for anything from it.

"Kids," the medic says after a moment.

Daniel nods again. "Yeah."

The word lands differently than the others. Not patients. Not victims. Kids. It shifts the frame without changing the facts.

Daniel exhales, longer this time, the breath pulling something upward that does not release.

"I couldn't get to all of them," he says.

The words come out before he decides to speak them. They hang in the air between them, not heavy, not light, simply present.

The medic does not answer right away. He looks out at the same scene Daniel is watching, as if measuring something before responding.

"No one could," he says finally.

The sentence is true. Completely true. It carries the weight of experience, the kind that knows the limits before they are reached.

Daniel hears it.

Understands it.

Knows it.

And still—

it does not land where the sentence inside him lives.

Because his sentence is not about everyone.

It is about specific.

A voice. A hand. A moment.

"My friend is still in there."

Daniel closes his eyes briefly. The memory does not need prompting. It is already present.

"You did what you could," the medic says.

Daniel nods. "Yeah."

True.

Still not enough.

He opens his eyes and looks back toward the building, toward the doors that now stand open but unreachable in a different way.

"I stayed," he says.

The medic nods. "You had to."

Daniel's jaw tightens, almost imperceptibly. Because had to suggests inevitability, removes the weight of choice, places the decision outside of him.

And yet—

it still feels like one.

"I could have—" he starts, then stops. The sentence fractures before it can form because there are too many possible endings and none of them are real.

The medic shakes his head, not sharply, not dismissively.

"Don't," he says.

Daniel looks at him.

"You start pulling that thread," the medic continues, "it doesn't stop."

Daniel exhales, because the thread is already there, already pulled, already running through everything he is holding. It connects the moment to every version of what might have been different, and none of those versions can be reached.

The medic pushes himself up to standing.

"Grab water, Reyes," he says.

Daniel nods. "Yeah."

The medic walks off, absorbed back into the movement of the scene, into the structure that continues whether or not anything inside Daniel settles.

Daniel stays.

The noise around him continues—voices, radios, footsteps—but it feels distant now, like something happening adjacent to the space he occupies.

"I couldn't get to them."

The sentence returns again, quieter, less sharp, but deeper, embedded now in a way that does not rely on repetition.

He realizes something in that moment.

It is not leaving.

Not because it is unresolved.

But because it is true.

And truths like that do not resolve.

They remain.

He sits there a little longer, watching movement reorganize itself into something manageable, something that can be documented, reported, closed.

But what he is carrying does not follow that process.

It does not file.

It does not clear.

It stays in the space between what he did and what he could not do, and that space does not shrink with time.

Eventually, he stands.

Not because he is ready.

Because staying seated does not change anything.

The ground remains solid beneath him.

The scene remains active around him.

And the sentence remains exactly where it settled.

"I couldn't get to them."

He does not say it again.

He does not need to.

It is already part of him now.

Part III—The Line That Stays

By the time Daniel leaves, the scene has already begun to close around itself, not finished, not resolved, but contained. Tape holds the perimeter, vehicles idle in ordered lines, and voices lower as if volume itself might disturb what has already settled. The building stands behind it all, unchanged from a distance, carrying everything inside it without showing any of it. From here, it looks intact, almost ordinary, and that dissonance presses quietly against the edges of Daniel's awareness.

He signs out because someone tells him to. Name. Time. Unit. The pen moves in his hand without thought, letters forming in a line that looks complete, final, something that can be filed and accounted for. The form receives what he gives it without resistance. It accepts the version of the day that can be written down.

It looks like closure.

It isn't.

"Get some rest, Reyes," someone says as he hands the clipboard back.

Daniel nods. "Yeah."

The word comes easily now, the same way it has all afternoon, shaped correctly, placed where it belongs, doing its job without touching anything underneath it.

He walks toward his car. Each step feels normal, measured, controlled. His body knows how to leave a scene. It has done this before, many times, stepping away from what just happened and moving toward what comes next. There is a rhythm to it, a sequence that usually holds.

But this time something does not follow the pattern.

Usually, there is separation. The call ends. The scene stays. You leave, and what happened remains where it occurred, contained by distance, by time, by the fact that you are no longer inside it. It might return later, in fragments, in memory, but it does not travel intact.

This does.

He reaches his car, opens the door, then stops. His hand rests on the frame, fingers curled slightly against the metal, feeling its solidity, its certainty. He does not get in, not yet. The pause is not intentional. It happens before he can move past it.

The sentence is already there.

I couldn't get to them.

It does not arrive.

It is waiting.

Not sharp anymore. Not pressing.

Fixed.

He leans his forehead briefly against the top of the door frame and closes his eyes. The parking lot continues around him—engines idling, doors closing, voices crossing distances—but it feels separate, like a layer he is no longer fully inside.

Behind his eyes, the hallway remains.

Not all of it.

Not the full sequence.

Just enough.

A voice.

"My friend is still in there."

A hand on his sleeve.

The pull of that moment, the direction it offered, the direction he did not take.

He opens his eyes, straightens, and gets into the car. The door closes with a solid, contained sound that feels louder than it should, sealing the space around him. Inside, everything is still. The world narrows to the interior of the car, the wheel beneath his hands, the dashboard, the windshield framing what remains outside.

He does not start the engine.

There is a moment where nothing is required of him. No one is calling his name. No one is asking him to decide, to act, to move. The absence of demand should feel like relief.

It doesn't.

Because what remains has no task attached to it.

He looks at his hands again, resting lightly on the wheel. Clean. Steady. They do not show what they held, what they pressed, what they could not reach. There is no visible trace of the difference between what he did and what he could not do.

He tightens his grip slightly, enough to feel resistance, something solid pushing back.

I couldn't get to them.

The sentence expands, not louder, but wider. Not just one voice, not just one moment. Others attach themselves to it—not fully formed, not clearly remembered, but present in the same way, part of the same pattern.

Unreached.

He tries, without fully deciding to, to answer it.

You did what you could.
You followed protocol.
You made the right calls.

Each statement arrives complete, accurate, supported by everything he knows about the work, about training, about how decisions are made when time is limited and need is not.

Each one is true.

Each one passes through him without changing anything.

Because the sentence is not arguing with those truths.

It exists alongside them.

Parallel.

Unresolved.

He exhales slowly, the breath leaving him without release.

This is not something to solve.

There is no correction to apply, no alternative path to retrace, no version of events he can re-enter and alter. The decisions are fixed. The moments are closed.

And still—

they remain open inside him.

A car pulls out nearby, tires moving across pavement, a normal sound, part of the ordinary world continuing as it always does. Daniel watches it pass through the windshield, the motion smooth, uninterrupted, unmarked by what has just occurred.

He reaches forward and starts the engine. The vibration runs through the car, through the wheel, through his hands, grounding and mechanical, something that responds predictably.

He sits there a second longer, then shifts into gear and pulls out slowly.

The road away from the scene is familiar. He has driven it before, after other calls, other endings, other moments that required leaving. The route does not change. The turns come where they always do. The signals operate on their own timing.

Today, everything along that road feels sharper, more defined. Each intersection holds its shape more distinctly. Each car passing carries a separation he cannot step into yet. The distance between his experience and everything else feels precise, measurable, and unmoving.

He stops at a light and waits. The engine idles. A pedestrian crosses in front of him, head down, phone in hand, moving through the space without awareness of what remains behind him.

Normal.

The word forms without weight.

The light changes.

He drives.

The sentence remains.

Not as interruption.

As presence.

I couldn't get to them.

He does not repeat it.

He does not push it away.

It stays where it is, aligned with everything else he knows to be true.

At the next turn, he signals. The indicator clicks steadily, a small, contained rhythm—left, right, stop, go. These systems hold. These patterns remain intact. They respond in ways that make sense.

He turns onto his street and slows. His house comes into view, familiar, unchanged, a place that belongs to another part of his life, one that exists outside the structure of calls and responses.

He pulls into the driveway and puts the car in park. The engine continues for a moment, then he turns it off.

Silence.

Not the same silence.

This one is ordinary.

It does not press.

It does not hold.

But inside him, the other silence remains—the one from the hallway, the one after the last sound, the one where the decisions settled and did not move.

He sits there, hands still resting on the wheel, and understands something he does not yet have language for.

This will not fade the way adrenaline does.

It will not dissipate the way noise does.

It will remain.

Not overwhelming.

Not constant.

But present.

A line he will carry.

Between what he did.

And what he could not do.

He opens the car door, steps out, and closes it behind him. The house waits. The door is where it has always been. The path to it is unchanged.

He walks toward it.

And the line moves with him.

Unseen.

Unnamed.

But already part of everything that comes next.

Chapter 11—This Is the Job

Part I—What I Signed Up For

Evan had imagined his first real call differently, not easier, not simple, but contained. He had trained for this in classrooms and simulations, controlled chaos with instructors watching from the edges, ready to pause, reset, explain. He had learned the steps—scene safety, triage, airway, breathing, circulation—and practiced saying the words, "I'm here to help," "Stay with me," "Look at me," until they came without thinking. He had believed those words would carry him, that they would bridge the gap between training and reality.

And at first, they did.

When the call came in, his body moved the way it had been taught—gear, check, radio, respond. The siren had felt like confirmation, like a line being crossed into the role he had been preparing for, the moment where preparation becomes action. This is it. This is what it's for.

Evan had been riding third under Daniel Reyes that shift, close enough to follow, not close enough to understand everything yet. He had watched how Reyes moved, how decisions seemed to form without hesitation, how his voice stayed steady even when everything else didn't. In training, decisiveness had been framed as clarity, as confidence, as knowing what to do next. Watching Reyes in the hallway, Evan had believed that was what he was seeing—certainty.

Now he wasn't sure.

Because the moment had not arrived the way he expected. It had not been one moment. It had been many, stacked, overlapping, unfolding faster than he could name them. A building. A hallway. Too many people. Too many directions. Too many voices asking for help at the same time, each one carrying urgency that felt absolute.

He had seen Reyes turn toward one voice, commit fully, anchor himself there.

Then stay.

While something else happened somewhere else.

And not move.

That had been the moment Evan didn't know what to do with.

Evan stands now near the back of the ambulance, his hands resting on the edge of the open doors. He is not doing anything, not actively, not visibly, which feels wrong, because everything inside him is still moving. The urgency has not left his body, even though the scene around him has begun to slow, even though the structure of response is beginning to reassert itself.

"You okay?"

Evan turns. A medic stands nearby, older, posture steady, movements economical in a way that suggests familiarity with this kind of aftermath, the part of the work that comes after the visible crisis has passed.

Evan nods. "Yeah."

The word comes out quickly, too quickly.

The medic studies him for a moment, not challenging the answer, just taking its measure. "Drink some water," he says.

Evan nods again, reaches for a bottle sitting beside him, opens it, drinks. The water feels strange, like it belongs to a different version of the day, one where things make more sense, where actions and outcomes align more cleanly.

He lowers the bottle and looks at his hands. They are steady, cleaner than they had been inside, but he remembers what they felt like then—the pressure of holding, the urgency of deciding, the weight of being told where to be and when to move. He had done things. Real things. Not practice. Not simulation. He had followed instructions, given them when someone looked to him, moved where he was told, and sometimes moved where no one told him because there was no one left to ask.

He replays it in fragments. A patient. A call. A voice from somewhere he couldn't see. He had turned toward it, just slightly, enough to register that it existed, enough to feel the pull of it, the instinct to move toward need.

Then another voice.

Closer.

Clear.

"Stay here."

Reyes.

Evan had stayed, because that was the rule. Stay with your patient. Do not leave. Do not split. Do not abandon the one in front of you for the one you cannot see. He had followed that exactly, because following it was what it meant to do the job correctly.

And now he is not sure what that means.

"This is the job."

Evan looks up. The medic is still there, watching him, not closely, but with a kind of awareness that does not require intensity.

"What?" Evan asks.

The medic shrugs slightly. "Days like this."

The words are simple, flat, not unkind, not comforting. They do not soften anything or sharpen it. They simply place what happened into a category that already exists.

Evan nods. "This is the job," he repeats.

He hears himself say it and tries to understand it.

In training, the phrase had meant something else. It had meant commitment, purpose, a willingness to step into situations other people could not or would not face. It had meant helping, stabilizing, making a difference in the narrow window where difference was still possible. Watching Reyes, it had meant something else too. It had meant knowing.

Now it feels different.

This is the job means you will not get to everyone. It means you will choose. It means you will stand in one place while something else happens somewhere you cannot reach. It means that doing it right does not mean reaching everything.

Evan feels something shift inside him, not outward, not visible, but real.

He had imagined becoming this—a responder, someone who runs toward, who helps, who makes a difference. That part is still true. He had helped. He knows that in the same way he knows his hands had moved correctly, his voice had stayed steady, his actions had followed the sequence he was taught.

But something else has attached itself to that identity, something he had not expected.

Limits.

He leans back against the ambulance. The metal is cool, solid, grounding in a way that nothing else has been for the past hour, something that does not move, does not shift, does not require interpretation.

"I thought—" he starts, then stops.

The medic waits, does not fill the silence, does not offer the word Evan cannot find.

"I thought it would feel different," Evan says finally.

The medic nods. "Yeah."

No explanation. No correction. Just agreement.

Evan looks out across the lot. Parents are finding children. Children are not finding parents. Responders move between them, guiding, redirecting, holding space where something has broken but not yet settled into a shape that can be understood.

Near the edge of the crowd, a girl stands alone, looking toward the building, waiting for something that has not reached her yet.

Evan feels it again.

The pull.

To go.

To help.

To close the distance between where he is and where he feels he should be.

But no one calls him.

No one directs him.

He stays where he is.

Because that is also the job.

"This is the job," he says again.

The words sound different this time, heavier, more specific, no longer a statement of purpose but a recognition of what the role actually contains.

Something in him resists it.

Because if this is the job, then the job includes what he could not do—the hesitation, the turning, the staying, the voices he did not reach.

He feels it press against the edges of how he sees himself, the outline of the person he thought he was becoming.

He had imagined a line, clear, between who he was before and who he would be after this moment.

But the line is not clean.

It is fractured.

Because the person he is becoming includes things he did not choose.

He looks at the medic. "Does it always feel like this?" he asks.

The medic considers the question, not rushing to answer it.

"No," he says, then pauses, "not always."

Evan nods, waits.

"But sometimes," the medic adds.

Evan exhales.

Sometimes.

The word does not comfort him.

It places this moment in a category, one he will enter again.

He straightens, pushes off the ambulance.

There is still movement around him, still things to do, even if they are smaller now, less urgent, less defined.

He picks up a piece of equipment and carries it to where it belongs.

The motions are familiar.

Ordered.

But inside—

the shift continues.

This is the job.

He understands it now.

Not fully.

Not all at once.

But enough.

Enough to know that the person he thought he would be and the person he is becoming are no longer the same.

And that difference is not something he can put down when he leaves.

Part II—Where It Breaks

Evan does not leave right away. Even when someone tells him, "You can clear when you're ready," he nods, but he does not move. Ready feels like a word from a different system, one that assumes something has finished, something has settled into a form that can be named and left behind. Nothing about this feels finished, not in a way that matches the word.

So he moves instead without deciding to move, drifting through the edge of the response as if proximity might give shape to what he is holding. From the ambulance to the command table, from the command table toward the taped perimeter, then back again as if the path itself might resolve something. Each movement is small, contained, responsive rather than intentional.

He picks up a bag and carries it to where someone gestures. He hands off gloves. He grabs a roll of tape and holds it longer than necessary before someone else takes it from him. Tasks. Small ones. They give his hands something to do, something that begins and ends in a way he can follow.

They do not touch what is happening underneath.

A group of responders stands near the side of a truck, their voices low, steady, already shaping what just happened into something that can be spoken about later.

" . . . multiple entry points . . . "

" . . . response time was good . . . "

" . . . we got who we could . . . "

Evan slows as he passes, not enough to stop, just enough to hear.

We got who we could.

The phrase lands with a kind of finality that feels out of place this close to the moment itself.

He keeps walking.

But the words stay with him.

He stops near the edge of the taped perimeter and looks toward the building. It feels farther away now, held behind barriers and bodies and roles that exist to maintain distance. He can no longer see the hallway, no longer see where Reyes had stood, where Evan had been told to stay, where the moment had fixed itself in him.

Only the outside remains.

Which should be easier.

But isn't.

Because now everything that happened inside has to exist somewhere else.

Inside him.

A parent approaches the tape, voice unsteady. "Please—I just need to know—"

An officer steps forward, calm, practiced. "We're working on that."

The parent nods but does not move away. Their hands shift without purpose—open, close, open again—as if trying to hold something that is not there.

Evan watches their hands.

Watches the repetition.

The lack of resolution.

He feels something shift.

Not sudden.

Not sharp.

A recognition forming slowly.

The job does not end at the doorway.

It moves outward.

Into people who were not inside.

Who did not see.

But still carry it.

He steps back from the tape, not because anyone tells him to, but because something in him needs the distance.

“You okay?”

He turns. The same medic from earlier stands nearby, watching him with the same steady presence.

Evan nods. “Yeah.”

The word feels thinner now, stretched across something it cannot fully contain.

“First one like this?” the medic asks.

Evan nods again. “Yeah.”

The medic exhales slightly. “Yeah.”

That’s all.

No explanation.

No expansion.

Just recognition.

Evan looks down at his boots. Dust clings to them, small and unremarkable. There is nothing visible that reflects where he has been, what he stepped through, what he stood in. The surface tells nothing.

"I did what I was supposed to," Evan says.

The sentence comes out uncertain, balanced between statement and question.

The medic nods. "You did."

Evan waits.

Because it doesn't feel complete.

The medic watches him for a moment, then says, "That doesn't always feel like enough."

Evan looks up.

The words land closer than anything else has.

"Yeah," he says.

He doesn't elaborate.

He doesn't need to.

The gap is already there.

He replays the moment again, not the whole scene, just the part that won't release.

The voice.

The direction it pointed.

The way he had turned.

And then stopped.

"I stayed," he says.

The medic nods. "You had to."

Evan hears that.

Understands it.

Recognizes it as true in the way training defines truth.

But something inside him pushes back.

Had to.

The phrase removes choice.

And yet—

it still feels like one.

Because he remembers the moment before the staying.

The fraction of time where movement was still possible.

"I could have—" he starts.

Then stops.

Because the sentence opens into too many endings.

And none of them are real.

The medic shakes his head slightly, not dismissing, not correcting.

"Don't," he says.

Evan looks at him.

"You start pulling that thread," the medic continues, "it doesn't stop."

Evan nods.

Because the thread is already there.

Already pulled.

He can feel it running through the moment, through the memory, through the version of himself that stepped into that hallway believing he understood what the job required.

"I thought I knew what this was," Evan says.

The medic watches him.

"And now?" he asks.

Evan exhales, long, the breath moving through him without clearing anything.

"Now I don't know what to call it."

The medic nods.

"That's part of it," he says.

Part of it.

Not the whole.

Evan looks back toward the building.

"This is the job," he says again.

But the words do not settle the way they had before.

They shift.

From statement to question.

From identity to uncertainty.

Because if this is the job, then the job includes not knowing—not knowing who he could have reached, not knowing what would have changed, not knowing how to carry what remains when the work itself is finished.

He feels something give.

Not break.

Move.

A small separation between what he thought being a responder meant and what it actually is.

It is not dramatic.

Not visible.

But it is real.

And once it opens—

it does not close again.

The medic reaches out, pats his shoulder once. "Go home," he says.

Evan nods.

This time, he moves.

But as he walks away, the words stay with him, not loud, not urgent, but present in a way that does not fade.

This is the job.

And he is no longer entirely sure what that means for who he is.

Part III—Who That Makes Me

Evan doesn't turn on the radio when he gets in the car. He usually does—music, news, something to fill the space between the call and whatever comes next—but this time he leaves it off. The silence feels closer to what he's carrying than anything else would, closer to the shape of the day as it actually unfolded.

He sits for a moment with his hands on the wheel, not starting the engine, not moving. Around him, the parking lot continues to thin, vehicles pulling out one by one, responders stepping away in small groups, the structure of the scene loosening now that the urgency has passed. He watches one unit leave, then another, their departure unremarkable, part of a process that happens after every call, no matter what the call contained.

At some point, Reyes had disappeared into that movement.

Evan realizes he didn't see him go.

The thought lands quietly, not sharp enough to demand attention, but present enough to remain.

Reyes had been everywhere inside—moving, deciding, holding the shape of the work in place. Evan had followed him when he could, watched when he couldn't, assumed that understanding would come just from being close enough, from observing how experience translated into action.

Now Reyes is gone.

And whatever Evan thought he was following feels less defined without him.

He starts the engine. The vibration fills the car, low and steady, something predictable, something that responds in a way the rest of the day has not. He shifts into gear and pulls out, the motion automatic, practiced, something his body knows how to do even when his thoughts do not settle.

The road away from the scene is familiar. He has driven it before, on other days, after other calls, none of which stayed with him like this. The turns come where they always do. The signals change without regard for what just happened a few miles behind him. The world continues without adjustment.

He notices everything.

The way the streetlights reflect across the windshield.

The rhythm of the tires against the pavement.

A car braking too quickly at the intersection ahead.

All of it sharper, as if something inside him has narrowed its focus, stripping away anything that does not belong to the immediate moment.

He stops at a red light and waits. The engine idles, steady, contained. A family crosses in front of him, moving from one side of the street to the other. A child holds an adult's hand, swinging slightly as they walk, their movement loose, unguarded, uncontained.

It is an ordinary moment.

It should not mean anything.

But it does.

Because he cannot stop seeing it in relation to something else.

Something missing.

Something unfinished.

The light turns green.

He doesn't move right away.

The car behind him honks, short and impatient, a sound that belongs to a world that expects motion, expects continuity.

Evan presses the gas and moves forward. The moment passes as if nothing had interrupted it.

The world continues.

He understands that now in a way he did not before.

It does not stop.

It does not pause.

Even when something should be enough to make it.

He turns onto his street and slows. The houses are familiar, lights on in windows, shapes he recognizes without effort. This part of his life remains exactly where it was, unchanged by what happened elsewhere, unaffected by the weight he is carrying back into it.

He pulls into his driveway, puts the car in park, and turns off the engine. Silence fills the space immediately, not the same silence as before, not the kind that holds tension or expectation.

This one is ordinary.

It does not press.

It does not hold.

It simply exists.

He stays there, hands still on the wheel. There is no next instruction, no voice telling him where to go or what to do. No one is asking him to decide anything. The absence of direction feels unfamiliar, almost disorienting after the constant movement of the scene.

"This is the job."

The words come back, not from the medic this time, but from him.

He says them quietly, testing them, trying to understand what they mean now.

Before, they had been something he reached for—a reason, a way of explaining why he chose this path, why it mattered, why the difficulty would be worth it.

Now they feel like something that has been placed on him.

A definition he did not fully understand when he accepted it.

He leans back in the seat and closes his eyes. The hallway returns, not in full detail, not as a complete sequence, but in fragments that carry more weight than the whole ever could.

Reyes's voice.

"Stay here."

Another voice.

"My friend is still in there."

The two moments overlap, not in time, but in meaning, forming a single point of tension that does not resolve.

Evan feels it again.

The hesitation.

The pull.

The decision.

He had stayed.

Because that was the rule.

Because that was the training.

Because Reyes had said it.

Because leaving would have meant stepping outside the structure that was supposed to guide him, stepping into something uncertain, something that could have made everything worse.

He opens his eyes and looks at the dashboard, the familiar shape grounding in a way that feels incomplete.

"I did it right," he says.

The words come out quietly, almost as if saying them too loudly might expose something he cannot defend.

He hears them.

Waits for them to settle.

They don't.

Because something else is already there.

And still—

He exhales, long, the breath moving through him without releasing what it carries.

There is no one to say it to.

No one to confirm it.

No one to correct it.

This part belongs to him.

He opens the car door and steps out. The air is still, familiar, unchanged. His house stands in front of him exactly as it always has, the door closed, the lights on inside, the structure of his life intact in a way that feels almost disconnected from what he just left.

He walks toward it, each step steady, normal, part of a routine that has not shifted.

He reaches the door and stops.

His hand hovers over the handle.

Because something has shifted.

Not outside.

Inside.

The person who left this morning and the person standing here now are not the same.

Not completely.

The difference is not visible. No one will see it when he walks inside. No one will name it. There will be no marker for it, no acknowledgment that something fundamental has moved.

But it is there.

A fracture.

Small.

But real.

He opens the door and steps inside. The house smells like something cooking. A television plays somewhere in another room. Voices move through the space in familiar patterns, unchanged, unbroken.

"Hey," someone calls.

Evan answers automatically. "Hey."

His voice sounds the same.

He takes off his shoes and sets them by the door. Everything is where it should be, everything in place, everything aligned with the version of his life that existed before today.

And yet—

nothing feels entirely in place.

He moves through the house, responding when spoken to, answering questions the way he is expected to.

"I'm okay."

"Yeah, it was a lot."

"I'm home."

The sentences come easily.

Too easily.

No one asks the question that matters.

Not because they don't care.

Because they don't know it exists.

Evan goes to his room and closes the door behind him. The quiet returns, different from the car, different from the scene, but still holding something that does not settle.

He sits on the edge of the bed and leans forward, elbows on his knees, hands clasped together as if holding them still might contain what is moving inside him.

"This is the job."

He says it again.

This time it feels like something he is trying to accept rather than something he believes.

Not something he chose.

Something he is becoming.

And in that becoming, there is something he cannot ignore.

That being this person means carrying what he could not do alongside what he did.

Not instead of.

Not separate.

Together.

He sits there, not moving, letting the realization settle fully, not resisting it, not resolving it, just allowing it to take its place.

This is the job.

And it is not just what he does.

It is what it does

to him.

Chapter 12—The Questions Begin

Part I—Why Them

The questions do not arrive all at once. They begin quietly, not as words at first, but as pressure, something present before it is understood. Evan notices it the next morning, not when he wakes, not in the first clear moment of consciousness, but in the spaces between things—in the pause between brushing his teeth and looking at his reflection a second too long, in the moment between pouring coffee and remembering to drink it, in the gap between picking up his phone and forgetting what he meant to check. Something is there, unfinished, unsettled, resisting the normal rhythm of the day.

He tells himself it's normal. It was a hard call. People say that. He has already heard it. "You good?" "That was a tough one." "Take care of yourself." The language is familiar, rehearsed in the culture of response, designed to acknowledge difficulty without opening it too far. It fits. It belongs. But it does not reach what is actually happening inside him.

The questions begin as fragments. Not full sentences. Pieces.

Why them.

Why not me.

Why at all.

He doesn't say them out loud. Not yet. They move through him without needing permission, forming and reforming in the background of everything he does. He is sitting at the kitchen table when the first one fully takes shape.

Why them?

It doesn't sound like a question. It sounds like something that expects an answer.

He thinks about the hallway, not in sequence, not clearly, just enough. A face. A voice. A moment that could have gone another way, or at least feels like it could have. That one made it. That one didn't. The line between them does not make sense.

He tries to reconstruct it. Who was closer. Who was first. Who had a chance. Who could wait. Who couldn't. He can explain it in terms of triage, in terms of timing, in terms of what was possible in a moment where everything demanded more than anyone could give. He knows how to say it. He knows how to justify it. He knows how to stand in front of someone and explain why one person was treated before another.

But none of that answers the question.

Why them?

Because the question is not about process.

It is about worth.

The thought lands and he immediately resists it. That is not how it works. That is not how decisions are made. He knows that. The system exists precisely to remove worth from the equation, to focus on survivability, on immediacy, on what can be done now to save the most lives possible.

And still—

the question moves there anyway.

Why them and not someone else?

Why that person and not—

He stops the thought before it completes, because he knows where it leads, and he is not ready to follow it all the way through.

Why them and not me?

This one lands differently. Sharper. Closer. More personal.

He feels it physically, a tightening in his chest, not quite fear, not exactly anxiety, something closer to exposure. He had been there. In the same space. Close enough to hear. Close enough to respond. Close enough to be part of whatever determined who walked out and who didn't.

And yet—

he walked out.

Others didn't.

There is no clean explanation for that. Not one that holds at the level the question is asking from.

He leans back in his chair, the room suddenly feeling smaller, not because anything has changed physically, but because something inside him has shifted its sense of space. He looks around. Everything is where it should be. The table. The counter. The light coming through the window. Normal. Unchanged.

That feels wrong.

Not because it shouldn't be normal, but because part of him expected something to reflect what happened, some visible marker that the world itself had registered the event and adjusted accordingly.

But nothing has.

And that disconnect begins to settle in.

The question shifts again.

Why at all?

This one is different. Less about comparison. Less about who and more about why. Why does something like that happen? Why does it exist in the first place? What kind of world allows it?

He doesn't have a framework for that. Not one that fits what he saw, what he felt, what he cannot stop replaying in fragments that refuse to organize into something coherent.

Training doesn't answer that.

Training explains response.

Not reality.

He stands up, not because he needs to go anywhere, but because sitting still makes the questions louder. He moves through the room, picks up his coffee, sets it down again, walks to the sink, turns the water on, then off. The actions are disconnected from intention, movements without direction.

The questions move with him.

They are not loud.

They do not overwhelm.

But they do not leave.

Later, he hears someone use the word trauma. Not directed at him. Just in passing. "That kind of trauma stays with you."

He recognizes the word. He knows what it means, at least in the way it is usually explained. Something overwhelming. Something the body reacts to. Something that leaves a mark in the nervous system, in memory, in the way a person responds to threat.

That fits.

Part of it.

He had felt that. The urgency. The intensity. The way his body moved without thinking, the way his focus narrowed, the way everything outside the immediate need disappeared.

But this—

this feels different.

Because it isn't just about what happened.

It's about what it means.

He sits down again, the thought forming more clearly now, taking shape in a way it hadn't before.

Trauma is about what you experienced.

This—

is about what you can't make sense of.

About what doesn't fit.

About what feels wrong even when everything was done right.

He remembers what he said in the car.

"I did it right."

And how it didn't land.

Because something else had already been there.

And still—

That space.

Between doing it right and it not being enough.

That's where the questions live.

Why them?

Why not me?

Why at all?

They are not looking for information.

They are looking for meaning.

And meaning is not something he can apply the way he applied pressure or followed protocol or moved from one patient to the next.

Meaning does not respond to instruction.

It resists.

He feels that resistance now, not as confusion, but as tension, something held between what he knows and what he cannot accept, between what happened and what it means about the world he thought he understood.

He exhales slowly.

He doesn't try to answer the questions.

Not yet.

Because he can already tell—

they are not going away.

They are just beginning.

And whatever this is—

it is not just something he went through.

It is something

he is now carrying.

Part II—What Doesn't Fit

The questions do not stay contained. They follow Evan into places that used to feel separate, into work, into conversation, into silence, moving with him in a way that makes it impossible to assign them to a single moment or location. He notices it first when someone tries to explain what he is feeling, when the language meant to make sense of it brushes against something deeper and fails to reach it.

"Adrenaline crash," a coworker says. "Your body's just coming down."

Evan nods.

That makes sense.

It fits something.

The fatigue.

The heaviness.

The way his body feels slower than it should, like it is catching up to something it moved through too quickly to fully register.

That part is real.

But it isn't the whole thing.

Because even when his body settles—

the questions don't.

He tries to name it the way he has heard it named.

Trauma.

It is the word people use, the one that shows up in trainings, in conversations, in the quiet shorthand that signals understanding without requiring explanation.

"That's trauma," someone says. "You'll feel it for a while."

Evan nods again.

Because part of that is true.

He had felt overwhelmed.

He had felt the intensity.

The way everything moved too fast.

The way his body reacted before he could think.

But what he is feeling now—

does not feel like that.

Because it isn't about what his body did.

It is about what his mind will not stop doing.

He is standing in the grocery store when it surfaces again, not triggered by anything obvious, not connected to a sound or a smell or a specific memory, just there, present in the same way it has been present since the moment began to settle into something that could be remembered.

A person in front of him reaches for something on a shelf.

Ordinary.

Unremarkable.

And the thought forms anyway.

Why them?

It does not connect to the person directly.

It connects to the fact of them.

The fact that they are here.

Standing.

Reaching.

Continuing.

Unaware.

The question widens.

Why them here—

and someone else not?

He grips the handle of the cart, harder than he needs to, the pressure grounding in a way that feels necessary even though there is no immediate reason for it.

This is not about danger.

There is no threat here.

And yet—

the question feels just as present.

That is when he realizes something.

This is not tied to the moment anymore.

It has moved.

From the event

into everything.

He finishes shopping, moves through the store, pays, leaves. All of it automatic, all of it unchanged, all of it functioning the way it always has.

But inside—

something is shifting.

He gets into his car and sits, not starting it right away. The space around him is quiet, contained, separate from the movement outside. The thought returns.

Why at all?

He says it this time.

Out loud.

The words sound different when spoken, more defined, more real.

But no more answerable.

He leans back in the seat and closes his eyes. He tries to approach it the way he was trained to approach everything else.

Break it down.

Understand the components.

What happened.

Why it happened.

What could be done differently.

But this—

does not break down.

Because there is no clear cause that satisfies the question.

No action that explains the outcome.

Even if there are reasons—

they do not feel like answers.

He opens his eyes and looks out through the windshield. People move. Cars pass. Everything continues, structured, predictable, operating within systems that still make sense.

The world is intact.

That feels wrong.

Not because it should not be.

But because part of him expected something to change.

Something visible.

Something that would match the weight of what he experienced.

But nothing has.

And the disconnect settles in.

Between what happened

and everything that continues as if it didn't.

He realizes that is part of it too.

Not just the event itself.

But the way the world absorbs it

and moves on.

Leaving him holding something

that does not have a place.

He thinks about Reyes.

About the way he moved.

The way he stayed.

The way he did not hesitate.

Evan had thought that meant something.

Clarity.

Certainty.

Now he wonders—

if it meant something else.

If it meant carrying this

without showing it.

If it meant knowing

that the questions do not go away.

He exhales slowly, the breath moving through him without easing the tension that has settled into place.

The word comes back again.

Trauma.

He turns it over.

Feels where it fits.

Trauma explains reaction.

Explains the body.

Explains the intensity.

But this—

this is not only reaction.

This is interpretation.

Meaning.

And the meaning does not hold.

Because what he saw

does not fit

with how things are supposed to work.

People are supposed to be safe.

Children are supposed to be safe.

There is supposed to be a line

between ordinary

and something like that.

But there is not.

And now he knows that.

Not as information.

As reality.

That is what will not settle.

Not the memory.

Not the sound.

Not even the fear.

But the shift.

In how the world works.

He grips the steering wheel again, not because he needs to drive, but because it is something solid, something that responds to pressure, something that confirms that at least some things remain predictable.

The question comes back.

Not loud.

Not demanding.

Just present.

Why them?

And underneath it—

something deeper.

What does that mean about everything else?

He does not try to answer it.

Because he can feel it now—

the shape of it.

This is not something that resolves.

It is something that remains.

Not in the same way as fear.

Not in the same way as memory.

But as a question

that changes everything around it.

He starts the car, pulls out, moves forward. The road is the same. The turns are the same. The signals operate the same way they always have.

But the questions do not stay behind.

They move with him.

Not attached to the scene anymore.

Attached to him.

And he understands now—

whatever this is—

it is not just about what happened.

It is about what it means.

And that meaning

is still breaking open.

Part III—The Wound Beneath the Wound

By evening, Evan understands that the questions are not only his. He hears them everywhere, not always directly, not always spoken in full, but present beneath conversation, beneath silence, beneath the practical language people use when they are trying to survive the first shape of what has happened. At the station, someone says, "Nothing makes sense anymore." Someone else answers, "It never did." The words are meant to sound hard, experienced, like something learned over time, but Evan hears the tremor underneath them, the unspoken question that holds them in place.

Why at all?

He sits at the edge of the room with a cup of coffee he does not want, listening to people talk around the thing none of them can fully approach. They talk about response time, about entry points, about what worked, about what should have happened sooner, about what will have to change next time. All of that matters. Evan knows it matters. Procedures matter. Training matters. Timing matters. But beneath every practical sentence is another one, harder, less contained.

What kind of world lets this happen?

No one says it that way. Maybe they cannot. Maybe saying it too clearly would make the room stop functioning, would disrupt the fragile structure that allows them to keep talking, to keep moving, to keep working.

So they stay with what can be measured.

Minutes.

Routes.

Radio traffic.

Staging.

Access.

Sequence.

Things that can be reviewed.

Things that can be improved.

Things that can make the next time less terrible.

The next time.

Evan feels the phrase catch inside him, because there it is again, the quiet assumption built into the job. There will be a next time. Not maybe. Not theoretically. Eventually.

The thought does not frighten him the way he expects it to. It does something else.

It makes him tired.

A fatigue deeper than lack of sleep, deeper than physical exhaustion, something that settles into meaning itself and weighs it down.

Reyes walks in later. Daniel Reyes. Not moving fast now, not issuing direction, not holding the shape of the room together the way he did in the hallway. Just entering. He looks older than he did earlier, not in his face, not physically, but in the way he occupies space, as if something invisible has shifted around him.

Evan watches him from across the room. Reyes pours coffee but does not drink it right away. He stands there with it, looking down into the cup as if it holds something more than what it is.

For a moment, Evan thinks Reyes might say something to the room, might step into the space the way experienced responders sometimes do, offering a summary, a frame, something that helps organize what just happened.

He does not.

He takes the coffee and sits alone.

No one bothers him.

That tells Evan something.

Experience has its own silence.

People recognize it.

They make room for it.

They respect it.

Or they avoid it.

Evan is not sure which.

After a while, Reyes looks over. Their eyes meet, not long, just enough. Evan looks away first, not out of embarrassment, but because he does not know what Reyes can see when he looks at him now.

The questions keep moving.

Why them?

Why not me?

Why at all?

By now, Evan understands that the questions are connected, but not identical. Why them reaches toward the victims, toward the randomness, toward the terrible unfairness of who stood where, who turned when, who was seen, who was missed. Why not me reaches inward, toward survival, toward the strange discomfort of still being here when others are not. Why at all reaches beyond the event, toward the structure of the world itself, toward whether anything can still be trusted to hold.

Trauma explains part of this. Evan knows that now. Trauma explains the body's alarm, the way sound startles, the way sleep breaks, the way memory returns without permission. It explains the intensity, the way the moment imprints itself on the nervous system.

But this is different too.

This is the wound beneath the wound.

Not only fear.

Not only memory.

Meaning.

Trust.

The collapse of what he thought was true.

That help would be enough.

That doing the right thing would feel right.

That surviving would feel only like gratitude.

That the job would make sense because the job mattered.

Now all of that feels less certain. Not gone, but cracked, as if something foundational has shifted just enough to be felt but not enough to be clearly named.

Reyes stands to leave.

Evan speaks before he can think better of it.

"Reyes?"

Daniel stops.

Turns.

The room continues around them, low voices, the hum of lights, the quiet rhythm of people trying to stay inside something manageable.

Evan almost takes it back.

Instead, he asks, "Does it ever make sense?"

Reyes does not answer right away.

That helps.

A quick answer would have felt false.

Finally, Reyes says, "Some parts do."

Evan waits.

Reyes looks down at the cup in his hand.

"The work can make sense," he says. "The protocol. The choices. The sequence."

He looks back at Evan.

"But the thing itself?"

A pause.

"No."

The honesty lands harder than comfort would have.

Evan nods.

Reyes adds, "Don't confuse those."

"What?"

"The work making sense and the harm making sense."

Evan holds the distinction, feels it settle beside the questions, not as an answer, but as a boundary.

Reyes continues, quieter now. "If you need the harm to make sense before you can keep doing the work, it'll break you."

Evan looks at him.

"And if the work doesn't feel like enough?"

Reyes' expression shifts slightly, not surprise, not confusion, something closer to recognition.

"Then you tell the truth about that too."

That is all he says.

Then he leaves.

Evan stays seated. The room keeps moving. The questions do not disappear, but something has shifted. Not relief. Not resolution. A small separation.

The harm does not make sense.

The work still matters.

Both can be true.

That does not heal the wound.

But it gives it shape.

And sometimes shape is the first mercy.

Evan looks down at his coffee. Cold now. Untouched. He lifts it anyway, takes a sip. It tastes bitter, ordinary, real. Around him, people continue talking, about routes, about timing, about what will change, about what must change.

And beneath all of it, the questions remain.

Why them?

Why not me?

Why at all?

They do not leave.

They do not resolve.

But Evan begins to understand something.

These questions are not signs that he is weak.

They are signs that something in him is still intact.

Something that knows this should not be normal.

Something that refuses to let what happened become just another call, just another report, just another sequence to review and improve.

That refusal hurts.

Maybe that is part of the wound.

Maybe that is where moral injury begins.

Not only in what happened.

But in the collision between what happened

and what should never have been possible.

Evan sits with that.

Not comfortably.

Not completely.

But honestly.

The questions have begun.

And he knows now they will not be answered quickly.

Maybe not ever.

But they can be carried differently.

Not as failure.

Not as weakness.

As testimony.

As refusal.

As the part of him that still insists the world should be more than this.

And because it should be—

the work still matters.

Chapter 13—**Guilt, Shame, and Betrayal**

Part I—What I Carry (and Why)

Evan doesn't have words for it at first, not precise ones, not the kind that separate one feeling from another or give shape to what is pressing against him from the inside. It all arrives together, heavy and unsorted, a convergence of reactions that feel connected but indistinguishable, like layers that have not yet been pulled apart. He just knows something feels wrong, not only about what happened, but about himself, and that difference matters even if he cannot name it yet.

It begins with replay, not the whole scene, not in sequence, just moments, specific ones that return without invitation. The turn he didn't take. The voice he didn't follow. The place he stayed. "I could have—" The sentence forms again, stops again, because there is no version of it that resolves anything, no ending that settles what it opens. But the feeling attached to it stays, persistent, returning in slightly different forms but always anchored to the same point. That feeling is guilt, even if he does not call it that yet, even if it has not been named.

Guilt asks a simple question: What did I do? Or more precisely, what didn't I do? Evan sits with that, replays the moment again, feels the structure of it as he experienced it. He had followed protocol. He had stayed with the patient. He had done exactly what he was trained to do. The steps had been clear. The decisions had been consistent with everything he had learned. And still—"I could have gone." The thought presses in, even though he knows that if he had gone, something else would have been left behind, someone else would have been unattended, another need would have gone unmet.

That does not stop the feeling. Because guilt is not logical. It is relational. It measures action against outcome, not intention, not structure, not constraint. When the outcome is loss, guilt looks for a place to land. Evan feels where it lands. On him. Not fully, not completely, but enough to feel like weight that belongs, even if it cannot be justified in the way he would justify any other decision.

But something else is there too, quieter at first, less defined, more diffuse. Not about what he did. About what it says about him. The thought comes slowly, then more clearly. "What kind of person—" He stops, but the sentence finishes anyway, internally, without permission. What kind of person hears that and stays? This feels different. Not tied to the moment alone. Tied to identity.

This is shame.

Guilt says: I did something wrong.

Shame says: I am something wrong.

Evan feels the shift between them, subtle but significant. Guilt still holds to the moment, still returns to the scene, to the decision, to the alternative that was not taken. Shame expands beyond it, moving outward into how he sees himself, how he imagines others might see him, how he evaluates his own response in a way that goes beyond action.

Guilt can be argued. Explained. Contextualized. It can be placed within a framework and examined.

Shame resists all of that.

Because it does not ask what happened.

It decides what that means about you.

Evan stands in front of the mirror again later that night, the same place as the morning before, the same reflection looking back, unchanged in every visible way. He studies it longer this time, as if something might reveal itself if he looks closely enough. There is no mark, no visible difference, nothing that signals the shift he feels internally. But he feels it anyway, a question embedded under the surface, not fully formed but persistent.

What kind of person are you now?

He looks away.

The third feeling comes later, not as immediate, not as internal, but no less present. It begins when he listens, really listens, to what others are saying, to the way people try to make sense of what happened using the language available to them. At the station. In passing conversations. In the spaces where explanation and frustration overlap.

"They should have had better security."

"Someone should have seen something."

"There should have been more protection."

The phrase repeats.

Should have.

Should have.

Should have.

Evan notices how often it appears, how quickly it surfaces, how naturally people reach for it when trying to understand something that resists understanding. And something in him responds, not simple agreement, not immediate alignment, but something sharper, something more pointed.

Because the "should have" directs attention somewhere.

To systems.

To people.

To decisions made before he ever arrived.

The thought forms slowly, then clearly enough to hold.

Someone failed.

Not him.

Not in the moment.

Before the moment.

This feeling is different from guilt and different from shame. It does not pull inward. It does not attach itself to identity. It moves outward, toward structure, toward responsibility beyond the immediate scene.

This is betrayal.

Betrayal asks: What should have protected us and didn't? What should have been prevented and wasn't? What failed before the moment that made the moment possible?

Evan feels that question settle, and with it, a shift in how responsibility is distributed, how the weight of what happened is carried.

Guilt says: I didn't do enough.

Shame says: I am not enough.

Betrayal says: This should not have been mine to carry at all.

The three sit together, not separate, not clean, interwoven in a way that makes them difficult to distinguish if he is not paying attention. He feels all of them at once—guilt pulling him back into the moment, shame pressing inward toward identity, betrayal pushing outward toward systems and failures beyond his control. Each one points in a different direction. None of them resolve.

He sits on the edge of his bed, hands clasped, still, trying to hold them apart, to name them, to understand them, because without names they blur, and when they blur, everything feels like fault, everything collapses into a single weight that is heavier than any one of them alone.

He exhales slowly.

Guilt.

What I did.

Shame.

Who I am.

Betrayal.

What others failed to do.

He repeats it, not as a solution, not as an answer, but as a distinction, something that allows him to begin separating what he is feeling into parts that can at least be seen clearly, even if they cannot yet be resolved.

Because something about separating them feels important, even if none of them go away, even if all of them remain.

He leans back and stares at the ceiling. The questions from before are still there.

Why them?

Why not me?

Why at all?

But now they have weight attached to them, direction, movement.

Guilt answers: Maybe because I didn't do enough.

Shame answers: Maybe because I'm not who I thought I was.

Betrayal answers: Maybe because something bigger failed.

None of those answers settle the questions.

But they change how the questions feel.

More specific.

More personal.

More complicated.

Evan closes his eyes, not to sleep, just to stop looking, to give himself a moment without visual input, without the need to interpret anything outside himself.

The feelings do not disappear.

But they begin to separate.

Just enough for him to see

that not all of them belong

to him.

And that matters.

Even if he doesn't yet know

what to do with it.

Part II—Where It Lands

The words help, but they do not fix anything. Evan notices that almost immediately. Naming it—guilt, shame, betrayal—creates space, but it does not remove weight. If anything, it makes the weight clearer, more defined, less diffuse. What had been a single, overwhelming pressure now has edges, and those edges make it easier to see where each feeling begins and ends, even if none of them lessen.

He starts to recognize where each one shows up, not in theory, not in reflection, but in real moments that unfold without warning. Guilt is the easiest to find. It attaches to memory, specific and repeatable, returning to the same point again and again with slight variations that do not change its core.

He is washing his hands when it returns, the same moment, the same voice.

"My friend is still in there."

His hands pause under the water. He watches them, remembers what they were doing instead, where they were placed, why they stayed where they were. The pressure, the position, the decision that was not made but enforced by everything around it.

"I could have gone."

The sentence feels automatic now, practiced in a way that makes it feel more real, even though it leads nowhere new.

Guilt speaks in alternatives, in versions of the past that feel possible even when they were not. It reconstructs moments with different outcomes, rearranges choices as if time were flexible, as if the structure that held him in place could have been stepped outside of without consequence.

He knows the logic. He knows the training. He knows why he stayed.

But guilt does not care about that.

It cares about the gap between what happened and what feels like it should have happened.

He turns off the water and dries his hands slowly, as if the pace of his movement might influence the pace of the thoughts, as if slowing down might stretch time enough to change something that has already closed.

But the moment does not change.

It never does.

Shame shows up differently, less tied to a single memory, more attached to how he moves through the present. He notices it when someone asks him a question, something simple, something routine.

"How are you doing?"

He answers automatically. "I'm fine."

But something in him tightens, because the answer feels like performance, not a lie exactly, but not true either. It feels like a version of himself he is presenting rather than something he is actually experiencing.

Shame lives there, in the gap between what is felt and what is shown. It asks a different kind of question.

If they knew—would they see you differently?

He finds himself watching his own behavior, measuring it, evaluating it in real time.

Am I acting normal?

Am I saying the right things?

Am I holding this the way I'm supposed to?

That last question lingers longer than the others, because he does not know what "supposed to" means anymore. The framework he thought he understood no longer applies in the same way, or at least not in a way that feels complete.

He thinks about Reyes, about the way he carried himself after the call, quiet, contained, not withdrawn but not open either. Evan studies that memory carefully, looking for something he can replicate, something that will tell him how to be.

Is that strength?

Or is that just practice?

Shame leans into that question.

You're not like him.

The thought is subtle, not loud, but it lands in a way that makes it difficult to dismiss. It settles into place alongside everything else, reinforcing the sense that there is a standard he is not meeting, even if he cannot clearly define it.

He pushes it away, but it stays close.

Because shame is not satisfied with moments.

It looks for identity.

And once it finds a crack, it widens it.

Betrayal takes longer to recognize, not because it is weaker, but because it points away from him, and he is less practiced at looking outward when something feels wrong inside.

He notices it when someone starts listing failures, not his, not immediate, but systemic, structural, embedded in how things were arranged before anyone ever arrived.

"They should have had more security."

"There were warning signs."

"Someone missed something."

The words are sharp, directed, carrying a different kind of energy than the quiet, inward pull of guilt or the evaluative pressure of shame.

Evan feels something rise in him.

Unexpected.

Anger.

Not explosive, not expressed, but present in a way that demands attention. It sits differently than the other feelings, less tangled, more pointed.

Because something about the "should have" feels true.

And something about it feels dangerous.

Because if it is true—

then what happened was not only tragic.

It was preventable.

That realization shifts the ground beneath everything else.

He leans back in his chair and listens as the conversation continues, people naming gaps, failures, missed opportunities, each one pointing somewhere, each one suggesting that the moment they responded to was shaped long before they entered it.

Not at him.

At something larger.

Systems.

Processes.

Decisions made in rooms he was never in.

Betrayal sits there, quiet but heavy.

It asks: Why were we put in that position? Why did it come down to that moment? Why did it become ours to carry?

Evan feels the shift clearly now.

Because this is different from guilt.

Guilt pulls him inward.

Betrayal pushes outward.

And the two do not cancel each other.

They coexist.

That is what makes it complicated.

He can feel responsible and wronged at the same time.

He can feel like he failed and like something failed him.

There is no clean line between them.

He exhales slowly.

The room feels heavier now, not because anything has changed externally, but because he can feel more of what is happening internally, more of the layers that were present before but not yet distinguished.

Later, he sits alone, trying to hold the distinctions in place.

Guilt.

Shame.

Betrayal.

He repeats them again, not as definitions, but as locations, as ways of orienting himself within what he is feeling.

Where does this feeling belong?

He closes his eyes.

The moment returns again.

But this time he watches it differently.

He sees himself staying.

Feels the pull to go.

Hears the voice.

"I could have—"

Guilt.

Then the next layer.

What kind of person does that?

Shame.

Then the wider frame.

Why was this even happening?

Why was anyone there at all?

Betrayal.

He opens his eyes, breath steady.

The moment has not changed.

But his relationship to it has shifted slightly.

Not resolved.

Not healed.

But clearer.

And in that clarity, something important happens.

He begins to see that not every feeling is telling the same truth.

Some are about action.

Some are about identity.

Some are about the world.

And if he does not separate them, they collapse into one, into something heavier than it needs to be, something that feels absolute when it is actually composed of parts.

He leans back and stares at the ceiling.

Guilt says: You should have done more.

Shame says: You are not enough.

Betrayal says: This should not have been yours.

He lets them sit.

Does not argue.

Does not resolve.

Just holds them.

Separately.

And for the first time, it feels like maybe he does not have to carry all of them the same way.

That realization is small.

Fragile.

But it is there.

And it matters, even if everything else still feels the same.

Part III—What Is Mine (and What Is Not)

It takes time for Evan to realize that naming something is not the same as knowing what to do with it. Guilt, shame, betrayal—he can say the words now, can recognize them when they surface, can feel where they attach and how they move. But recognition does not tell him where they belong or how much of each is his to carry. That question begins quietly, not as defiance, not as relief, but as uncertainty.

What is mine?

He sits with that longer than the others because it feels different, less reactive, more deliberate, a question that does not rush toward conclusion but instead waits for something deeper to surface. He starts with guilt because it feels the most justified, the most earned, the most clearly connected to something he can point to.

He returns to the moment again, not because he wants to, but because it continues to draw him back. The hallway. The voice. "My friend is still in there." He sees himself staying, feels the pull to go, the tension between movement and restraint that defined the moment in a way that cannot be undone.

"I could have—"

This time he lets the sentence form fully. He does not stop it.

"I could have gone."

The words land and remain. He does not argue them, does not correct them, does not soften them. He lets them exist as they are, without interruption. Then something else follows, not automatically, not easily, but intentionally.

"If I had gone—"

He pauses, because this is where his mind usually fills in the rest, usually moves toward a different ending, a rescue, a version of events that justifies the impulse he felt in that moment.

But this time, he does not let it go there.

Instead, he continues honestly.

"If I had gone, someone else would have been left."

The sentence lands differently. Not lighter, not relieving, but more complete. It holds more of the truth than the earlier version did, includes what had been left out when guilt narrowed the focus to a single absence.

He sits with that.

Because guilt had been holding only one side of the moment, focusing on what he did not do and ignoring what he did instead.

He stayed.

He treated.

He held.

He followed the structure that made survival possible for someone else.

Guilt had erased that, reduced the moment to a single perceived failure, rather than the complex set of actions that actually occurred.

He exhales slowly.

This does not remove the guilt.

But it changes its shape.

Makes it more accurate.

Less absolute.

Maybe that matters.

Shame is harder.

Because shame resists correction.

It does not respond to logic or to completion.

It attaches itself to identity, to how he sees himself and how he imagines others might see him.

He feels it when he thinks about Reyes.

The comparison comes automatically.

Reyes moved without hesitation.

Reyes knew what to do.

Reyes did not stop.

Evan had hesitated, even if only for a moment.

Shame builds from that difference.

You're not ready.

You're not strong enough.

You're not who you thought you were.

The thoughts are quiet, but persistent, returning without needing to be invited.

He sits with them.

Does not push them away immediately.

Lets them speak fully, lets them complete their logic.

Then he asks something different.

Not are they true.

But where do they come from?

He traces them back.

To expectation.

To the version of himself he believed he would be.

Calm.

Decisive.

Certain.

Untouched by doubt.

That version did not exist.

Not really.

It was built in training.

In imagination.

In distance from reality.

And now that version has been disrupted.

Shame is trying to fill the gap, not with truth, but with judgment.

He exhales again, slower this time.

Because this matters.

Shame is not pointing to something he did.

It is reacting to something that was never real to begin with, an expectation that could not have been met because it was never grounded in what the moment actually required.

He thinks about Reyes again, but differently now.

Not as perfection.

More carefully.

Reyes had moved, yes.

But he had also stayed.

He had also chosen.

He had also left things undone.

Because that is the nature of the moment.

Not failure.

Limit.

Evan feels something shift.

Small.

But important.

Shame had been built on comparison, on a false version of what strength looks like.

If that version is not real, then maybe the judgment is not either.

Betrayal is the most complicated.

Because it does not feel like something he is supposed to question.

It feels justified.

Someone should have prevented this.

Someone should have seen it coming.

Someone should have made it impossible.

He feels the anger again.

Quiet.

Controlled.

But present.

And he lets it be there.

Because unlike shame, betrayal is not about distortion.

It is about rupture.

Something that should have held did not.

Something that should have protected failed.

But even here, something shifts.

Because he notices what happens next.

The anger begins to attach.

Not just to systems.

To people.

Someone should have done something.

Someone failed.

The thought sharpens, becomes more specific, more directed.

He pauses.

Because this matters too.

Betrayal can clarify.

But it can also consume.

It can point to failure.

Or it can turn everything into blame.

He sits with that tension.

Because not everything that failed was within reach.

Not everything that broke was visible beforehand.

Not everything that could have been done was known.

This does not erase the betrayal.

But it complicates it.

Moves it out of absolutes.

Into something more difficult.

Shared limitation.

Systemic fragility.

Human imperfection.

He exhales again.

Slow.

Guilt.

Shame.

Betrayal.

He looks at them now differently, not as a single weight, but as separate layers.

Guilt—partly his, but incomplete.

Shame—less his than it felt.

Betrayal—real, but not simple.

He leans back and closes his eyes.

The moment is still there.

The hallway.

The voice.

The choice.

But something has changed.

Not the memory.

His position inside it.

He is no longer only the one who failed.

He is also the one who acted, who stayed, who carried something impossible in a moment that did not allow for completeness.

That does not make it right.

But it makes it real.

He opens his eyes.

Breath steady.

The feelings do not disappear.

They do not resolve.

But they are no longer indistinguishable.

And because of that, he can begin to ask a different question.

Not just what happened.

But what belongs to me—

and what does not?

He does not have the full answer.

Not yet.

But he has enough to know that everything he feels is not his to carry in the same way.

And that—

is the beginning of something shifting.

Chapter 14—**Systems Under Strain**

Part I—When the Structure Fails

Evan had been trained to trust the system, not blindly, not without question, but functionally, in the way that allows action to happen without hesitation. The system was what made the work possible. Dispatch. Communication. Chain of command. Protocols that turned chaos into sequence. You didn't have to understand everything. You had to trust that what you were stepping into was held by something larger than you, something structured, coordinated, and reliable enough to support decisions made under pressure.

That trust had felt solid.

Until it didn't.

The cracks didn't show all at once. They revealed themselves in fragments, small moments that didn't fit, delays that felt longer than they should have been, instructions that didn't align, voices overlapping on the radio—not coordinating, but competing. Evan hadn't noticed it clearly in the moment. There hadn't been time. Everything had been immediate, focused, narrowed to what was directly in front of him. But now, in memory, the gaps begin to stand out.

He remembers waiting. Not long. But long enough to feel it. Standing in place while something else was still unfolding somewhere beyond reach, somewhere just outside the boundaries of what he could see or act on.

"Hold."

The word had come through the radio, clear, authoritative, leaving no room for interpretation.

So he held.

Because that's what the system required.

But now he replays it.

What was happening during that hold?

Who was still waiting?

What was still moving without response?

The question unsettles him, because it shifts something fundamental. It moves the focus from individual action to collective function, from what he did in the moment to what the system did—or didn't do—around him.

It wasn't just about him.

It was about what surrounded him.

He hears it again later, not in memory, but in conversation.

"There was a delay in entry."

"Communication broke down."

"Units weren't aligned."

The words are clinical, measured, delivered in the tone of analysis rather than emotion, but Evan hears what they mean beneath the surface.

Time was lost.

Direction was unclear.

People moved without full information.

And in a moment like that, those things matter, not abstractly, not theoretically, but directly, shaping what was possible and what was not.

He feels something tighten in his chest, because this is different from guilt.

Guilt lives in the moment of choice.

This lives in the structure that shaped the moment before the choice.

He sits at the edge of the debrief, listening as the event is reconstructed, not emotionally, but operationally.

"What time was entry confirmed?"

"Where were units staged?"

"Who had command at that point?"

Each question attempts to map the sequence, to restore order after the fact, to create a version of events that can be understood, evaluated, and improved.

But something doesn't sit right.

Because the map feels cleaner than the experience.

The lines are clearer.

The timing more precise.

The roles more defined.

But inside the moment, it hadn't felt that way.

It had felt fragmented.

Uncertain.

Held together, but not fully.

Evan shifts in his seat, because this realization carries weight.

If the system wasn't fully holding, then what was he standing inside?

The thought unsettles him more than anything else so far.

Because training assumes structure.

Even in chaos, there is supposed to be coordination, a framework, a logic, something that ensures you are not alone in what you are doing, that your actions are part of something larger that connects, aligns, and supports.

But what if that wasn't fully true?

What if parts of it broke?

Not completely.

Not visibly.

But enough to matter.

He thinks back again.

The radio.

Voices overlapping.

Someone asking for confirmation and not getting it.

Someone giving direction that didn't quite match what he was seeing.

He had adjusted.

Followed what was clearest.

Stayed where he was told.

But now he sees the edges.

Where clarity thinned.

Where certainty wasn't complete.

Where decisions were made inside incomplete information.

That realization lands differently.

Because it reframes the moment, not as a single point of responsibility, but as something distributed, across people, across systems, across structures that were supposed to hold but didn't fully.

He exhales slowly.

This is where something shifts again.

Because moral injury is no longer only about what he did or didn't do.

It is about what he was part of.

A system that did not fully function the way it was supposed to.

That thought is harder to hold.

Because it is less defined.

Less contained.

Guilt has edges.

You can point to it.

System strain is harder to locate.

Where does it begin?

Where does it end?

Who carries it?

He looks around the room at the others listening, nodding, taking notes. Everyone is trying to understand, to improve, to prevent it from happening again. That matters. It does. But it doesn't erase what already happened, and it doesn't answer what it means to have been inside it.

Evan feels the tension building, because this is where betrayal returns, not as accusation, but as realization.

Something that should have held—

didn't fully.

Not completely.

But enough.

Enough that the moment felt different from what it was supposed to be.

Enough that the burden shifted in ways he didn't fully understand at the time.

He leans forward, hands clasped, still, trying to hold the thought without letting it scatter into something unmanageable.

Because this changes something.

Not just about the event.

About the job.

About what it means to trust the structure you are working inside.

He had believed the system would hold.

Now he knows it can strain.

That it can falter.

That it can leave gaps.

And in those gaps, people make decisions they were never meant to carry alone.

He exhales, long and steady, grounding himself in the present as the debrief continues, more questions, more answers, more attempts to restore order to something that resisted it in real time.

But Evan sits with something else, a quieter realization that moves beneath the conversation.

That what happened was not only the result of one moment, but of many things not aligning the way they were supposed to.

And that is harder to resolve.

Because it doesn't end with him.

It extends outward.

Into systems.

Into structures.

Into trust.

And now that trust is no longer untouched.

It is still there.

But altered.

Because he has seen what happens when it strains.

And he knows now that being inside the system does not mean being fully protected by it.

And that knowing stays.

Part II—The Weight of the Gaps

The system doesn't collapse all at once. That's what unsettles Evan most. It doesn't announce failure, doesn't stop functioning, doesn't break in a way that is immediately visible or undeniable. It continues, but not completely, not in the way it is meant to, not in the way it needs to when everything depends on it working as intended. That is what makes it difficult to recognize in the moment, difficult to name, and even harder to trust afterward.

Evan notices it more clearly now, not during the call, but in the space that follows, when everything is being reviewed, reconstructed, and explained. He listens as timelines are drawn, as sequences are clarified, as decisions are placed in order, each one assigned a time, a position, a rationale that makes it appear connected and coherent.

"Dispatch received the call at—"

"Units were mobilized at—"

"Entry was confirmed at—"

Everything has a place in the sequence, a defined position in a timeline that appears continuous, structured, and complete. On paper, it looks like continuity. It looks like control. It looks like a system that functioned, even if imperfectly.

But Evan remembers the feeling inside it.

He remembers the pauses that were not accounted for, the uncertainty that was not named, the moments that did not fit cleanly into the timeline that is now being constructed. Those are the gaps, and the gaps carry weight.

He leans forward slightly, listening more carefully, because this is where the system tries to make sense of itself, not emotionally, but operationally, in a language designed to identify breakdown and prevent repetition.

"What caused the delay?"

"Where was the breakdown?"

"How do we prevent this next time?"

The questions are necessary. They matter. They are part of how the system learns, adapts, improves. But they also simplify. They assume that breakdown can be located, defined, corrected, that failure can be isolated to a point and addressed in a way that prevents it from happening again.

Evan isn't sure it works that way.

Because what he experienced wasn't a single failure. It was accumulation. Small misalignments stacking on top of each other until something essential became unclear, until the structure that was supposed to hold began to strain in ways that were subtle but consequential.

He remembers the radio again, not the specific words, but the tone. Overlap. Urgency without direction. Someone asking. Someone answering.

But not always the same conversation, not always aligned, not always integrated into a single, coherent flow of information.

He had followed what made sense, stayed where the instruction was clearest, acted within the part of the system that felt most stable. But now he wonders what others were hearing, what instructions they were following, what information they did not have access to in the moment.

That thought widens the experience.

Because it means no one was fully seeing the whole.

Everyone was acting from a partial view.

And the system, which was supposed to integrate those views into something unified, didn't fully succeed.

That realization lands heavily.

Because it shifts responsibility again, not away from individuals, but across them, distributing it in a way that is harder to hold. When responsibility is shared, the weight does not disappear. It becomes harder to locate, harder to assign, harder to release.

He can feel that now.

Not lighter.

More complex.

Because there is no single place to put it down.

Evan exhales slowly.

This is where something else begins to take shape, not just awareness of the gaps, but awareness of what those gaps required from the people inside them. They required individuals to make decisions without full clarity, to act without complete information, to carry outcomes that were shaped by more than their own choices.

That is where moral injury deepens.

Not in the action alone, not in the isolated moment of decision, but in the realization that the action was never fully contained within individual control, that it was influenced, constrained, and shaped by a system that was not functioning completely in the way it was intended to.

He feels that now.

Because it changes the question.

From: What did I do?

To: What was I part of?

And that question does not resolve the same way.

It does not lead to correction.

It leads to complexity.

He looks around the room again at the others listening, responding, trying to make sense of what happened, each one engaging with the process in a way that reflects commitment, responsibility, and the desire to improve.

Everyone is engaged.

Focused.

Committed to making the system better.

That matters.

But something inside him resists the idea that improvement alone is enough.

Because improvement looks forward.

And what he is carrying is still tied to what already happened.

The system will adjust.

Protocols will change.

Communication will be reviewed.

But none of that undoes the moment when the system strained.

It does not remove what was carried inside that strain.

Evan shifts in his seat.

Because this is where the tension sharpens.

He wants to trust the system.

He still does, in many ways.

But now that trust includes something new.

Awareness of its limits.

Awareness that it can falter.

That it can leave spaces where individuals must compensate, must fill in the gaps, must act in ways that extend beyond what they were prepared to carry.

And those spaces are where the weight accumulates.

He thinks about future calls, about stepping into the next moment with this knowledge, about how it might change the way he listens, the way he responds, the way he trusts what he is told.

Will he trust the radio the same way?

Will he hesitate more?

Will he question what he is hearing?

The thought unsettles him.

Because hesitation has its own cost.

And trust, even imperfect trust, is what allows action to happen.

If that trust fractures, what replaces it?

He does not have an answer.

Only the awareness that something has shifted.

Not broken.

But altered.

He leans back and stares at the ceiling as the conversation continues around him, plans being made, adjustments suggested, lessons identified, all of it part of the system trying to hold itself together, trying to respond to what it has revealed about itself.

All of it necessary.

All of it important.

But Evan sits with something quieter.

The understanding that systems are not static.

They are human.

Built by people.

Run by people.

Dependent on people.

Which means they carry the same limitations.

The same vulnerabilities.

The same potential to strain under pressure.

He exhales slowly.

This does not mean the system failed completely.

It means it did not hold perfectly.

And in that imperfection, people carried more than they were meant to.

That includes him.

That includes everyone in that room.

And that realization does not resolve the weight.

But it explains why it feels the way it does.

Not just personal.

Structural.

Not just about what happened.

About how it happened.

And that distinction matters.

Even if it does not make it easier to carry.

Part III—Trust After Fracture

What unsettles Evan most is not that the system strained. It is that he had believed it wouldn't, not completely, not in the ways that matter most. There had always been an underlying assumption, never fully stated but consistently reinforced, that while individual moments might be chaotic, the structure itself would hold, that even if everything felt uncertain at ground level, there was something above it organizing, guiding, making sense of what no single person could fully see.

Now that assumption feels different.

Not gone.

But fractured.

He notices it the next time he hears the radio, not during a major call, not in a moment of crisis, but in something routine, a minor dispatch that does not carry the same urgency or weight. And still, he listens differently, more carefully, more critically, not only to what is said, but to how it is said, to the pauses, the overlaps, the slight hesitations that he would not have registered before.

Nothing is wrong.

Not exactly.

The call proceeds.

Units respond.

The system functions.

But something in him has changed.

He is no longer only receiving information.

He is evaluating it.

Not out of defiance.

Out of awareness.

And that awareness comes with a cost.

Because it introduces doubt.

And doubt, in this work, is complicated.

Too much of it slows action, creates hesitation, interrupts the flow that allows people to move quickly and effectively in high-pressure situations.

Too little of it means trusting something that may not fully hold, relying on a structure that can strain in ways that are not always visible until it matters most.

Evan feels that tension now, between trust and doubt, between structure and uncertainty, between what he was taught to rely on and what he has now seen with his own experience.

He does not know yet how to balance them.

Only that he cannot return to what it felt like before.

The system still works.

But now he sees its edges.

And once you see the edges, you cannot unsee them.

He thinks about Reyes again, not just how he moved during the call, but how he held himself after, the quiet, the containment, the way he seemed to carry something without showing it fully. At first, Evan had interpreted that as strength, as control, as a kind of composure that came with experience.

Now he sees something else in it.

Accommodation.

Not resignation.

Adjustment.

Reyes knows the system, not just how it is supposed to work, but how it actually works, including where it does not, where it falters, where it leaves space that must be filled by the people inside it.

Evan wonders how long it took to learn that.

How many moments like this it required.

How many times Reyes stood inside something that did not fully hold and still had to act, still had to decide, still had to carry the outcome.

That realization changes how Evan sees him.

Not as someone unaffected.

But as someone who has learned to function within imperfection.

That feels more real.

But also heavier.

Because it suggests something about the future.

That this is not an exception.

It is part of the work.

The thought settles in slowly.

Systems will strain again.

Not necessarily in the same way.

Not necessarily in the same place.

But somewhere.

And when they do, people like him will be inside that strain, making decisions, carrying weight that they did not create but must still hold.

Evan exhales slowly.

This is where something shifts again, not in what happened, but in how he understands his place within it.

He is not just responding to events.

He is operating within systems that shape those events.

And those systems are not perfect.

They are functional.

Often effective.

But not flawless.

That realization removes something.

Not trust entirely.

But certainty.

And in its place comes something more complex.

Conditional trust.

Trust with awareness.

Trust that includes the possibility of failure.

He sits with that.

Because it changes how he will move forward.

He will still respond.

Still follow protocol.

Still rely on the structure.

But now he will also watch for the gaps, listen for misalignment, pay attention to what does not fit, not to challenge the system, but to understand it more fully, to be ready when it strains.

That readiness feels necessary.

But it also feels like weight.

Because it adds something to every future moment, an extra layer of awareness, an additional responsibility.

Not just to act.

But to notice.

Not just to follow.

But to interpret.

Evan feels the complexity of that, because in a perfect system, that would not be required, but this is not a perfect system, and now he knows that in a way he cannot undo.

The thought returns, not as a question, but as a realization.

Moral injury is not only about what individuals do.

It is about what they are asked to carry when systems do not fully hold.

That lands differently.

Because it expands the scope.

Moves the weight outward without removing it.

He is still part of it.

Still inside it.

But not alone in its origin.

That distinction matters.

Even if it does not make the experience easier.

He leans back and closes his eyes.

The moment returns again, but now it includes more than before, not just the hallway, not just the voice, but the structure around it, the signals, the delays, the misalignments, all of it shaping what was possible in ways that were not fully visible at the time.

He exhales slowly.

This does not remove responsibility.

But it redistributes it.

And in that redistribution, something shifts.

Not relief.

But recognition.

That what he carries is not only his.

That the weight has sources beyond him.

And that understanding, even if incomplete, changes how it sits.

He opens his eyes.

The room is quiet.

Still.

Nothing outward has changed.

But inward, something has settled differently.

Not resolved.

But named.

The system strained.

He was inside it.

And now he has to learn how to trust again, without pretending it will never happen the same way.

Part III—**The Weight**

Chapter 15—The Replay

Part I—It Doesn't Stay Past

The moment doesn't end when it's over. It changes form. It returns, not as a full memory, not as a clear sequence, but as pieces—uninvited, unordered, carrying fragments of what happened without the structure that would make them manageable. Evan notices it first in the quiet, not during activity, not when he's moving, but when he stops, when there is nothing immediate demanding his attention. That is when it begins again.

He is sitting on the edge of his bed, not thinking about it, not trying to remember, not reaching for the past in any intentional way. And suddenly he's back in the hallway. Not completely, not in a way that replaces the present, but just enough. The sound returns. A voice. "My friend is still in there." It doesn't play like a story. It hits like a fragment, sharp and contained, something that arrives fully formed and then disappears just as quickly.

He exhales, but his body doesn't settle, because it is already anticipating the next one. The replay does not wait for readiness. It does not ask permission. It moves on its own timing, independent of his intention, appearing in the gaps where his guard is lowest.

Across town, a woman stands in her kitchen holding a plate she hasn't set down. She hears a noise, something ordinary, something that would not have registered before, and her body reacts before her mind can interpret it. A flinch. A tightening. A shift in breath that happens automatically. Then it comes, not the whole day, not a complete sequence, but one image. A door. A moment just before something changed. She closes her eyes, but that doesn't stop it, because this is not about seeing. It is about remembering without permission.

In a classroom down the street, a child sits at a desk with a pencil unmoving in their hand. The teacher is speaking. Words are being said. But they are not landing. Something else is happening, internal and unspoken. A sound, not even real, just close enough to echo something familiar, and suddenly the room is not the room anymore. It becomes that place again, that moment, that feeling. The child doesn't move. Doesn't react. Just stops. From the outside, it looks like stillness. From the inside, it is anything but.

Evan stands up and starts pacing, not because he has somewhere to go, but because sitting still makes it worse. The fragments keep coming, not connected, not ordered, arriving as isolated pieces that refuse to form a complete picture. A hand. A voice. The weight of the decision. Each one complete in itself. Each one unfinished.

He presses his hands against his face, as if that might interrupt it, as if physical pressure could break the sequence or redirect the flow. It doesn't. Because this isn't something he is choosing to remember. It is something that keeps remembering him, something that returns without his involvement, something that insists on being present even when he is not inviting it.

At the station, Reyes sits alone with a cup of coffee he has not touched. He is not replaying it, not intentionally revisiting the moment, not searching for it. But it is there, beneath everything else. He hears something—a radio call, routine, unrelated—and for a split second, it overlaps. Two moments trying to exist at the same time. He doesn't react. Doesn't show it. But his grip tightens slightly around the cup before releasing again. Practice. Not prevention.

The replay is not the same for everyone. That is what makes it difficult to name. For Evan, it comes as fragments, moments of decision, points where something almost changed. For the woman in the kitchen, it is anticipation, the moment before, the sense that something is about to happen again. For the child, it is confusion, the inability to separate then from now. For Reyes, it is overlay, the past threading itself through the present without replacing it.

But the effect is shared.

The moment does not stay contained.

It moves.

Into ordinary spaces.

Into quiet.

Into places that used to feel safe.

Evan stops pacing and leans against the wall, breathing slower now, trying to anchor himself in something present, something stable, something that confirms where he actually is. But even that feels unstable, because the present does not feel separate in the way it used to. It feels thin, easily crossed, as if the boundary between what is happening now and what has already happened is no longer fully intact.

He looks around the room. Everything is the same. The bed. The chair. The light coming through the window. Nothing has changed. And yet it doesn't feel the same, because something has shifted in how he experiences it. The past is not staying past. It is moving into now, into moments that have no direct connection to what happened but become connected anyway.

He says it out loud, quietly, more to hear it than to explain it.

"It's not stopping."

The words do not fix anything, but they name it, and naming it matters, because without that, it feels like something else, like losing control, like something breaking. But this has a shape. A pattern. The replay.

Across town, the woman finally sets the plate down. Her hands steady again, but her eyes are still somewhere else, still holding something that has not fully released. In the classroom, the child blinks and looks up. The teacher's voice returns, but something lingers, a gap that does not close immediately. At the station, Reyes stands, takes a sip of coffee that has gone cold, and sets it down without reacting.

The replay fades.

For now.

That is what it does.

It comes.

It takes.

Then it leaves.

Not gone.

Just waiting.

Evan sits back down, still, the room settling around him again, the quiet returning, but not in the same way as before. He knows now this is not about remembering in the way he understood it before. It is about something that has not finished, something his mind is still trying to resolve, still trying to process, still trying to place somewhere that makes sense.

But there is no resolution.

Not yet.

Maybe not ever.

The thought lands not as fear, but as recognition. This is part of it. Not just what happened, but what keeps happening after. He exhales slowly as the room steadies, the moment passing again, but not completely, not in a way that suggests it is finished.

Because now he knows it can return at any time.

And that knowing changes something, not just about the past, but about how the present is lived. The replay does not ask permission. It does not wait. It does not stay contained. It moves through all of them, different in form but shared in effect.

And this—

is how it continues.

Part II—When It Comes Back

It doesn't come back the same way twice. That's what makes it hard to prepare for, hard to anticipate, hard to manage in any predictable way. If it followed a pattern, if it gave warning, if it signaled its arrival, Evan could brace for it, create distance, build something around it. But it doesn't. It arrives without sequence, without respect for where he is or what he's doing, interrupting the present with something that does not belong to it.

He is halfway through a conversation when it happens again. Someone is talking, words moving between them in a normal rhythm, and suddenly he is not fully there. Not gone, not disconnected in a way that would be obvious, but split. Part of him is still listening, nodding, responding in small ways that maintain the appearance of presence. Another part is back inside the moment.

He hears it again.

Not the whole sentence.

Just the part that stayed.

"My friend—"

The rest doesn't come, but it doesn't need to. His body fills it in, reconstructing the rest from what it already knows. He blinks, forces his focus back to the person in front of him, tries to re-anchor himself in the present.

"Yeah," he says, but the timing is off. Too late. Or too early.

The person across from him hesitates.

"Sorry—what?"

Evan shakes his head. "Nothing."

But it isn't nothing.

It is the replay interrupting the present, inserting itself into a moment that has no connection to the original event except that he is in it.

Across the room, Reyes hears a sound. A door closing. Sharp, distinct, ordinary. For a fraction of a second, it becomes something else. Not a door. Not here. Then it shifts back. He doesn't move. Doesn't react. But his body registers it—a tightening, a pause, a subtle recalibration before release.

He has learned that rhythm.

Not control.

Accommodation.

Let it pass.

Don't follow it.

Stay here.

The child sits at the kitchen table now, homework in front of them, pencil moving across the page in slow, uneven lines. Then it stops. A word—just a word—triggers something, not because of its meaning, but because of its sound, the way it lands in the air.

And suddenly the room shifts.

Not completely.

Just enough.

The child stares at the paper, not seeing it, hearing something else, something that does not belong to this moment but is present anyway. They don't say anything. They don't move. They just stop.

From the outside, it looks like distraction.

From the inside, it is something else entirely.

The woman in the kitchen has started avoiding certain things. She doesn't notice it at first. It appears as small changes, adjustments that feel reasonable on their own. She turns the television off before certain segments. Avoids certain streets. Doesn't answer calls from unfamiliar numbers. Each choice makes sense individually. Each one feels protective, manageable, justified.

But together, they begin to shape her world.

Narrow it.

Without her fully deciding to.

Evan notices something similar in himself, though it takes a different form. Not avoidance exactly, but adjustment. He keeps moving. Keeps busy. Because stillness invites the replay. He stays in motion, finds things to do, even when they don't need doing, even when the activity itself feels unnecessary.

Movement creates distance.

Or at least the illusion of it.

From the fragments.

From the interruptions.

From the moments that keep returning.

But the distance doesn't last.

It never does.

Later that night, it comes back differently. Not as a fragment, not as a brief interruption, but as a loop. He is lying in bed, eyes closed, the room quiet around him, and the moment begins again.

The hallway.

The voice.

The pause.

But this time it doesn't stop.

It resets.

Plays again.

And again.

Each time slightly different.

A different choice.

A different turn.

A different outcome.

In one version, he moves.

In another, he calls out.

In another, someone else arrives sooner.

The loop continues, not as memory, but as simulation, his mind trying to find a version that resolves it, a version where the outcome changes in a way that justifies the repetition.

But none of them do.

Because the real moment does not change.

He opens his eyes, sits up, breaking the loop through movement, through interruption. The sequence stops, but the feeling remains, lingering beneath the surface, waiting for another opportunity to return.

Because even when the replay stops, the question underneath it doesn't.

What if—

The sentence never completes.

It doesn't need to.

He exhales slowly, understanding something now that he did not understand before.

The replay isn't just remembering.

It is searching.

For a different ending.

For a way to make sense of something that doesn't resolve.

At the station, Reyes finishes his shift and walks outside. The night air is quiet, still, carrying none of the urgency that defined the earlier hours. He pauses, not because something triggered it, but because he knows it will come.

Not if.

When.

That is the difference time creates.

Not prevention.

Prediction.

He breathes in slowly, grounding himself in the present, and when it comes, he lets it pass through, not resisting, not engaging, not following it into the depths it offers.

Just allowing.

Because fighting it only deepens it.

Evan doesn't know that yet.

He is still trying to stop it.

Still trying to control it.

Still trying to make it behave like something that can be managed.

But it isn't.

Not yet.

Maybe not ever.

He lies back down, the room quiet again, but not empty. Because now he knows the replay is part of what follows. Not just a symptom. A process. Not just an interruption. A continuation.

And that changes something.

Not the experience itself.

But his understanding of it.

It's not random.

It's not weakness.

It's what happens when something has not found a place to settle, when the mind continues to circle an event that has not been integrated into the rest of experience.

He closes his eyes, not to sleep, just to rest, to allow the moment to pass without engaging it fully. The replay does not return immediately. The quiet holds for now.

But that doesn't mean it's gone.

It means it's waiting.

And now he is beginning to understand that waiting goes both ways.

Part III—What the Mind Keeps Asking

The replay is not always fear. Sometimes it is a question wearing the shape of memory. That is what Evan begins to understand, not quickly, not completely, but enough to notice that what returns is not only image or sound, but something searching beneath it. The fragments come back—the hallway, the voice, the pause—but underneath each one is something unresolved, something that does not settle when the memory fades.

What else could I have done?

The question is not spoken. It does not need to be. It is built into the loop itself, embedded in the way the moment reappears, always returning him to the point just before the outcome fixed itself into something permanent. His mind brings him back to where things still feel changeable, where possibility still exists, where the ending has not yet been decided.

Except it has.

The past does not open.

It only repeats.

Evan sits at the kitchen table, hands wrapped around a mug he has not lifted. Morning light filters through the window. The room is quiet. Nothing is happening. That is when it comes. The hallway. The voice. "My friend is still—" He closes his eyes, not in anticipation but in resistance.

No.

Not now.

But resistance does nothing. The fragment continues, not as sound exactly, but as pressure, as a physical echo that settles into his chest. His head turns slightly, as if the voice is still somewhere to his left, as if responding to it is still an option.

Then Reyes's voice.

Stay here.

The two voices meet inside him, not in sequence, but at once, occupying the same space. Need and instruction. Compassion and protocol. Human pull and system order. The replay holds them together and refuses to resolve the tension between them.

That is what makes it unbearable.

It does not simply show him what happened.

It asks him to judge it again.

And again.

And again.

Across town, Lila sits in the back seat of her mother's car, looking out the window as houses pass in a steady rhythm. Her mother is speaking into the phone, using the tone adults use when they are trying to sound normal, controlled, steady in a way that reassures more than it explains.

Lila is not listening.

She is watching the sidewalk.

A bird lifts suddenly from a patch of grass, its movement quick, almost silent. Still, her body reacts. A tightening. A subtle shift in posture.

The closet returns.

Not all of it.

Just the rule.

Stay quiet.

Her foot moves slightly inside her shoe, and the memory attaches itself immediately to the sensation. The scrape comes back. Small. Barely there. Enormous.

She looks down quickly, as if the sound might have happened again. It hasn't. Her feet are still. The car continues moving. Her mother is still talking.

Nothing has changed.

Everything has.

The replay for Lila is not a complete memory. It is a question.

Did I do something wrong?

It comes with the smallest details, the things that seemed insignificant at the time but now carry disproportionate weight. Adults have told her she was brave. They have told her she did exactly right. But the replay does not repeat their voices.

It repeats the scrape.

Because that is where the question lives.

Marcus experiences it differently. For him, the replay comes in public spaces, places that used to feel neutral but now carry a layer of awareness that he cannot remove. A grocery aisle. A parking lot. The doorway of a building he has entered a hundred times without thinking.

He notices exits now.

Not because he chooses to.

Because the replay teaches him to.

His memory does not return first as sound or image. It returns as awareness.

Where would I go?

Who would I leave?

Who would I not see?

He stands in line at a pharmacy and watches a man step near the entrance. There is nothing threatening about him. He is holding a bag and a set of keys. Still, Marcus feels something rise in him.

Not fear.

Anger.

Because the replay returns him to the same realization.

Someone chose this.

The memory gives him fragments—doors, movement, sirens, a stretcher he tried not to focus on. Underneath all of it is the same question, the same refusal.

They didn't have to.

His replay is not searching for a different outcome.

It is searching for a place to put the outrage.

At the station, Reyes does not name it the same way. He has other words for it, quieter ones. Afterimage. Echo. Residue. Sometimes he has no word at all. He is cleaning equipment when it comes, a strap slipping through his fingers, the sound soft but enough to carry him, briefly, back into the hallway.

A hand on his sleeve.

A voice.

A direction he did not go.

His body stills, but only for a moment. Then he continues. That is the difference experience has made. Not that the replay stops. Not that it loses its impact entirely. But that he has learned not to follow it all the way down.

He knows the mind can turn memory into a courtroom. It will call witnesses, produce evidence, reconstruct timelines, ask the same question in different forms until repetition begins to feel like proof. He sets the strap down carefully and breathes once, then again.

"I couldn't get to them," he thinks.

The sentence remains.

But another one follows.

"I got to who I could."

It does not erase the first.

It does not resolve the tension.

It simply stands beside it.

Sometimes that is all there is.

Evan begins to understand something similar when he speaks with Reyes later, not formally, not in a structured conversation, but in passing, in the space between tasks where words feel less constructed.

"It keeps coming back," Evan says.

Reyes nods. He does not ask what.

He already knows.

"Yeah."

Evan looks away, toward the open bay doors, the light shifting as the day moves forward.

"It feels like my mind is trying to find another way through it."

Reyes considers that.

"That's what it's doing."

"Does it help?"

"Sometimes."

"And when it doesn't?"

Reyes meets his eyes.

"It just hurts."

There is no attempt to soften it.

No reassurance.

Just truth.

Evan lets that settle, because it feels more accurate than anything else he has been told.

"So what do you do?" he asks.

Reyes looks out again.

"You learn to notice when the question doesn't have an answer."

Evan turns that over.

"And then?"

"You don't have to answer it every time."

The simplicity of it stays with him.

He had assumed the replay required engagement, required participation, required him to follow it wherever it led.

Maybe it doesn't.

Maybe noticing is different from obeying.

That night, when the hallway returns, he tries something different. He does not push it away. He does not follow it completely. He lets it appear, recognizes it for what it is.

Replay.

Then he recognizes the question beneath it.

What else could I have done?

He does not answer.

Not because there is no answer.

Because the question has already taken enough.

The room remains around him. The bed. The chair. The window. The present holds, not strongly, but enough.

The replay fades.

Not gone.

Not finished.

But less consuming.

Evan exhales.

Across town, Lila lies awake, staring at the line of light beneath her door. Marcus checks exits without thinking. Reyes rinses a cup he never really used.

Each of them carries a different loop.

A different question.

A different unfinished moment.

The replay does not mean they are broken.

It means the mind is still circling something the rest of them cannot yet place.

It means the past has not found its boundary.

It means the wound is still asking where it belongs.

For now, that is enough to know.

Not enough to resolve.

But enough to begin.

Chapter 16—The Empty Chair

Part I—Where They Should Be

Loss does not arrive all at once. It becomes visible slowly, not in the moment of crisis, not in the noise or urgency, but in what follows, in what remains missing when everything else has settled. Evan notices it first in a place that has nothing to do with the event, a diner in the early morning where the rhythm of routine continues without interruption, where people sit in the same booths at the same times without needing to think about it.

He is halfway through his coffee when he sees it. Not something new. Something absent. A chair. Empty. At a table meant for two. One plate. One cup. One person sitting across from space that should be filled.

He doesn't know them. Doesn't know who is missing. But he knows.

The recognition is immediate, not because of context, but because absence has a shape now. It is no longer abstract. It is a place where someone should be and isn't, a presence defined by what is not there rather than what is.

Across town, a mother stands in her kitchen holding two plates. She sets one down, then hesitates. The second plate stays in her hand longer than it should. There is nowhere to put it. Or rather, there is. A place at the table that has not changed. The chair is still there. Pushed in. Waiting.

She places the plate down anyway, not because it makes sense, but because not placing it feels worse. She sits across from it, not looking directly at it, but feeling it. The presence of absence. There is no conversation, no exchange of words, and yet something in her posture holds the shape of it, a question, an answer, a pause where laughter should be.

Lila notices it differently, not as a space, but as a disruption. She walks into the classroom and stops, not because anything obvious has changed, but because something is wrong in a way she cannot immediately name. The teacher is moving. The lesson continues. Everything looks the same. But then she sees it.

A desk.

Empty.

She stares at it longer than anyone else does. The room moves forward, the rhythm of the day continuing, but she does not sit right away. Because the room is different now, even if nothing in it has visibly changed. She takes her seat carefully, as if the empty desk might mean something she does not yet understand.

She does not ask.

No one does.

But everyone knows.

Marcus sees it in motion. At a stoplight, cars idling, waiting for the signal to change. A bus passes, children inside, talking, moving, alive in the way children are when nothing has interrupted them. He watches them, not intentionally, but because his attention catches on something that feels familiar.

Then he sees it.

A seat.

Empty.

It shouldn't matter. Seats are empty all the time. But now it does. Because it is not just a seat. It is a space that could have been filled, a space that was filled, and now is not.

His jaw tightens. He looks away. But the image stays.

At the station, Reyes moves through routine. Equipment checks. Reports. Everything in order. Everything functioning as it should. And still, even here, it appears. A locker. Closed. Unused. Not permanently. Just not used right now. Still, he notices it. Because his mind has learned to look for what isn't there.

Evan finishes his coffee and pushes the cup away, but he does not leave. Something about the diner feels different now, not unsafe, not unstable, but altered. He looks again at the table, at the empty chair. The person sitting across from it has not moved much, has not spoken, just sits with hands wrapped around a cup that has long since cooled.

Evan feels something shift, because this is not the moment. This is after. This is what remains when everything else is over.

He stands, moves to the counter, pays, but even as he leaves, he carries it with him, not the chair itself, but what it represents.

Loss is not always loud. It does not always announce itself. Sometimes it sits quietly in ordinary places, at tables, in classrooms, on buses, in homes, waiting to be noticed.

He steps outside. The air is cold, clear. The world continues. Cars pass. People move. Everything functioning as it always has. But now he sees it differently, because he knows what is missing, even when no one says it.

The empty chair is not just absence. It is evidence. Of someone who was there. Of a life that intersected with others, that occupied space, that belonged somewhere specific in the pattern of daily life.

Evan exhales slowly, because this part is harder than he expected. Not the moment itself, not the intensity of what happened, but the aftermath, the quiet, the way loss enters everyday life and stays.

He walks to his car, opens the door, then stops, because for a moment he imagines it, a seat beside him, someone who isn't there. The thought is brief, but it holds, enough to make him close his eyes, not to escape it, but to acknowledge it.

Then he gets in, starts the engine, drives.

But the awareness does not leave.

Because now he sees it everywhere.

The spaces where people should be.

And aren't.

Across town, the mother clears the table. She takes both plates, washes them, dries them, places them back where they belong, even though one of them does not anymore.

In the classroom, Lila glances at the empty desk again, just once, then looks forward, trying to follow, trying to stay.

Marcus drives past the bus, does not look again, but he does not need to. The image is already there.

Reyes closes the locker room door, does not pause, but he noticed it.

The empty chair is not just a symbol. It is a reality that moves into every space they enter, not always visible, but always present.

And this is how loss becomes part of the world again, not by leaving, but by staying in everything that continues without it.

Part II—The Space That Stays

The first time they notice it, they think it's temporary, a pause, a gap that will eventually close, something that belongs to the early days and will fade as time moves forward. That is how absence begins, not as permanence, but as interruption, something out of place that the mind assumes will correct itself.

The mother keeps setting two plates. Not every meal. Not every day. Just sometimes, without deciding to, without planning to. Her hand reaches for the second plate before her thoughts catch up, before she allows herself to remember why the motion no longer fits the reality of the room.

She places it on the table anyway, then stands there, looking at it, not really seeing the plate, but seeing who should be sitting in front of it.

She doesn't speak. There is no one to answer. But something in her posture holds the shape of conversation, the expectation of it, the rhythm of exchange that has not fully disappeared from her body. A question. An answer. A pause where laughter should be.

Then she sits.

Eats.

Across from the space that does not fill.

Lila begins to notice patterns, not consciously, not in a way she could explain if asked, but through small shifts in how she moves through her day. She chooses a different seat in the classroom, not the one she used to take. She doesn't know why, only that sitting near the empty desk feels wrong, too close to something she does not have words for, too exposed to something she does not understand.

The teacher rearranges seating a week later, calls it routine, calls it normal, a change that happens without deeper meaning. Lila does not question it. But when she sees someone else sit at that desk, she freezes, not visibly, not in a way that draws attention, but internally, where the shift registers.

Because the space was supposed to stay empty.

Not forever.

But longer.

Long enough for something to make sense.

She looks down, doesn't raise her hand, doesn't say anything. But something changes, because now even the absence is changing, and that feels like another loss layered on top of the first.

Marcus tries to avoid certain places at first, not as a decision, not as a conscious act of withdrawal, but as a quiet adjustment. He goes to the grocery store at different times. He skips the park on weekends. He chooses routes that keep him away from spaces where the absence feels louder, where the awareness of what is missing presses in more directly.

But avoidance has limits.

Life does not rearrange itself to accommodate it.

Eventually, he has to go back.

The first time he does, it feels wrong, not because anything has changed, but because everything has stayed the same. People are laughing, talking, moving through their routines without awareness of what has been lost, without carrying the same weight he feels in every step.

He stands in the middle of it, disoriented, not angry, not exactly, but unsettled by the fact that the world has continued. That it has not paused. That it has not marked the loss in a way that matches its impact.

How can this still exist?

The question does not demand an answer. It sits there, unresolved, reflecting the gap between his internal experience and the external world that continues without interruption.

Evan notices something similar, not in others, but in himself. He goes back to work, answers calls, moves through routine. Everything functions. He functions. But something does not align. The work continues as if the moment has been completed, logged, processed, finished.

But it does not feel finished.

Not to him.

He is restocking supplies when the realization comes, not as a replay, not as a fragment, but as a shift in understanding.

This is still happening for them.

Not the event.

The absence.

He pauses, hands still, because this part was not in the training. What happens after. What remains. How long it lasts.

At the station, Reyes fills out a report, precise and complete, every detail accounted for. Time. Action. Outcome. He finishes, signs it, sets it aside. That is how the system holds it—contained, documented, closed.

But Reyes knows better.

Because he has seen what does not close.

What continues outside the report, in homes, in routines, in the quiet after everything else is done.

The mother clears the table again, this time with only one plate. She stands at the sink longer than necessary, water running, hands still, because the silence is louder here, because there is no conversation to fill it, no movement to interrupt it.

She turns off the water, dries her hands, looks at the table before leaving the room, as if checking that it is still there.

The empty space.

Lila walks past the desk again. This time, someone is sitting in it, talking, writing, living in the space that used to hold something else. She does not stop. But she notices.

And noticing is enough.

Marcus sits in his car outside the grocery store, hands on the wheel, not moving. He is not avoiding it. Not exactly. He is preparing, for the feeling that will meet him inside, for the awareness that will not be contained once he steps through the door.

He exhales, opens the door, steps out.

Because eventually, everything requires re-entry.

Evan finishes his shift and walks out. The sky is dim, fading. He pauses before getting into his car, because now he sees it, not one chair, but many, everywhere, spaces where someone should be and is not.

He exhales slowly, because this part is not dramatic, not loud, but constant, the way absence moves into daily life and stays, shaping it without announcing itself.

Loss is not only what is taken.

It is what remains unfilled.

And the unfilled does not disappear.

It becomes part of the structure, part of the room, part of the routine, part of the people who keep living around it.

Evan gets into his car, closes the door, sits for a moment, because leaving does not leave it behind. Nothing does.

He starts the engine, drives.

But now he understands something he did not before.

The empty chair is not temporary.

It is not waiting to be filled.

It is part of what remains.

And learning to live around it—

is part of what comes next.

Part III—Learning to Sit With It

At first, they try to fix it, not consciously, not with a plan, but through instinct, because something is missing and instinct says it should be restored, adjusted, made whole again in whatever small ways are available. The mother rearranges the table one afternoon, not dramatically, just enough to change the shape of the space. She moves the chair slightly, turns it at an angle so it no longer faces directly into the place where someone used to sit.

It looks different.

Less exact.

Less like a position waiting for someone specific.

She steps back and studies it, taking in the small alteration as if it might shift something deeper, as if changing the arrangement could change the feeling attached to it. For a moment, it helps. The space feels less defined, less fixed, less anchored to a specific absence.

But only for a moment.

Because absence does not depend on position.

It depends on memory.

And memory does not move when furniture does.

She exhales and moves the chair back, returning it to where it was, because even altering it feels like another loss, like removing something that still holds meaning, even if that meaning is painful.

Lila tries something similar, not with objects, but with attention. She learns not to look at the desk, to keep her focus forward, on the board, on the teacher, on anything that keeps her from noticing the space that no longer holds what it used to. If she does not look, maybe it will not feel as real, maybe the absence will soften or fade at the edges.

Sometimes it works.

For a while.

Until someone mentions a name casually, without thinking, without realizing what it does to the room. The space returns immediately, not through sight, but through feeling, through the sudden awareness of what is not there.

She tightens her grip on her pencil, holds herself still, because this is the part she cannot understand, how something can be gone and still present, how absence can occupy space as fully as presence once did.

Marcus tries to outrun it, not physically, not in a way that would be visible, but through pace, through movement, through filling his time with enough activity that stillness becomes rare. Work, errands, small tasks that extend into larger ones, anything that keeps him from stopping long enough to feel what settles in when everything else quiets down.

Because stillness lets the absence settle.

Movement keeps it at a distance.

Or at least makes it feel that way.

But movement has limits.

At night, it finds him, in the quiet, in the pause between one thought and the next, in the space where there is nothing left to distract him from what remains. He sits in the dark, not turning on the light, because the darkness feels more honest, less structured, less demanding of normal behavior.

There is no pretending here.

No need to appear steady.

Just the space.

And the awareness that it is not going anywhere.

Evan approaches it differently, not because he understands it more clearly, but because he has seen it in all of them, the empty chair appearing in different forms, not just at tables, but in classrooms, in cars, in conversations that do not complete the way they once did. He recognizes it now even when no one names it, in pauses that last half a second too long, in sentences that shift direction midway through, in glances toward places that no longer hold what they used to.

This is how loss speaks without words.

He sits at his own table, just one chair, nothing visibly missing, no second place set, no absence marked in a physical way. And still he feels it, not personal, not tied to someone he knew, but present, because once you see it, you do not stop seeing it.

At the station, Reyes does not try to fix it. He does not move chairs or avoid spaces or redirect his attention away from what is missing. He acknowledges it quietly, moves through a room, notices the absence, and lets it be there without trying to alter it.

Not resisting.

Not reshaping.

Just allowing it to exist alongside everything else.

That is what experience has given him.

Not resolution.

Capacity.

The ability to hold presence and absence at the same time without needing to collapse one into the other.

Evan watches that, not directly, not as something being taught, but over time, in the way Reyes moves through space without trying to correct it, without trying to make it something other than what it is. There is something in that, something that feels closer to what might be possible than the attempts to fix or avoid.

One evening, Evan sits in a waiting room, not working, just waiting, occupying space that is not his, watching the way others move within it. A family sits across from him, three people, close together, and a space between them, not large, not obvious, but noticeable.

No one sits there.

No one mentions it.

But everyone adjusts around it, leaning slightly away or toward each other to compensate, to account for what is not being filled.

Evan sees it immediately.

The empty chair without the chair.

He looks down, not because he wants to avoid it, but because seeing it feels like witnessing something that does not belong to him to name, something that exists in the space between people without needing to be spoken.

But it is his to recognize.

He understands something now.

The goal is not to fill the space.

It cannot be filled.

The goal is not to remove it.

It will not go.

The goal, if there is one, is to learn how to live with it.

Not around it.

With it.

The mother sits at the table again, this time with only one plate. She does not reach for the second, does not rearrange the chair, does not try to change what is there. She just sits, the space present, felt, acknowledged without being altered.

That is new.

Small.

But new.

Lila looks at the desk, just once, then back to the front. She does not freeze this time, does not stop moving forward, even though the awareness is still there.

Marcus stands in the store, not at the edge, but inside, still noticing exits, still aware, but not leaving immediately, not retreating from the space.

Reyes finishes his shift, walks out, does not pause, but carries it with him.

All of them do.

Evan sits in his car, engine off, hands resting on the wheel, the world moving around him in its usual rhythm. Nothing has changed externally.

Everything has changed internally.

He exhales slowly, because this is the part no one prepares you for, not the crisis, not the moment, but the continuation, the way loss integrates itself into ordinary life and stays there, not as interruption, but as presence.

The empty chair is not something to move past.

It is something that moves in.

And learning to sit with it is how life begins again, not the same, never the same, but still life.

Chapter 17—**Anger Has a Target**

Part I—Where It Lands

Anger does not stay general for long. It looks for somewhere to land. At first, it is everything, too large, too undefined, too overwhelming to hold in a single direction. But that doesn't last, because anger needs shape. It needs a point of contact, something to absorb its force, something to carry the weight of what has been broken.

Keisha stands in the briefing room, hands braced against the table, eyes fixed on a map that has already been studied too many times. The room is quiet, but not empty. Officers, supervisors, voices that carry authority without offering resolution. Someone begins speaking.

"This is what we know."

The words are measured, careful, constructed to sound complete. But Keisha hears what isn't being said. This is what we can say. The distinction forms immediately, sharp and undeniable, and something in her tightens. Because the space between those two things is where anger begins.

Across town, Marcus doesn't try to contain it. His anger has already found its first target. The shooter. It is clean, direct, uncomplicated. There is no confusion here. Someone chose this. That fact does not shift, does not soften, does not invite interpretation. It holds. And because it holds, Marcus holds onto it, letting the anger attach to something that does not move.

"They didn't have to."

The sentence returns without variation. It doesn't ask. It declares. And in that declaration, everything else becomes secondary, at least for now.

The mother's anger moves differently. It does not arrive as a clear line. It surfaces in moments, small disruptions that carry more weight than they should. Someone says the wrong thing. Silence lingers too long. A memory surfaces at the wrong time. She grips the edge of the counter, knuckles whitening, breath held without realizing it.

"Why?"

The word escapes before she can direct it. It does not land anywhere specific. Not yet. It hangs in the space, searching for something to attach to, something that can absorb it.

Lila's anger does not look like anger from the outside. She sits still, quiet, her behavior altered in ways that do not immediately register as resistance. She doesn't laugh the same way. She hesitates before answering. She watches more than she speaks. But something in her has shifted. Something pushes back, not loudly, not visibly, but persistently.

This shouldn't have happened.

The sentence is not fully formed in her mind, but it exists, shaping her responses, altering her sense of what is safe, what is predictable, what can be trusted.

Evan feels it tangled, not clean like Marcus's, not contained like the mother's, not hidden like Lila's. His anger arrives mixed with guilt, mixed with questions, difficult to isolate from everything else he is carrying. He hears a report on the television, a voice summarizing, framing, reducing what happened into something structured and digestible.

Something in him reacts immediately.

Not to the facts.

To the distance.

To the way it is being turned into something manageable.

Something contained.

He turns it off too quickly, the motion sharper than he intends. Because the anger does not want containment. It wants something else. Something closer to what it felt like in the moment, something that reflects the reality rather than reshaping it.

Back in the briefing room, Keisha listens as timelines are reviewed.

"Response time was within expected range."

"Communication followed protocol."

"Units acted appropriately based on available information."

Each sentence is technically correct. Each one constructed to hold under scrutiny. And yet none of them feel complete. None of them carry the gaps she remembers, the delays that stretched longer than they should have, the misalignments that were subtle but consequential.

She feels it rise, not directed at the speaker, but at the structure itself, at the need to present something whole when she knows it strained.

"This isn't the whole picture."

The words leave her before she can filter them. The room shifts, not dramatically, but enough. Eyes turn. Someone clears their throat.

"We're working with confirmed information."

Keisha nods, but the anger does not recede. Because confirmed is not the same as complete. And complete is not something they have.

Anger moves again. It shifts direction, expands beyond its initial target. From the shooter to the systems. From the act to what surrounded it. What failed to prevent it. What did not hold.

Marcus feels that shift later. After the clarity of blame, after the initial certainty, the questions begin to change.

"How did this happen?"

"Where was everyone?"

"What was supposed to stop it?"

The anger does not leave the first target. It builds around it, adding layers, complicating what once felt simple.

The mother's anger turns differently. Not toward the shooter. Not toward the system. Something harder. Something less visible. She stands in the quiet of her home, hands still, breath uneven.

"God."

The word is barely spoken, but it lands heavily. Because this is where the question turns, from human action to divine absence.

"Where were you?"

There is no answer. And the silence feels like something.

Lila does not name it, but she feels it in the quiet moments, in the spaces where something should be and is not. The trust she had in adults, in safety, in the predictability of the world has shifted. Something in her resists what she is told now, not loudly, but with a quiet withdrawal, a hesitation that was not there before.

Evan sits alone, tracing where his anger lands. It does not stay in one place. It moves. The shooter. The system. Himself. And something beyond that, something harder to define but no less present.

He exhales slowly, because this is what he understands now. Anger does not stay still. It searches. It finds targets and then finds more.

Keisha steps out of the briefing room, the door closing behind her. The hallway is quieter, but the anger does not leave. It sharpens, takes on clearer form. Not just frustration. Not just reaction. Conviction.

Something did not hold.

Something was not said.

Something still is not being said.

She walks forward, steps steady, because this is where her role begins to change. Not just to represent, but to question.

Anger has a target.

But it rarely has just one.

And once it begins to move, it does not stop easily. It travels through all of them, different in form but connected in source, shaping how they see what happened and what must come next.

And this is how it begins to speak.

Part II—Where It Spreads

Anger does not stay where it starts. It moves, expands, gathers weight as it travels. What begins as clarity becomes complexity. What begins as certainty becomes fracture. Because once anger finds one target, it begins to look for others, not to replace the first, but to add to it, to widen the scope of what must be accounted for.

Marcus thought it would stay simple. The shooter. That was enough. It gave his anger direction, gave it a place to land without hesitation. There was no confusion in that, no ambiguity, no competing explanation. Someone chose this. That truth did not shift.

At first, that was enough.

But time changes that. Not by removing the first target, but by introducing others that demand attention. He stands outside the building now, watching people move in and out, their routines intact, their conversations uninterrupted. It feels wrong, not because they are doing anything incorrect, but because it should not feel this easy.

"How did this happen here?"

The question comes sharper now, more demanding than before.

"Who was watching?"

"Who was responsible?"

The anger expands, not away from the shooter, but beyond them. Because one person should not have been enough to cause this. And if they were, then something else failed, something larger, something that should have intervened and did not.

In her home, the mother feels the shift differently. Her anger does not move outward first. It circles, returning to the same place, the last conversation, the last moment, something small, something ordinary that now carries unbearable weight.

"Why didn't I . . . "

She stops, because that path leads somewhere she cannot follow without breaking something she cannot repair. But anger does not stay contained. It redirects, moving from herself to the world, to the people who should have protected, to the structures that were supposed to hold.

"Why didn't they?"

The question lands harder, because it demands something beyond her control, something that cannot be answered in a way that satisfies what she is feeling.

At school, Lila experiences it in smaller, quieter ways. Not as an explosion, not as something that draws attention, but as resistance. A teacher corrects her gently, a normal interaction, something that would not have mattered before. But now something in her reacts too quickly, too strongly.

She pulls back, does not answer, does not engage.

Because something in her no longer trusts that correction means safety, that authority means protection. The anger is there, but it has no clear direction, no obvious place to go. So it settles into distance, into quiet refusal, into a shift in how she relates to everything around her.

Evan feels it when he returns to the station. Not in the work itself, but in the spaces between it. A conversation that stops short. A look that does not fully land. A silence that stretches too long. Something is unspoken, something present but unacknowledged.

That is where his anger goes.

Not at the job.

At the gaps inside it.

The things that are known but not said.

The things that are felt but not named.

He leans against the wall, arms crossed, listening, waiting for someone to say it out loud, to bridge the space between what happened and how it is being discussed.

No one does.

And that absence becomes its own kind of failure.

Back at the station office, Keisha sits across from a supervisor. The conversation is controlled, professional, measured in a way that prioritizes stability over honesty.

"We have to be careful about how this is communicated."

She nods. She understands that. She has lived that. But something in her resists.

"Careful isn't the same as honest."

The words come out before she can reshape them into something more acceptable. The supervisor exhales, choosing his response carefully.

"We're working with what we know.

Keisha holds his gaze.

"And what we don't?"

Silence follows. Because that is where the tension lives, not in the confirmed facts, but in the missing pieces, the things that do not fit neatly into reports, the gaps that resist closure.

Anger moves again. From institutions to community. To the people who were there, who saw something, who noticed something, who might have acted differently.

Marcus feels it when someone says, "I had a feeling something was off."

The sentence lands wrong, too late, too distant from the moment where it could have mattered. He does not respond, but the anger sharpens, because now it has another direction, another layer.

The mother hears something similar, fragments of conversation about warnings, about signs, about things that could have been noticed.

"Why didn't anyone . . . "

She does not finish it. She does not need to. The anger fills the space where the answer should be.

Lila does not hear those conversations directly, but she feels the shift in how adults speak, in the tension they try to conceal, in the way their voices change when they think she is not listening. She absorbs it without understanding it fully, and it becomes part of how she sees the world now.

Unstable.

Uncertain.

Not as safe as it was supposed to be.

Evan sits alone again, tracing where the anger goes. It does not settle. It keeps moving, from person to system to silence, to the things that did not happen the way they should have.

He exhales, because this is what he understands now. Anger is not just reaction. It is information. It points to rupture, to expectation that was not met, to something that should have held and did not.

Keisha stands outside the building, the air still, the city moving around her in its usual rhythm. But inside her, nothing is still. She looks out at the people, at the systems continuing as if they can absorb what has already shown their limits.

She feels it all.

The shooter.

The failure.

The silence.

The continuation.

Her jaw tightens, because this is where her anger settles, not in a single place, but in a refusal to let it be simplified, to let it be reduced to something that fits comfortably within explanation.

Anger has a target.

But it also has reach.

It spreads across people, across systems, across belief.

And once it moves, it changes everything it touches.

Part III—What It Demands

Anger does not only point. It demands. It asks for something in return, an answer, a change, a reckoning that matches the weight of what has been broken. At first, the demand feels simple. Someone should pay. Someone should answer. Someone should be held in a way that restores balance, even if only symbolically.

That feels right.

Proportional.

Contained.

But anger does not stay contained, because once it begins asking, it keeps asking, and the first answer, no matter how clear, no matter how justified, does not fully satisfy what it is trying to resolve.

Marcus feels that shift first. The initial demand was clear, the shooter, accountability, consequence, something that names what happened and assigns responsibility in a way that feels concrete. That mattered. It still matters. But now it does not feel complete. Even if justice comes, it does not restore what was taken, does not return what is missing, does not answer how it was allowed to happen in the first place.

He leans against his car, hands pressed into the metal, breathing uneven, because the question has changed.

"What else?"

It is not directed. It does not settle on a single person or system. It searches, because something in him knows that one answer is not enough to hold what he is carrying.

The mother feels the demand differently, not as a question, but as a pressure that builds without release, a need for the world to be different than it is, for something to interrupt the finality of what has already happened. She moves through her home, touching objects that have not moved, a chair, a doorframe, a jacket still hanging where it was left.

Each one demands something.

Not logically.

Emotionally.

This should not be here without them.

The world should have changed.

Something should have stopped.

She stands still, because the demand has nowhere to go, no one to receive it, no structure large enough to answer it. And that absence of response becomes its own form of harm, a second rupture layered onto the first.

Lila's anger asks in a quieter way, not outward, not directed, but inward, shaping how she receives what she is told. She watches the adults, listens to their explanations, their reassurances, the words meant to restore stability.

"You're safe."

The sentence does not land the way it used to. It feels incomplete, misaligned with what she knows now. Her anger does not reject it loudly. It withdraws. It refuses to accept something that no longer fits. It changes how she listens, how she trusts, how she moves through spaces that once felt certain.

Evan sits with it longer, tracing what anger is asking of him. It would be easier if it stayed external, if it remained directed at the shooter, at the system, at something outside of him. But it does not. It turns.

"What should I have done?"

The question returns, but now it carries the weight of expectation, the demand for resolution in a place where resolution is not available. He exhales slowly, because this is where anger becomes something else, something heavier, something that does not dissipate when it cannot be answered.

At the station, Reyes leans back in his chair, watching the room without focusing on anything specific. He has felt this before, the shift from anger to expectation, from expectation to frustration, from frustration to something that settles deeper. He knows the pattern, not because he has mastered it, but because he has endured it.

He watches Evan across the room, sees the tension in how he holds himself, how he carries something he does not yet know how to set down. Reyes does not interrupt. He does not offer advice. Because this part cannot be explained into resolution. It has to be experienced, understood from within.

Keisha feels it most sharply, because her anger does not remain separate from her role. It collides with it. She stands in front of a mirror, uniform partially on, badge resting in her hand. The weight of it feels different now, not heavier, but more defined, more specific in what it represents.

Protection.

Order.

Safety.

The words used to feel solid, stable, anchored in something reliable. Now they feel conditional, dependent on factors that are no longer theoretical. She looks at her reflection, not critically, but directly.

"What does this mean now?"

The question is not rhetorical. It is immediate, pressing, because anger has moved into her identity, into what she represents to others, into what she is expected to uphold even when she is not sure it held in the way it was supposed to.

She exhales, because this is where the demand sharpens, not just for answers, but for truth, not just for accountability, but for honesty, even when honesty complicates everything, even when it challenges the structures she is part of.

She walks back into the station. The room shifts slightly as she enters. People look up, sensing something, not confrontation exactly, but a change in tone, a shift in what might be said.

She does not raise her voice.

"What are we not saying?"

The question lands heavily, because everyone knows there is something, something incomplete, something unresolved. No one answers immediately, because answering it requires stepping outside what is safe, outside what is controlled, outside what is expected.

Marcus stands alone, the anger still present, but changed, less sharp, more insistent, because it is no longer satisfied with one target. It wants more explanation, more acknowledgment, something that reflects the scale of what has been lost.

The mother sits again, hands folded, the house quiet. Her anger does not move now. It settles, not because it is resolved, but because it has nowhere else to go. In that stillness, it becomes something deeper, something that does not leave when the moment passes.

Evan looks up, across the room, at Reyes, at Keisha, at the others carrying their own versions of the same weight. He sees it now. Anger is not just reaction. It is a demand for a world that did not happen, a world that should have been.

And because it was not, something in all of them keeps asking, not once, but continuously, returning to the same place, the same need for something that does not yet exist.

Anger has a target.

But what it wants is restoration.

And when restoration is not possible, it searches for something that can stand in its place, truth, accountability, meaning, something that acknowledges what was lost and refuses to let it be reduced or forgotten.

But for now, none of that is complete.

And so the anger remains, not as an explosion, but as a presence, a pressure that does not disappear, because it is still asking, and no one has fully answered.

Chapter 18—**Faith After the Gunfire**

Part I—What Still Holds

Faith does not disappear in a moment. It fractures, not always visibly, not all at once, but in ways that alter how it is experienced. Something that once felt certain no longer settles the same way. Something that once moved easily between question and trust now hesitates, pauses, resists completion.

Evan notices it in silence, not the absence of sound, but the absence of response. He sits alone, hands resting loosely in his lap, head lowered, not in prayer exactly, but in the shape of it. The posture remains. The expectation does not.

There was a time when silence meant listening, when quiet suggested presence, when stillness held the possibility of response. Now it feels different. Not empty. Not entirely. But distant. As if something that once felt near has shifted just out of reach.

He exhales slowly, because this is where the question forms. Not loudly. Not with urgency. But steadily.

Are you there?

The words do not leave his mouth, but they settle in the space between breath and thought, where language begins but does not fully form. He does not push them away. He lets them remain, unfinished, because finishing them would require something he does not have.

Across town, the mother stands at the edge of her bed, hands pressed into the mattress, eyes fixed on nothing in particular. She has prayed here before. The words were familiar. Memorized. Structured in ways that made them easy to reach, easy to use, easy to trust.

Now the words do not come.

Not because she has forgotten them.

Because they do not fit.

She tries anyway.

"God . . . "

The word breaks before it completes. It falters, not because of uncertainty in pronunciation, but because of uncertainty in meaning. The name that once held comfort now holds a question. Not about existence, but about presence.

She does not try again immediately. She stands there, feeling the absence of the words as much as their failure, aware that something has changed in a way that cannot be reversed by repetition.

Lila hears it differently. Not in silence, but in absence, in what is said and what does not land. She listens when adults speak about God, the same words, the same reassurances, phrases that once felt stable.

"He's watching over us."

"He's with you."

She does not argue. She does not question them out loud. But something in her does not accept them in the same way. Because if that were true, something does not make sense. Her mind does not form the theology. It forms the contradiction.

And the contradiction stays.

Marcus rejects it outright. Not gradually. Not carefully. Directly. He stands outside the church, doors open, people moving in and out, voices inside rising in song. It sounds wrong to him, not because of the music itself, but because of the timing.

How can this still be happening?

How can people stand and sing as if something has not broken?

He turns away, not ready, not willing to step into something that feels disconnected from what he knows, from what he has seen, from what he cannot reconcile.

At the station, Reyes does not speak about it. He carries it instead, in quiet moments, in the spaces between calls, in the places where thought is not occupied by immediate need. He has seen this before, not the same event, but the same question.

What holds when everything else doesn't?

He does not rush to answer it. He knows what happens when you do. You settle too quickly. You reach for something that sounds right but does not sustain. And when it fails, something else fractures.

So he does not offer answers, not to Evan, not to anyone. Because this part is not about resolution. It is about allowing the question to exist without forcing it into something it is not.

Evan sits with it longer, not trying to resolve it, not pushing it away, just letting it exist. Because something in him knows that this part matters, not the answer, but the asking.

He remembers words, not as comfort, but as echo.

"My God, my God, why have you forsaken me?"

He does not think about where they come from. He only knows that they fit, not as explanation, but as expression. They name something he cannot otherwise say. Not disbelief. Not rejection. Distance.

The mother feels it too, in different words, carrying the same weight.

"How long?"

The question does not complete. It does not need to. Time has changed. Days stretch. Moments linger. Nothing resolves the way it used to. The question remains in the room, unanswered, not dismissed, not resolved.

Lila hears fragments, not full prayers, but pieces, lines from songs, phrases spoken in passing. They sound familiar, but they do not land, because something in her is waiting for them to match what she feels. They do not.

Not yet.

Marcus drives past the church again, slower this time, not stopping, but not looking away either. He hears the music through the open doors. It does not make sense to him. But it does not anger him the same way. Now it feels distant, like something that belongs to another world, one he is not part of.

Faith does not disappear. It changes. It becomes less certain, less immediate, more fragile, but also more honest. Because what existed before does not fully fit now, and forcing it would feel like ignoring the fracture.

Evan feels that. Because what he had before does not hold in the same way. And trying to make it hold feels wrong, like placing something broken back together without acknowledging that it has been broken.

At the station, Keisha sits alone, her badge set on the table in front of her. Not removed, not rejected, just set aside. She looks at it, then looks away, because this question reaches into everything, not just belief, but identity, responsibility, what she represents, what she trusts.

She does not speak. She does not pray. But she stays, in the question, because leaving it feels like giving up something she is not ready to release.

Evan lifts his head and looks around the room. Nothing has changed. And yet everything has. The silence is still there, but it feels different now. Not empty. Unanswered.

And that distinction matters.

Because unanswered means something could still be there, even if he cannot feel it.

Faith after this is not resolution. It is refusal. Refusal to pretend nothing changed. Refusal to accept easy answers. Refusal to stop asking.

"My God . . . why?"

The question remains, not as failure, but as presence, something that stays when certainty does not.

And this is where faith begins again, not in clarity, but in the willingness to remain in the question.

Part II—The Words That Don't Hold

The problem is not that there are no words. It is that the words come too quickly, too easily, forming themselves into sentences that sound complete before anything inside has had time to catch up. They arrive shaped like answers, offered with care, meant to comfort, meant to stabilize. But when they land, they do not hold.

Evan hears them first from someone who means well. They always mean well. The tone is gentle, the timing careful, the intention clear.

"I'm just grateful God was watching over you."

He nods, because that is what is expected, because rejecting it in the moment would create a different kind of disruption. But something inside him resists. Not loudly, not in a way that shows on his face, but enough to create distance between what is said and what is felt.

Watching over me.

The phrase repeats, turning over in his mind, and almost immediately something else follows.

Then where was He for the others?

He does not say it. He does not even look like he is thinking it. But the question forms anyway, settling beneath the surface, where it does not disappear, where it becomes part of what he carries forward.

Across town, the mother hears a different version, but it carries the same shape.

"God has a plan."

She is standing in her kitchen when it is said, hands resting against the counter, body still. The sentence lands, but it does not settle. It hovers, disconnected from everything around it.

If this is a plan—

she does not want it.

The thought comes quickly, sharper than she expects, and immediately something else follows. Guilt. Because she knows what she is supposed to believe, what she is supposed to say, what she is supposed to trust. But the anger has already made space for something else, and now that space cannot be closed.

She does not respond. She cannot. The sentence does not give her anywhere to stand.

Lila hears it in simpler forms, phrases that are meant to organize the world, to give it meaning that can be understood.

"Everything happens for a reason."

She turns the sentence over in her mind, not analyzing it, not debating it, just holding it against what she knows. She looks for the reason. She searches for it in what happened, in what she remembers, in what she cannot stop remembering.

It is not there.

And because it is not there, the sentence does not help. It creates distance, a gap between what she is told and what she feels, between the explanation offered and the reality she experienced.

Marcus does not internalize it the same way. When someone says to him, "God is still in control," he reacts immediately.

He laughs.

Not because it is funny.

Because it is not.

"Then I don't want that kind of control."

The words come out before he can soften them, before he can reshape them into something more acceptable. The person in front of him steps back, hurt, surprised, unprepared for that response. Marcus feels it, sees the impact of what he said, but he does not take it back.

Because something in him refuses to soften it.

Not yet.

At the station, Reyes hears the phrases as they pass through different conversations, different voices, each one attempting to do the same thing, to bring closure, to create meaning where none has settled yet.

"Everything happens for a reason."

"God won't give you more than you can handle."

He does not respond. Not because he agrees, but because he understands what is happening. People are trying to close something that should not be closed yet. They are trying to resolve something that has not had time to unfold.

He has learned what happens when you rush that. The words fail. They collapse under the weight they are asked to carry. And when they collapse, people feel it, even if they cannot name why.

So he does not offer them. Not to Evan. Not to anyone.

Because this part is not about answers.

It is about space.

Space for the question to exist without being forced into something that does not fit.

Evan sits with the phrases longer than he wants to. He turns them over, tests them against what he experienced, against what he knows cannot be reduced.

"God is in control."

It sounds stable, something that should anchor him. But when he places it next to what happened, it fractures. It does not disappear. It does not lose meaning entirely. But it does not hold in the same way.

"Everything happens for a reason."

It sounds complete, like something that should bring resolution. But when he asks what that reason could be, it empties. There is nothing there that matches the scale of what occurred.

He exhales slowly, recognizing that something has shifted, not necessarily belief itself, but the language that once carried it. The words he used before no longer carry what they once did. They have not disappeared. They have lost weight.

And that is its own kind of loss.

The mother stops trying to use them, not as a decision, but as a response. They do not fit, so she lets them go, not faith itself, but the words that once held it. What remains is something quieter, less defined, more difficult to articulate.

Lila listens less, not because she is disengaged, but because the words do not connect. They remain above what she feels, and she stays below them, in the place where things do not yet make sense.

Marcus avoids those conversations when he can, not always, but enough to keep the tension from escalating. Because every time someone tries to explain it, something in him pushes back harder, not against the person, but against the explanation itself.

Explanation feels like reduction.

And what happened cannot be reduced.

Reyes understands that, not as theory, but as experience. He has seen what happens when people are given answers too soon. They either reject them or pretend to accept them. Neither holds.

So he allows the questions to remain.

Evan does the same, though he does not realize it at first. He sits in the space without trying to close it, without forcing the words to work again before they are ready.

He remembers the words that came to him earlier.

"My God, my God, why have you forsaken me?"

They do not explain anything.

They do not resolve anything.

But they fit.

Because they do not pretend.

They name what is actually there.

Absence.

Distance.

Question.

He exhales, because maybe this is what remains, not answers, not explanations, but words that are honest enough to stay when everything else falls away.

Faith after this is not built on certainty.

It is built on what does not hold and what remains when it doesn't.

The words may change, fall away, break under pressure, but the need to speak, to ask, to name what is real does not disappear.

And maybe that is where something still lives.

Not in what explains.

But in what refuses to pretend.

Part III—What Remains Without Answer

What replaces certainty is not clarity. It is endurance, not the kind that feels strong or resolved, but the kind that remains when nothing else settles, when answers do not arrive, when the questions continue without resolution. Faith does not rebuild itself quickly. It does not return to what it was, because what it was no longer fits the world as it is now experienced.

Evan understands that, not as a conclusion, but as a condition he finds himself living within. He sits in the same chair, in the same room, in the same posture he once used for prayer, but the experience has changed. Before, there was movement, a sense that something was being heard, that something might respond, that silence contained presence rather than absence.

Now the silence feels different. Not empty, not entirely devoid of meaning, but unresolved, carrying no clear sense of return. He does not speak, not because he has nothing to say, but because speaking feels uncertain, like sending something outward without knowing if it will land anywhere at all.

Still, he remains.

Because leaving would feel like another kind of loss.

Across town, the mother sits in the dark. No lights, no movement, just presence. She has stopped trying to make sense of what happened, stopped trying to locate meaning that would justify something that cannot be justified. That effort exhausted her, took more from her than it gave, leaving her with less certainty than she began with.

Now there is something else. Not acceptance. Not peace. But a kind of stillness that does not argue, that does not attempt to resolve what cannot be resolved. She speaks once, quietly, without structure or expectation.

"If you're there . . . "

The sentence does not complete. It does not need to. Completion would require certainty, and certainty is not available. She does not repeat it, does not build on it, does not try to shape it into something more formal. She lets it remain unfinished.

And that feels more honest than anything she has tried before.

Lila carries it differently, without naming it, without forming it into words. She notices the change in how adults speak, the hesitation that was not there before, the way certainty has softened, the way answers take longer to form or do not form at all. She does not analyze it. She absorbs it.

She waits differently now.

Not expecting explanation.

Not expecting resolution.

Just noticing that it is not there.

And in that noticing, something forms, not belief, not disbelief, but something in between, something unfinished, something that does not require immediate definition.

Marcus returns to the church, but he does not go inside. He stands near the steps, hands in his pockets, watching people enter. There is no music now, no voices rising, just the building, still, unchanged in its structure even as everything else has shifted.

He looks at the door longer this time. Not with anger. Not entirely. With distance. He does not step forward, but he does not turn away immediately either. Something in him is no longer pushing against it with the same force.

Not ready to move toward.

But no longer resisting in the same way.

At the station, Reyes finishes his shift, moving through the routine as it has always been, each step familiar, each action expected. On the surface, everything continues as it should. But inside, he carries the same question he has carried before, in different forms, in different moments.

What holds when answers do not?

He no longer tries to resolve it. Not because it lacks importance, but because he understands that resolution is not always available. Instead, he allows it to remain, present without being solved, acknowledged without being closed.

Keisha sits in her car, engine off, hands resting on the wheel. She has not turned the key. She is not ready to move yet. This is where everything meets, her role, her belief, her understanding of what should have happened, all of it altered.

She looks out at the street, at people moving, at life continuing in the same patterns that existed before, patterns that now feel different because of what they carry.

Continuation without resolution.

She closes her eyes, not to pray in the way she once did, not to form words or structure thought, but to sit in the space where prayer used to form. There are no words. Only awareness.

Of absence.

Of question.

Of something that has not been answered

She exhales slowly, recognizing that this is where she is now, not outside of faith, not fully within it as it once was, but somewhere between what was and what has not yet been defined.

Evan lifts his head and looks around the room. Nothing has changed. The same walls, the same objects, the same space. And yet everything feels different, because what once felt certain now feels open, unfinished, not in a way that demands immediate closure, but in a way that resists it.

He does not try to close it. He does not try to define it. Something in him recognizes that doing so would be premature, would force something into place that is not ready to hold.

Instead, he remains.

In the question.

In the silence.

In the space where something may still exist, even if he cannot feel it.

Faith after this is not about answers. It is not about resolution. It is not about returning to what was before. It is about what remains when answers do not come, when words fail, when certainty breaks under the weight of reality.

What remains is not clarity.

It is presence.

Not the kind that is proven.

The kind that is endured.

Held.

Carried.

Even when it does not respond.

"My God . . . "

The words return, not completed, not resolved, but still spoken, still present, still reaching into something that may or may not answer.

And maybe that is what faith becomes.

Not knowing.

Not understanding.

But continuing to reach into silence.

And refusing to stop.

Chapter 19—The Child Who Doesn't Talk About It

Part I—What Shows Without Words

Not all wounds speak. Some shift behavior. Some move into the body and stay there, changing how a child moves through the world without ever becoming language. Lila does not talk about it, not because she can't, but because nothing she says feels like it fits what happened. The questions adults ask don't match what she feels.

"Do you want to talk about it?"

She shakes her head, not in defiance, but in recognition that talking about it would require something she does not have. Words would make it smaller, or wrong, or incomplete. So she doesn't try.

Instead, she changes.

At first, it is small, barely noticeable unless someone is paying attention. She takes longer to get ready in the morning, standing in front of her shoes without moving, choosing one pair, then another, then back again. It is not about preference. It is about decision. Decision feels heavier now, as if every small choice carries more weight than it should.

At school, she sits differently. Not slouched, not distracted, but still, too still, her body held in a kind of quiet tension that looks like control from the outside. Her teacher notices and interprets it the only way she knows how.

"She's doing really well."

"She's so strong."

The words are meant as praise, but they miss something essential, because stillness is not the same as strength. Stillness can be holding, holding too much without release.

Lila does not raise her hand as often. Not because she does not know the answer, but because attention feels different now. Being seen feels like risk. Something in her has learned that without explanation, without language, without anyone needing to say it out loud.

At recess, she stays closer to the building. No one tells her to. No one instructs her to remain there. But she does, watching more than she plays, tracking movement, listening for changes in sound. The other children run freely, their attention moving from one game to another without calculation. Lila stays aware, not consciously, but automatically, her body remembering something her mind cannot fully organize.

At home, it shows in quieter ways. She does not ask for help the way she used to. She does not call out from another room. If she needs something, she gets up and retrieves it herself, moving through the house without announcing where she is or what she is doing. Sound feels different now, as if making noise might invite something she cannot name.

Her mother notices, not all at once, but over time, through the accumulation of small absences. The absence of requests. The absence of ordinary noise. The absence of the casual calling out that once filled the house.

"Do you need anything?" her mother asks gently.

Lila shakes her head, even when she does. Because needing feels like something that should be minimized, contained, kept from becoming visible.

At night, sleep changes, not dramatically, not in ways that would immediately alarm someone, but subtly. She takes longer to settle. She listens before closing her eyes, checking the room without turning her head, registering the door, the window, the hallway.

Nothing moves.

Nothing happens.

But the checking remains.

Because something in her has learned that stillness does not always mean safety.

She does not have nightmares in the way adults expect. She does not wake up crying or call out for comfort. Instead, she wakes quietly, eyes open, body still, listening for something that does not come. After a while, she returns to sleep, as if nothing has happened, as if the interruption does not count.

Evan sees it before he understands it. He visits, sits across from her, tries to find something to say, something that might open a door into what she is holding. But she does not offer anything to respond to. She answers questions, short, correct, contained, but she does not expand. She does not fill the space.

And he realizes this is not absence.

It is containment.

She is holding something that does not move outward, something that remains inside her, shaping how she responds without becoming something she can describe.

"What do you like doing?" he asks gently.

She shrugs.

"Reading."

"What kind of books?"

Another shrug.

"It doesn't matter."

The answer lands heavier than it should. It is not disinterest. It is detachment. The things that used to matter feel less defined, less important, because something else has taken their place, something larger, something that does not fit into ordinary categories.

Reyes notices it too, though he does not approach it directly. He sees it in posture, in movement, in what is not expressed. He has seen it before, children who carry what they cannot name, who adapt instead of speak, who survive by changing how they exist in the world rather than explaining what has happened to them.

He does not interrupt it. He does not try to draw it out, because forcing it can break something that is holding. Instead, he remains steady, predictable, safe in ways that do not demand response.

Lila sits on the floor, her back against the wall, a book open in her lap. She is not reading. The pages do not turn. But she stays there, still, contained, present without being expressive.

Her mother watches from the doorway, wanting to say something, to reach in, to offer something that might help. But she does not, because she does not know what would help, and saying the wrong thing feels like another risk.

The child who does not talk is not unaffected, not unaware, not healed. She is carrying, in her body, in her behavior, in the small shifts that others might miss but that are present in everything she does.

In how she sits.

In how she listens.

In how she moves through a world that no longer feels the same.

Evan exhales slowly, because this is different from what he expected. Not loud. Not visible in the ways people are trained to recognize. But real. Just as real.

He looks at her again, not trying to fix it, not trying to reach in, just seeing it.

And understanding that this is how it lives in her now, not spoken, but present, shaping everything that comes after.

And this is where the story continues.

Part II—The Body Keeps It

It does not stay in memory alone. It moves into the body, settling there when there are no words to carry it, shaping response before thought has time to form. Lila does not think about what happened the way adults expect. She does not replay the moment in full. She does not narrate it to herself. But her body remembers in ways she cannot explain.

She sits at her desk, pencil in hand, a simple assignment in front of her. Write three sentences. It should be easy. It used to be. But her hand pauses before it moves, not because she does not know what to write, but because starting feels different now. The pencil presses a little too firmly against the paper, the line darker than it should be. She erases and tries again. The same pressure returns, the same hesitation, as if her body is carrying something into the act of writing that has nothing to do with the assignment itself.

Her teacher walks by and glances down. "Take your time." The words are kind, meant to ease pressure, meant to reassure. But Lila's shoulders tighten slightly, because time does not change what her body is doing. The tension is not about speed. It is about something deeper, something that does not respond to instruction.

Across the room, another student laughs, a loud, sudden sound that cuts through the quiet. Lila flinches, small, barely visible, but real. Her head turns before she can stop it, her eyes scanning, locating the source, orienting herself to where the sound came from. Then stillness returns, as if nothing happened.

Her body resets quickly.

But not completely.

Something remains beneath the surface, a readiness that does not fully release.

At recess, it shows differently. She stands with the other children, close enough to belong, far enough to leave. The game shifts suddenly, someone running toward her without warning, fast, unstructured. Her body reacts immediately, stepping back too quickly, too far.

"Sorry," the other child says, confused by the response.

Lila nods.

Says nothing.

Because she does not know how to explain what just happened. It was not fear in the way people expect. It was response. Automatic. Immediate. Unchosen.

At home, her mother notices the smallest things. The way Lila holds a cup with both hands now, even when one would be enough. The way she sits closer to the wall during dinner, positioning herself in a way that feels contained. The way she turns toward the door every time it opens, no matter how quiet the sound.

None of it is dramatic.

All of it is consistent.

Patterns forming where there were none before.

"Are you okay?" her mother asks gently.

Lila nods.

Because she is.

And she isn't.

But there are no words for that difference, no language that captures both at the same time.

At night, her body stays awake longer than she does. She lies in bed, eyes closed, breathing steady, but something in her remains alert. She listens, tracks sound, registers the house settling, a car passing, a door closing somewhere in the distance. Each one is noticed, cataloged, checked.

Not consciously.

Automatically.

She turns over without fully waking, pulling the blanket tighter around herself, not because she is cold, but because containment feels necessary. Being held by something external helps her body settle, even when she does not understand why.

Evan sees it again when he visits. Not in what she says, but in how she sits, in how she moves between stillness and sudden awareness, in the way her eyes shift before her head does, tracking the environment before she consciously engages with it.

He does not comment.

Because naming it feels like exposing something she is not ready to share.

Instead, he adjusts himself. He moves more slowly, keeps his voice steady, predictable, because if her body is watching, then his movements matter.

Reyes understands it immediately. He has seen it before, in other children, in different contexts, but with the same underlying pattern. The body holding what the mind cannot organize, the nervous system learning something it cannot unlearn quickly.

He does not explain it in front of her.

Because explanation is not what she needs.

She needs space.

Consistency.

Time.

Time for the body to realize it is no longer there, even when it still feels like it is.

Lila sits on the floor again, a book in her lap. This time, she turns a page, then another. The movement is slow, deliberate, her breathing matching the rhythm of it.

Page.

Pause.

Page.

Something in her begins to settle.

Not fully.

Not permanently.

But enough.

Her mother watches, not interrupting, not asking questions, just noticing the small shift, the slight return of something that looks like ease.

The child who does not talk is not silent.

Not really.

She is expressing in a different language, one that lives in the body, in movement, in tension, in the way she exists in space.

Her story is not absent.

It is embedded.

In the way she flinches.

In the way she watches.

In the way she holds and releases and holds again.

Evan exhales slowly, because this changes how he sees it. Not something waiting to be spoken, but something already being lived.

He looks at Lila again, not expecting words, not needing them.

Because now he understands.

This is how she is telling it.

Without speaking.

And this is something that must be heard differently.

Part III—What Adults Miss

Adults are trained to listen for words. That is where they look for meaning, for evidence, for signs that something is wrong or beginning to heal. They ask questions because questions feel like care. They wait for answers because answers feel like progress. They listen for tears, for fear, for anger that can be named and responded to.

That is why they miss so much.

Lila does not cry in front of them. She does not refuse to go to school. She does not lash out or withdraw in ways that disrupt what is expected. She sits quietly, answers politely, follows directions, and because of that, people begin to say she is doing well.

Her teacher says it first.

"She's adjusting."

The word sounds gentle, responsible, something that suggests movement in the right direction. Lila is standing at the cubbies when she hears it, her coat half on, one sleeve caught at the wrist. She pauses for a moment, not because she understands the full meaning of the word, but because she feels it being placed on her.

Adjusting.

It sounds like something has already been decided.

She pulls her sleeve free and says nothing.

At home, her mother hears another version.

"She seems calm."

The counselor offers it carefully, not dismissing, not minimizing, just observing what can be seen from the outside. Her mother nods, because it is true in a certain way. Lila is calm. She does not make noise. She does not ask for much. She does not interrupt or demand attention.

But her mother has started to notice the difference between calm and contained.

Calm is what people see.

Contained is what Lila is.

Her mother watches the small things now, the way Lila chooses her seat at the table so she can see the door, the way she stops chewing when a car door closes outside, the way she answers "I'm fine" before the question is fully asked.

The counselor asks, "Has she talked about what happened?"

Her mother looks down the hallway, where Lila sits with a book open in her lap.

"No," she says.

Then, after a moment, "But she keeps her shoes by the bed now."

The counselor looks up, something in the detail registering.

"She never did that before," her mother adds, almost apologetically, as if the detail might sound too small to matter.

But the small things are where the story lives.

At school, Lila's silence becomes useful. It does not interrupt the lesson. It does not require additional attention. It does not demand that anyone stop and deal with something unresolved. So the day moves around her.

Morning work.

Reading group.

Lunch line.

Recess.

All the routines return, and because they return, adults hope the children will follow them back into normalcy.

Lila follows.

Outwardly.

She lines up when told. She sits when asked. She writes her name at the top of the page.

But something in her is always measuring.

How far to the door.

Who is behind her.

Whether the hallway is quiet.

Whether quiet is safe.

No one grades that.

No one comments on it.

No one sees the effort it takes.

At recess, another child asks if she wants to play. Lila almost says yes. The word forms, nearly spoken, but before it can leave her mouth, a voice shouts across the playground, sudden and sharp.

The yes disappears.

She shakes her head.

The other child shrugs and runs off.

A playground aide notices from a distance.

"Still shy?" she asks kindly.

Lila nods, because nodding is easier than explaining.

Shy.

Another word placed over something more complex.

Later, Evan watches from across the room as Lila sits beside her mother in a community gathering space. There are chairs arranged in a loose circle, a table with snacks, coloring pages spread out for children. The room is meant to feel safe, structured, supportive.

Lila does not color.

She holds a crayon, turning it slowly between her fingers.

Evan watches her eyes move.

Door.

Window.

Adult.

Door again.

Her mother's face.

Back to the door.

He feels something shift in him, because he recognizes it now.

She is not disengaged.

She is monitoring.

That difference changes everything.

Reyes stands beside him.

"She's quiet," Evan says.

Reyes nods.

"She's busy."

Evan looks at him, not fully understanding.

Reyes adds, "Quiet doesn't always mean nothing's happening."

Evan watches Lila again.

The crayon has stopped moving. Someone laughs nearby, not loudly, but unexpectedly. Lila's shoulders rise, just slightly, then settle.

No one else notices.

Except her mother.

And Reyes.

And now Evan.

Her mother places her hand on the couch beside Lila's, not touching, just close enough to be there if needed. Lila does not take it, but she shifts her hand slightly closer.

It is a small movement.

Easy to miss.

But it is communication.

The room continues. Adults talk about healing, about resilience, about community, about moving forward. The words are well-intentioned, carefully chosen, meant to offer direction.

Lila hears them.

But they do not reach her.

They move above what she is experiencing, too broad, too complete, too far removed from the way her body holds what happened.

Evan hears them differently now.

Resilient.

Strong.

Brave.

Adjusting.

He understands how those words can become a lid, how they can cover something that still needs space to exist.

Lila's mother leans toward her.

"Do you want to go?"

Lila looks at her.

"Yes."

The answer is immediate, quiet, but clear.

Her mother nods. No hesitation. No attempt to convince her to stay. No suggestion that leaving would mean failure.

They stand together.

Lila walks beside her.

Evan notices that her mother does not guide her physically, does not place a hand on her back or shoulder, does not direct her movement.

She simply stays beside her.

Reyes watches them leave.

"That helps," he says.

"What?" Evan asks.

"Letting her have a way out."

Evan considers that.

A way out.

It sounds simple.

But for a child whose body remembers being trapped, choice becomes something essential.

Outside, Lila pauses before getting into the car.

"Can I sit where I can see the street?" she asks.

Her mother nods.

"Yes."

No correction.

No reassurance that she does not need it.

Just yes.

Lila gets in.

The door closes.

Nothing is resolved.

Nothing is fixed.

But something is honored.

The child who does not talk about it is not silent.

She is communicating in a different language.

In posture.

In movement.

In the way she positions herself in space.

In the way she moves toward exits.

In the way she reaches for safety without naming it.

Adults miss it when they listen only for words.

But the body speaks.

Behavior speaks.

Silence speaks.

And if someone learns to listen differently, the child is not silent at all.

Chapter 20—The Responder Who Keeps Working

Part I—Still Showing Up

From the outside, nothing has changed. That is what people see first. Evan shows up on time, uniform in place, equipment checked, voice steady. He answers calls, moves with precision, does the job the way it is supposed to be done. No hesitation. No visible disruption. If anything, he looks sharper, more focused, more controlled.

"Good work out there," someone says.

He nods, because it's true.

And it isn't.

The job does not stop. That is part of what holds it together. Call follows call. Shift follows shift. There is no pause long enough to sit inside anything that does not have immediate function. Evan moves through it because movement is what the job requires. But something has changed, not in what he does, but in what stays.

The first call of the shift is routine. Chest pain. Vitals stable. Transport clean. Everything as expected. Evan performs each step without thinking about it because he doesn't have to. The training holds. The sequence is familiar. Nothing requires him to slow down.

But as they clear the call, something lingers. Not the patient. Not the outcome. A moment. A look. A question that was asked and not fully answered. He does not name it. He does not need to. It stays anyway.

The second call is different. More urgent. More complex. Adrenaline rises, focus sharpens, everything narrows to what needs to happen next. This part he knows. This part he trusts. And when it's over, when the patient is handed off, when the report is given, when the room empties, something else returns.

Not relief.

Not exactly.

Weight.

Not attached to one call, but accumulated, layered, carried forward from what came before.

Reyes notices it before Evan does, not in what he says, but in what he doesn't release. Most responders let something go between calls. A breath. A shift. A reset. Evan doesn't. He carries it forward, call to call, moment to moment, not intentionally, but automatically.

At the station, the others talk. Stories, fragments, pieces of the shift that get shared and then set down. Evan listens but doesn't add much. Not because he has nothing to say, but because saying it would require sorting it, and he is not ready to do that.

"You good?"

The question comes casually, routine, expected.

"Yeah."

The answer is immediate, automatic, and in one sense, true. He is functioning. He is doing the job. He is not falling apart. But that is not the same as being unaffected.

The next call comes in. They move. No pause. No space for what just happened to settle. Evan steps into it without hesitation because hesitation is not part of the job. And that is where the accumulation begins.

Not in the calls themselves.

In the lack of space between them.

Later, he sits alone, not intentionally, just where he ends up, hands resting on his knees, body still. For a moment, nothing is happening. No call. No demand. No immediate need. And that is when he feels it.

Not one thing.

Many things.

Layered.

Unsorted.

A voice. A face. A decision. A moment that passed too quickly. He exhales because this part is harder, not the action, but the holding.

Reyes sits across from him, not speaking right away, because he recognizes the moment, the space where everything that has been carried starts to surface.

"You don't have to figure it out tonight."

Evan looks up. The words land differently than most. Not dismissive. Not corrective. Allowing.

"I'm fine," Evan says.

Reyes nods.

"I know."

And he does, because fine is not the point.

The shift ends. Evan goes home. Routine continues. Shower. Food. Silence. From the outside, everything holds. Nothing breaks. Nothing signals that something is wrong. But inside, something is building.

Not explosively.

Gradually.

Call by call.

Moment by moment.

Each one adding something that does not leave.

He sits on the edge of his bed, hands still, trying to trace it, where it starts, where it gathers. But it does not begin in one place, and it does not stay in one form. It shifts, grows, becomes something harder to isolate, harder to name.

He leans forward, elbows on his knees, head down, not in collapse, but in containment, because this is what he knows how to do. Hold it. Keep moving. Stay functional.

But something in him recognizes the truth.

Function is not the same as freedom.

Working is not the same as releasing.

Showing up is not the same as processing what he carries when he leaves.

The responder who keeps working does not stop. That is what makes him reliable. That is what makes him strong. But it is also what allows the weight to accumulate quietly, without interruption, without being seen.

Evan exhales slowly, because he understands something now he didn't before. This does not leave when the call ends. It comes with him into the next call, into the next shift, into the spaces where nothing is happening, but everything is still there.

And this is where it begins to matter.

Part II—What Builds Without Notice

It does not feel like accumulation at first. It feels like continuity, like the job unfolding the way it always has. One call ends, another begins, the rhythm holding everything together. As long as that rhythm remains intact, nothing seems out of place. Evan relies on that structure, the sequence that gives shape to unpredictability. Dispatch. Response. Assessment. Action. Transfer. Clear. Each step leads to the next, each step has purpose, and within that purpose there is no room for what does not serve the immediate moment.

So he does not make room for it.

The next shift begins before the last one has fully settled. Coffee, equipment check, inventory, routine. Everything in order. Everything where it should be. Except something isn't, though he does not name it. He does not need to. It shows up in smaller ways, in pauses that last a second longer than they used to, in questions he asks twice to be certain, in looks he holds a fraction too long before moving on.

Nothing that disrupts.

Nothing that draws attention.

But enough to register, if someone is looking.

The first call is straightforward. A fall. Minor injuries. Reassurance. Transport. Evan moves through it with precision, every step correct, every action measured. But as he helps the patient onto the stretcher, something catches. A hand grips his sleeve tighter than expected. A look lingers longer than the moment requires.

"Don't leave me."

The words are quiet, almost lost in the movement around them, but they stay. Evan nods, responds the way he always does.

"I'm here."

And he is.

But the words follow him anyway.

Back in the ambulance, he checks vitals, records information, maintains the flow of the call. Everything routine. Everything as it should be. But the sentence repeats, not attached to the person anymore, but to something else, something that does not resolve when the call does.

At the hospital, they transfer care. Report given. Responsibility passed. That is where it is supposed to end. But nothing in him marks it as finished. It does not close. It moves.

To the next place.

Reyes watches him, not closely, not intrusively, but consistently. He has seen this pattern before, the responder who does not drop anything, who carries forward without noticing what is being added. He does not interrupt it, not yet, because interruption only works when someone is ready to feel what they are holding. Evan is not there. He is still moving.

The second call comes faster. A child. Difficulty breathing. Urgency rises, focus sharpens, everything narrows to the task. Evan moves immediately, no hesitation. This part he knows. This part he trusts. The child stabilizes. Breathing evens. The mother exhales, relief visible, immediate.

Evan registers it.

But he does not feel it the same way.

Because something else is already there.

Something that did not leave from before.

Back at the station, someone makes a joke. Light. Routine. Laughter follows. Evan almost joins. Almost. But something in him holds back, not intentionally, just enough to keep him slightly apart from the moment.

"You good?" someone asks.

Same question.

Same tone.

"Yeah."

Same answer.

But this time it feels thinner, less connected to what is actually there, more like something he says because it is expected.

He sits down, leans forward, hands clasped, not thinking about anything in particular, but not empty. Never empty. Because everything is still there, not as full memories, but as fragments that do not organize themselves into something clear.

A voice.

A grip.

A look.

A moment that ended but did not leave.

Reyes sits across from him again, same distance, same quiet.

"You don't have to carry all of it at once."

Evan looks up.

"What do you mean?"

Reyes does not rush the answer.

"Some of it can wait."

Evan nods, but he does not know how to do that. Waiting is not part of the job. Holding is.

The next call comes in. No time to sit. No time to sort. They move again. Evan stands, already shifting back into function, back into role. For a moment, everything aligns again, because the job gives him structure, gives him purpose, gives him something to do with his hands.

But not with what stays.

Later, alone again, the weight feels different. Not heavier. More present. Because now there are more pieces, more fragments, more moments that did not resolve when they ended.

He leans back, closes his eyes, not to sleep, but to pause. But even in the pause, it continues, not loud, not overwhelming, but persistent.

The responder who keeps working does not notice when the accumulation begins, because nothing breaks, nothing stops, nothing forces it into awareness. It builds in the background, quietly, steadily, without interruption.

Evan exhales slowly, because something in him is starting to recognize it. Not fully, not clearly, but enough to feel the difference between what he is doing and what he is carrying.

Between what ends and what stays.

And that difference is growing.

Part III—When It Follows You Home

It does not stay at the station. That is what Evan begins to understand, not all at once, but in the quiet moments when there is nothing left to do and nowhere left to direct his attention. For a while, it seems contained, held within the shift, bounded by the uniform, the vehicle, the call itself. But that boundary does not hold.

Not completely.

He notices it the moment he gets home, though not in a way that announces itself clearly. It is something smaller than that, something that feels like a shift in the air rather than a defined change. He sets his keys down in the same place he always does, kicks off his shoes, moves through the familiar routine that usually signals the end of the day.

Everything is the same.

But something is not.

He stands in the kitchen, opens the refrigerator, stares inside without reaching for anything. He is not hungry, but he knows he should eat. The thought is there, present, reasonable, but it does not translate into action. Something else occupies the space where decision usually happens.

He closes the door.

Walks to the living room.

Sits.

The silence feels different here, heavier, not because it is louder, but because there is nothing to interrupt it. At the station, there is always something. Movement, sound, conversation, the next call waiting to be answered. Here, there is space.

And in that space, everything that stayed begins to surface.

Not as a single memory.

Not as a clear sequence.

As fragments.

A voice.

"Don't leave me."

A moment.

A grip that held longer than expected.

A look that did not resolve before it ended.

They do not come in order. They do not connect into a single narrative. They exist separately, each one carrying weight, each one present in a way that does not depend on context.

He leans forward, hands on his knees, breathing steady. He is not overwhelmed. He is not losing control. But he is not unaffected. This is different from the shift. During the shift, everything has direction, purpose, a clear next step. Here, there is no action to take.

Nothing to fix.

Nothing to respond to.

Only what remains.

His phone buzzes. A message appears.

“Good work today.”

He reads it. Does not respond. Not because he disagrees, but because the words feel incomplete. Good work is true. It reflects what was done, what was accomplished, what was handled correctly.

But it does not include what it costs.

It does not include what follows.

He stands, moves to the bathroom, turns on the shower. The sound of the water fills the space, offering something else for his senses to hold onto. He steps in, lets the heat settle over him. For a moment, the fragments quiet, not gone, but less immediate.

He stays there longer than necessary, not because he needs the time, but because stepping out means returning to the silence.

When he does, the apartment feels the same as before.

Too quiet.

Too open.

He moves through it again, more deliberately this time, turning on a light that does not need to be on, switching on the television without paying attention to what is on the screen. He fills the space, not with intention, but with necessity.

Because empty space no longer feels neutral.

It feels like something will enter it.

Reyes told him once, “Pay attention to what follows you.”

At the time, it sounded like advice.

Now, it feels like instruction.

Because it is following him.

Not the calls themselves.

What stayed from them.

What did not end when the shift did.

He sits again, leaning back this time, trying to let it be there without reacting to it, without pushing it away, without pulling it closer. Just noticing.

But noticing is not neutral.

It brings things forward.

A child struggling to breathe.

A mother's face when relief did not reach him the way it should have.

A voice repeating, "Don't leave me."

He exhales slowly, because this is the part no one sees. The responder who keeps working does not stop when the shift ends. The work changes, from action to holding, from doing to carrying.

And carrying does not have a clear endpoint.

He lies down, closes his eyes, not expecting sleep, just rest. But rest does not come easily. His body stays alert, not in the sharp way of an emergency, but in a quieter, more persistent way, a readiness that does not fully release.

He shifts position.

Waits.

Eventually, sleep comes.

But it is lighter.

Less settled.

Easier to leave.

In the morning, he will get up, put the uniform back on, return to the station, continue. From the outside, nothing will look different. He will show up. He will function. He will do the job.

And he will.

But something in him will already be carrying what followed him home. And what he carries will go with him into the next call, and the next, and the next.

Evan opens his eyes in the dark, not fully awake, not fully asleep, aware of the room, of the silence, of what is still there. He does not move. He does not try to change it.

Because something in him understands now.

This is part of it.

Not failure.

Not weakness.

Part of the work that does not end when the shift does.

He exhales, slow, measured, and lets the silence remain.

Not empty.

Not resolved.

But real.

And still with him.

Chapter 21—The One Who Leaves

Part I—The Quiet Exit

No one announces it at first. There is no moment where it becomes official in the way people expect. It does not begin with a decision. It begins with a hesitation, a pause that lasts longer than it used to, a fraction of time that would go unnoticed by anyone else but does not go unnoticed by him.

Evan feels it on a call that should be routine. Not urgent. Not complex. Something he has done a hundred times before. He moves through it the way he always has, assessment, action, communication, everything correct, everything in place. No one questions him. No one hesitates. The call resolves the way it should.

But something inside him lags behind.

It is slight.

Almost imperceptible.

A delay between what he knows to do and the part of him that moves to do it. Not enough to disrupt the call. Not enough for anyone else to see. But enough for him to feel.

He notices it because he remembers what it used to feel like. Immediate. Instinctive. Unquestioned. There was no space between recognition and response. Now there is a space, small but undeniable, and once he feels it, he cannot ignore it.

Later, back at the station, he sits with his hands still, not tired in the way sleep would fix, not exhausted in the way that comes after a difficult shift, but something else. He watches the others move through the room, the same patterns, the same rhythm, the same unspoken coordination that comes from working together long enough to anticipate each other's movements.

Everything continues.

Everything functions.

And for the first time, he feels separate from it.

Not excluded.

Not pushed out.

But not fully inside it either.

As if the rhythm is still playing, but he is no longer aligned with it in the same way. He answers when spoken to. He participates when needed. He does not withdraw. But there is a subtle distance that was not there before.

"You good?"

The question comes the way it always does, casual, routine, more acknowledgment than inquiry.

"Yeah."

The answer comes just as easily, just as automatically. But this time, as he says it, he feels the gap between the word and what it is supposed to mean. He is functioning. He is performing. He is not breaking down. But the word no longer captures the whole of what is happening inside him.

The next shift feels heavier, not because the calls are worse, not because anything external has changed, but because the space between the calls feels different. Longer. More exposed. Less buffered by momentum. He starts to notice the moments he used to pass through without thinking, the seconds after a call ends, the quiet before the next one begins, the time when nothing is happening and everything he has just experienced is still present.

He had not realized how much the movement of the job had protected him from that.

Now, without the same immersion, those spaces widen.

They do not overwhelm him.

They reveal something.

Reyes notices it, not in what Evan says, but in how he holds himself, in the slight shift in presence, the way he is still engaged but not anchored in the same way. He has seen it before, not as a single moment, but as a pattern, the responder who begins to step back internally before any external change occurs.

"You ever think about taking a break?" Reyes asks.

The question is simple, open, not loaded with expectation.

Evan looks at him.

"What kind of break?"

Reyes shrugs. "Any kind."

The answer is intentionally undefined, because the question is not about logistics. It is about recognition.

Evan does not respond right away. The question lands differently than he expects. It does not feel like suggestion. It feels like something already forming being named out loud for the first time. Something in him has been moving in that direction, quietly, without language.

That night, at home, he sits longer than usual, not doing anything in particular, not avoiding anything either, just present in a way that feels unfamiliar. The apartment has not changed. The furniture is the same. The light falls the same way through the window. But his experience of it has shifted.

He looks at the space around him and realizes that the difference is not in the room.

It is in him.

He thinks about the next shift, the next call, the next moment that will require him to step forward without hesitation. For the first time, he is not sure he can do it in the same way. Not because he lacks the skill. Not because he has forgotten how.

Because something in him no longer moves toward it with the same certainty.

The thought comes quietly, without urgency, without panic.

Maybe I don't want to keep doing this.

He does not react to it immediately. He does not push it away. He does not follow it all the way through. He lets it exist, because something about it feels honest in a way that is difficult to dismiss.

He does not tell anyone. Not Reyes. Not the others. Saying it would make it more real, more defined, more immediate. He is not ready for that. For now, it remains internal, a recognition rather than a declaration.

The next morning, he wakes before the alarm and lies still, not dreading the day, not resisting it, but not moving toward it either. The uniform is where it always is, folded, ready, waiting. He looks at it longer than he usually would, not with resentment, not with rejection, but with distance.

At the station, everything continues as it always has. No one notices anything different, because nothing has changed on the surface. Evan moves through the routine, completes the tasks, answers the calls, functions in the way he always has.

But something in him is no longer fully invested in the continuation.

Not disengaged.

Not careless.

Just less anchored.

Reyes sees it in the smallest shift, not in performance, but in presence, the way Evan is there but not entirely, the way something in him has begun to pull back without fully leaving. He does not call it out. He does not force it into conversation, because this part cannot be rushed.

The decision to leave does not arrive all at once. It forms over time, in hesitation, in distance, in the quiet realization that something has already begun to separate. Evan stands at the back of the station, watching the others move through the space, talking, laughing, continuing as they always have.

He understands something now.

They are still inside it.

And he is beginning to step outside.

Not fully.

Not yet.

But enough to feel the difference.

The one who leaves does not always walk out in a single moment. Sometimes they begin by standing still, by noticing what no longer fits, by recognizing that staying is no longer the same as belonging.

Evan exhales slowly, because this is where it begins, not the leaving itself, but the awareness that leaving is possible. And once that awareness is there, it does not go away.

Part II—The Unspoken Decision

Evan does not decide all at once. A single moment of clarity would be easier to hold, easier to explain, easier to defend. But that is not how it happens. The decision gathers slowly, almost carefully, forming in the background of his days without demanding immediate attention. It appears in small shifts, in the way he sits in the parking lot a minute longer than usual, in the way he watches the station door before opening it, in the quiet awareness that something inside him is no longer moving in the same direction as everything around him.

He is not afraid to go in. That would be simpler. Fear has a shape, something recognizable, something that can be named and addressed. This is different. It is the slow loss of belonging, the sense that the place that once held him securely now feels slightly out of alignment with who he is becoming.

Inside, nothing has changed. Someone is making coffee. Someone is complaining about paperwork. Someone is laughing at a story that has been told too many times. The room holds its usual rhythm, the unspoken coordination of people who know how to work together without needing to explain themselves.

Evan used to feel part of that rhythm.

Now he observes it.

He still participates. He answers when spoken to. He completes the tasks in front of him. He checks equipment, restocks supplies, signs what needs to be signed. There is no visible difference in his performance. If anything, he is more precise, more deliberate.

That is what makes it harder.

He is still good at this.

Good enough that leaving feels difficult to justify.

The call that morning is routine. An older man short of breath, a worried daughter hovering nearby, a living room filled with familiar objects that have held a lifetime of ordinary days. Evan kneels, asks questions, listens carefully, checks oxygen levels, speaks with calm authority. His voice does not waver. His hands do not hesitate.

The daughter looks at him.

"Thank you," she says.

He nods.

"You're welcome."

He means it.

That is what unsettles him.

The care is still there. The instinct to help, to respond, to step into someone else's need without hesitation, has not disappeared. He is not numb. He is not indifferent.

And yet, when the call ends, something does not return.

There used to be a sense of completion, a feeling that the work had landed somewhere meaningful. Not perfect, not complete in every way, but enough. Now, the action ends, but the sense of resolution does not follow. The work stands on its own, disconnected from the internal response that once accompanied it.

Back at the station, Reyes finds him near the bay, wiping down equipment that has already been cleaned.

"You missed a spot?" Reyes asks lightly.

Evan looks down. The cloth in his hand is dry. He almost laughs.

"Guess not."

Reyes leans against the frame of the bay door. He does not press. He does not rush into questions. He lets the moment settle, allows the silence to carry what it needs to carry.

After a while, he says, "You're thinking about stepping back."

Evan does not answer immediately. He does not need to. The absence of denial is enough.

"I don't know," Evan says finally.

"That's usually how it starts."

Evan looks at him, searching for something to push against, some clear statement he can agree with or reject. But Reyes does not offer one.

“People think leaving starts with certainty,” Reyes continues. “Most of the time, it starts when certainty runs out.”

The words settle into something Evan has already been feeling but has not named. He wants to argue, to say that he is not uncertain, that he still knows how to do the job, that nothing has fundamentally changed.

“I’m not burned out,” he says.

“I didn’t say you were.”

“I’m not falling apart.”

“I know.”

“I can still do the job.”

Reyes meets his eyes.

“That’s not the only question.”

Evan looks away, because that is where the truth sits, just beyond what he is ready to say out loud. The issue is not capability. It is not skill. It is not even endurance. It is something deeper, something that asks not whether he can continue, but whether he should.

“You don’t owe the work your whole self,” Reyes says.

The sentence lands harder than Evan expects. It disrupts something he had not realized he believed, the idea that meaningful work requires complete surrender, that stepping back is a form of failure, that continuing is the only acceptable response to being needed.

Reyes straightens and walks back inside, leaving Evan with the thought.

Take your time.

The words are simple, but they carry weight. Time is not something the job often allows. Decisions are made quickly. Responses are immediate. Waiting is rarely an option.

But this is different.

This is not a call.

This is a shift in direction.

At home, the thought follows him. It appears in small moments, while he is standing in the shower, while he is walking through the grocery store, while he is answering a casual question about work.

"How's it going?" someone asks.

"It's good," he says.

The word feels insufficient.

Not false.

Incomplete.

He starts looking at job postings without fully intending to. Not as a plan. Not as a commitment. Just looking. Roles adjacent to the work, close enough to feel familiar, far enough to offer distance.

He tells himself it is nothing.

But he keeps looking.

One night, he folds his uniform more carefully than usual, smoothing the fabric, aligning the sleeves, paying attention in a way that feels deliberate. He expected resentment, or frustration, or some clear emotional response.

Instead, there is something else.

Respect.

Gratitude.

A quiet acknowledgment of what the uniform has meant.

It has given him access to people in their most vulnerable moments. It has allowed him to be present where presence mattered. It has also carried weight he did not know how to put down.

He sets it on the chair and sits across from it, recognizing something that feels both simple and difficult.

Leaving is not rejection.

It is not turning away from something meaningless.

It is acknowledging that meaning and cost can exist together.

And that sometimes, the cost changes what continuing requires.

The next shift, he arrives on time. Nothing is different on the surface. No announcement. No declaration. He moves through the routine, checks the rig, responds to calls, performs exactly as expected.

But something inside him has shifted.

Not away from care.

Not away from responsibility.

Toward honesty.

He is beginning to know.

And once that knowing begins, even quietly, it changes everything.

Part III—No Siren This Time

Evan tells Reyes first, not because he planned to, not because he had rehearsed the sentence, but because Reyes is there at the right moment, or maybe because Reyes knows how to wait until the truth finally comes close enough to speak. They are standing behind the station after a shift that has been strangely ordinary. No major calls. No chaos. No moment that would explain anything to anyone. Just a day of small needs, clean transports, routine decisions, and paperwork that took longer than it should have.

That is part of what makes it harder. If something dramatic had happened, leaving would have a reason people could understand. But nothing dramatic has happened. Only accumulation. Only distance. Only the quiet awareness that he cannot keep carrying the work in the same way.

Reyes leans against the wall, coffee in hand, watching the parking lot. Evan stands beside him. For a while, neither speaks.

Then Evan says, "I think I'm done."

The words are softer than he expected. Not dramatic. Not angry. Not final in the way he imagined. Just true.

Reyes does not turn immediately. He nods once, as if the sentence has not surprised him.

"As in done done?" he asks.

Evan looks down.

"I think so."

The quiet after that is not empty. It is full of everything the sentence means and everything it does not mean. It does not mean he stopped caring. It does not mean the work stopped mattering. It does not mean he failed. But it does mean something has ended.

Reyes takes a slow breath.

"Okay," he says.

That is all.

The simplicity of it nearly undoes Evan. No argument. No lecture. No reminder that the field needs good people. No attempt to turn the decision into weakness or wisdom before it has had time to be what it is.

Just okay.

Evan swallows.

"I thought you'd tell me not to."

Reyes looks at him then.

"No."

"Why?"

"Because I've seen what happens when people stay only because they think leaving means failure."

Evan looks toward the lot. A car passes on the street beyond the fence, ordinary and unaware.

Reyes continues, "That kind of staying has a cost too."

Evan nods, but it does not feel like relief yet. It feels like grief being given permission.

Later, the official version is quieter still. A conversation with a supervisor. A form. A timeline. Words like transition and availability and future opportunities. Everyone is kind. That almost makes it worse. No one says, You're abandoning us. No one says, You couldn't handle it. No one says what Evan had feared they might say.

But no one fully says what it costs either.

They tell him they understand.

Maybe they do.

Maybe they do not.

His last shift comes two weeks later. It is ordinary too. That feels unfair at first, then strangely merciful. No ceremony. No final heroic call. No perfect ending. Just the same routine. Coffee. Equipment check. A radio test. The inventory list with the pen that barely writes. The smell of the bay. The sound of tires against concrete.

The others know, but they do not make a scene. Someone jokes that he will miss the paperwork. Someone else says he can still come by. Someone claps him on the shoulder a little too hard and then looks away too quickly.

Everyone is trying.

So is he.

The first call is a lift assist. The second is a minor injury. The third is a welfare check that becomes a long conversation with an elderly woman who mostly needs someone to listen.

Evan listens.

Really listens.

There is no rush in him. No impatience. No detachment. Only a strange tenderness, as if knowing he is leaving allows him to feel the work more clearly for a moment.

At the end of the shift, he cleans the rig slowly. Not because it needs extra cleaning, but because his hands need something to do while the ending approaches. Reyes works beside him. Neither speaks much. They wipe surfaces already wiped, check compartments already checked, restock what has already been counted.

Finally, there is nothing left.

Evan stands at the open back doors of the ambulance. He remembers his first shift, how large the rig felt, how official, how full of possibility. He remembers wanting to be worthy of it.

He still wants that.

That is the part that hurts.

Reyes comes to stand beside him.

"You did good work," he says.

Evan closes his eyes briefly.

"Don't."

Reyes waits.

Evan opens his eyes.

"I know you mean it. I just don't know where to put it."

Reyes nods.

"Then don't put it anywhere yet."

Evan almost smiles.

"That your answer to everything?"

"Only the things that don't have one."

They stand together. No siren. No urgency. No one calling for them. Just the quiet of a bay at the end of a shift.

Eventually, Evan reaches into his pocket and takes out his keys. He separates the station key from the ring. The motion is small, ridiculously small for what it represents.

Metal sliding against metal.

A tiny sound.

A clean break.

He places the key on the counter inside. No speech. No announcement. Just release.

The others say goodbye in their own ways. Handshakes. Nods. Awkward jokes. One hug he does not expect. Evan accepts all of it, feeling both present and distant, grateful and hollow.

Then he walks outside.

The morning air is cool. The world is beginning again, indifferent and beautiful. He stands beside his car for a moment, looking back at the station. He expects certainty. Regret. Relief. Something clear.

None of it comes.

Only quiet.

Only the knowledge that he is leaving unresolved.

Maybe all real leaving is like that. Not clean. Not complete. Not free from love.

Reyes steps out behind him but keeps his distance.

Evan turns.

"Thanks," he says.

Reyes nods.

"Take care of what follows you."

Evan holds the words, then nods back.

"I'll try."

He gets into his car and starts the engine. No radio. Not yet. He pulls out slowly, watching the station shrink in the rearview mirror.

There is no siren this time. No urgency. No call pulling him forward. Only road. Only breath. Only the ache of something meaningful ending before it feels finished.

And as he drives away, Evan understands that leaving does not erase what he carried.

It only changes where he carries it from.

Chapter 22—The Anniversary

Part I—The Day That Returns

Time does not heal in the way people say it does. Or perhaps more accurately, it does not heal in the way people hope it will when they say it out loud. Some insist that time softens, that it creates distance, that it allows the sharpness of what happened to fade into something more manageable. Others say the opposite, that time only reveals what remains. But when the date returns, neither explanation fully holds.

The day arrives whether anyone is ready or not. It does not ask permission. It does not adjust itself to how people are feeling. It comes back marked, fixed, exact, carrying the same number on the calendar that it did before everything changed.

Evan notices it in his body before he looks at the date. Before anyone says anything. There is a heaviness that does not have a clear source, a restlessness that does not resolve no matter how still he stays. He wakes earlier than usual, not from a dream, not from noise, but from a kind of awareness that sits beneath thought. He lies still, staring at the ceiling, and then he knows.

It's today.

The recognition does not surprise him. It settles into place, like something expected that he had hoped might pass unnoticed. He does not reach for his phone right away. He does not need confirmation. His body has already named it.

Across town, the mother knows before she opens her eyes. She does not need a clock, does not need a reminder, does not need anyone to tell her what day it is. Her body has kept count in a way that cannot be interrupted. The days did not blur together the way people said they would. They did not soften into something indistinct. They stacked, one on top of the other, each one carrying forward what had not been resolved, until they led back here.

She sits up slowly, hands resting in her lap, the room unchanged. Everything looks the same. The same walls, the same furniture, the same morning light. And that sameness feels wrong, because the day is not the same. It cannot be.

Lila experiences it without naming it. She wakes and something feels different, not in a way she can explain, not in a way that would translate into words, but in a way her body recognizes. Her movements are slower. More careful. She stays closer to her mother without deciding to do so. She does not ask why. Her mother does not ask either. The closeness is enough.

Marcus sees it when he checks his phone. The date sits there plainly, without decoration, without emphasis, without any indication that it carries more weight than any other day. There is no notification. No reminder. Just the number. He stares at it longer than he intends to, then sets the phone down without unlocking it.

He does not need anything else to tell him what the day is.

The community marks it, because that is what communities do. There is a gathering, a vigil, a space where names are read aloud and candles are lit in an attempt to give shape to what cannot be contained by language alone. The structure is intentional. The order matters. The pacing matters. Everything is arranged to hold the moment in a way that feels respectful, careful, appropriate.

People arrive in small groups at first, then in larger numbers. Some come early, standing in clusters, speaking quietly, as if the volume of their voices might disturb something that needs to remain undisturbed. Others arrive just before it begins, slipping into place without drawing attention to themselves. There is no single way to enter a day like this.

Evan goes, though he is not sure what it means for him to be there now. He stands at the edge of the gathering, not fully inside the crowd, but not separate from it either. He listens as the names are read, each one spoken slowly, each one given space, as if the silence after each name is part of the name itself.

He recognizes some of them. Not all. Enough.

Faces return to him in fragments, moments that did not leave when the calls ended, pieces of memory that remain unorganized but persistent. He does not try to assemble them into something complete. He lets them be what they are.

The mother stands closer to the front. People approach her carefully, one at a time, offering words that are meant to acknowledge what cannot be fixed.

“I'm thinking of you.”

“I'm so sorry.”

She nods. She says thank you. She receives what is offered, not because it changes what she carries, but because the offering itself matters. The words do not reduce the weight. They recognize it.

Lila stands beside her, holding her hand, not tightly, not desperately, just enough to stay connected. She watches the candles, the way the flames move, the way people lower their heads at the same time, the way the air feels different from other gatherings. She does not fully understand the language, but she understands the tone, the weight, the quiet.

Marcus stands in the back, arms crossed, not resisting, not engaging in the same way as others. He listens to the names, but he does not move closer. Something in him does not trust that the collective language can hold what he carries individually. His grief does not align with the structure. It does not follow the pattern.

That is the difference.

Collective grief gathers. It creates space. It speaks in shared language, in ritual, in names and gestures that allow people to stand together in something that would otherwise isolate them.

Private grief does not move that way.

It remains in fragments, in moments that do not align with the script, in questions that are not answered by speeches or candles or the careful arrangement of words.

Evan feels both at once, the pull toward the gathering, the need for something shared, and the resistance to it, the awareness that what he carries does not fully fit inside what is being offered. He stands still between those realities, listening, holding what returns.

When the vigil ends, people linger. They speak softly. They touch shoulders. They say things that try to bridge the distance between what is shared and what is not. Evan does not stay long. He leaves quietly, without saying goodbye, because the day is not finished just because the event is.

At home, the silence returns, different from the morning, more defined, because now the day has been marked. Named. Acknowledged. And still, nothing is resolved.

He sits with his hands resting on his knees, the same posture as before, but now with the weight of the date fully present. Time does not heal in the way people promise. Time marks. It circles back. It returns to the place where something changed and asks not for resolution, but for recognition.

Evan exhales slowly, because this is what the anniversary is. Not closure. Not completion. A return. A reminder that what happened is still part of everything that comes after.

And this is how it continues to live.

Part II—What the Crowd Holds

The crowd gathers because it has to. It does not feel optional. It does not feel casual. It feels necessary, as if the day itself demands a place to be held, even if only for a short time. People arrive at different times, but with the same awareness. This is the place the day has been given. This is where what cannot be carried alone is, for a moment, placed into something shared.

Evan stands at the edge again, not fully inside, not fully outside, watching how it forms. Groups cluster before the vigil begins, small circles of familiar faces, people who have found one another in the aftermath of something none of them would have chosen. There are greetings, but they are quieter than usual, less about catching up and more about confirming presence.

You're here.

I'm here.

We made it to this day.

That is enough.

The organizers move with purpose, candles arranged carefully, the microphone tested, names printed in deliberate order. Everything is intentional, every detail meant to create a structure around something that resists structure. Evan watches as the first candle is lit. The flame catches slowly, then steadies. One by one, others follow, light building in small increments, a visual language for something that cannot be contained in words.

The speaker begins, voice steady, practiced, the cadence familiar. The words are chosen carefully, meant to hold the moment without overwhelming it.

"We gather today . . . "

The sentence unfolds in familiar patterns, language of community, of resilience, of remembering. Evan listens. He does not reject it. But he notices the distance, the way the words move across the surface of something deeper. They are not wrong. They are not empty. But they are not complete.

The mother stands near the front again. People approach her one at a time, not interrupting, not lingering too long. A hand rests briefly on her shoulder. A quiet voice offers something simple.

"I'm thinking of you."

"I'm so sorry."

She nods. She says thank you. She receives what is offered. But what she carries does not change with each interaction. It is not lessened. It is acknowledged. And that matters, even if it does not heal.

Lila stays close to her, closer than usual, her hand resting in her mother's. Not gripping, not clinging, but not letting go either. She watches how people move, how they lower their voices, how they pause before speaking, how they allow silence to exist between sentences. She senses the difference between this and other gatherings. This is not celebration. It is not routine. It is something heavier, something that requires quiet.

Marcus remains in the back. He has not moved since he arrived. He listens to the names being read, each one spoken separately, each one given its own space. The crowd responds in small ways after each name, a collective murmur, a shared breath, a subtle acknowledgment.

Marcus does not join in that rhythm.

Not because he disagrees.

Because his grief does not move in sync with the group.

That is the tension.

Collective grief creates a pattern, a shared cadence, a way to move together through something that would otherwise isolate. It offers a structure that people can step into, a language that can be spoken aloud.

Private grief does not follow that cadence.

It interrupts it.

Falls outside it.

Refuses to align in predictable ways.

Evan feels that as the vigil continues. He listens as stories are told, carefully chosen, measured, representing what can be said in public. He recognizes parts of them, pieces that connect to what he experienced. But not all of it is there. It cannot be. Some moments belong to individuals, to responders, to those who were present in ways that do not translate into shared language.

The final speaker steps forward, and the tone shifts slightly, less formal, less structured. There is a pause before the words begin, a hesitation that feels more honest than polished sentences.

"That day changed us."

The sentence lands with weight. It does not explain. It does not attempt to resolve. It simply names what is.

Evan feels it in a way the other words did not reach. Because it does not try to complete anything. It allows the incompleteness to remain.

The candles burn lower. The light shifts. People begin to move, not all at once, but gradually, as if leaving requires its own timing. Conversations begin in quiet tones. Some people stay. Some leave quickly. Some linger, unsure how to step away from something that feels unfinished.

Evan stays a little longer, watching as the crowd thins, as the structure dissolves, as what was held together begins to loosen. People return to themselves, to their own grief, to what does not fit inside the gathering.

He walks away without speaking, not because there is nothing to say, but because everything that matters has already been said and not said.

The anniversary is not the event. The vigil is only one part. The crowd holds what it can, but it cannot hold everything. It cannot carry the full weight of each person's experience. It cannot resolve what remains after the candles go out.

Evan understands that more clearly now. The collective gives shape to grief, but it does not contain it. Each person leaves with what they brought, and with what returned.

As he walks back to his car, the quiet settles again. Not empty. Full. Because the day has not passed. It has been marked. And what it marked remains.

That is what time does.

Not heal.

Mark.

Return.

And ask to be recognized again.

Part III—What Time Keeps

The day does not end when the vigil does. That is what Evan notices. People leave the gathering and return to cars, homes, restaurants, quiet rooms, lit kitchens, places where the public shape of grief dissolves back into private life. The candles are extinguished. The microphone is packed away. The printed programs are folded, tucked into pockets, left on chairs, carried home like small evidence that the day was witnessed.

But the day itself remains.

It follows them.

Across town, the mother places the program on the kitchen table. She does not read it again. She knows what it says. She knows the order of names, the poem, the printed phrase about hope and remembrance. Still, she smooths it with her palm, pressing out a crease that does not matter.

Lila stands beside her, coat still on.

"Can I keep mine?" she asks.

Her mother looks at her, surprised by the question.

"Yes," she says. "Of course."

Lila nods and carries the folded paper to her room. She does not know what she will do with it. She only knows she does not want it thrown away.

Some things must be kept, even when keeping them hurts.

Marcus drives home without music. The road is familiar, but the evening feels altered. The crowd had held something for a while, but now that he is alone, the old questions return with sharper edges.

Why them?

Why still?

Why does everyone get to leave?

He grips the wheel. The anger is not as hot as it once was. That almost troubles him. Part of him fears that if the anger softens, something sacred will be lost, as if rage has been guarding the truth that this should never have happened.

But beneath the anger there is grief.

And beneath the grief, love.

He does not know what to do with either.

At the station, Reyes sits in the locker room longer than usual. He had not gone to the vigil in uniform. He had stood near the back, civilian clothes, hands folded, listening while the names were read. Now the station is quiet around him, the kind of quiet that comes after people have tried to honor what cannot be repaired.

He opens his locker.

Inside, everything is arranged as always.

Order.

Routine.

Preparedness.

He looks at it and feels the distance between preparation and prevention, between response and restoration.

There are things the job can do.

There are things it cannot.

He closes the locker gently.

No slam.

No release.

Just closure.

Keisha does not go home right away. She sits in her car outside the station, the same way she has done too often since that day. The vigil gave the community language. But language in public is different from language in private.

In public, she stood still.

In private, the questions returned.

What did we know?

What did we miss?

What did we say because it was true, and what did we say because it was safe?

The anniversary has not answered any of it. It has only marked that the questions survived the year too. That realization sits heavily.

Time did not erase them.

Time preserved them.

Evan, no longer at the station, watches the evening from his apartment window. He had gone to the vigil without knowing whether he belonged there anymore. Former responder. Witness. Survivor of a different kind. Someone who left, but did not leave untouched.

He had stood at the edge and listened to the names.

Now he stands alone and feels the strange ache of distance.

The work continued without him.

The grief continued too.

Leaving changed his relationship to the wound, but not the fact of it.

He turns away from the window and sits at the table. On the surface in front of him is nothing connected to the event. No program. No candle. No uniform. Just a cup of water, his keys, an unopened envelope.

Ordinary things.

And still, the day is there.

That is what time keeps.

Not everything.

Not perfectly.

But enough.

Enough for the body to remember before the mind does. Enough for a mother to wake knowing the date without looking. Enough for a child to keep a folded program because throwing it away feels wrong. Enough for Marcus to feel anger soften and fear that softness means betrayal. Enough for Reyes to close a locker carefully. Enough for Keisha to sit with questions that official statements cannot hold. Enough for Evan to know that leaving did not remove him from what happened.

The anniversary does not bring closure.

It brings return.

Not the same return for everyone. For some, it is public. For others, private. For some, it comes with candles and names. For others, with silence, avoidance, anger, prayer, or the inability to pray.

But it comes.

The mother finally sits at the table. The program remains in front of her. She places one hand over it, not dramatically, not symbolically, just because her hand needs somewhere to rest.

In her room, Lila slides the folded program into a drawer beside drawings, hair ties, and small objects she has not explained to anyone.

Marcus pulls into his driveway and stays in the car until the engine noise becomes the loudest thing around him.

Reyes turns off the locker room light.

Keisha starts her car, then stops, then starts it again.

Evan takes a drink of water and lets the silence remain.

All of them carry the same day differently.

All of them have crossed a year.

But crossing a year is not the same as being done with it.

Time has not healed them.

Not in the way people promised.

It has marked them. It has given shape to before and after. It has taught them where the wound lives now—in dates, in rooms, in folded paper, in names spoken aloud, in names not spoken because they are too close, in public gatherings, in private pauses, in the ordinary return of a day that is anything but ordinary.

Night settles over the town. Lights go on in windows. Doors close. Dishes are washed. Children are put to bed. Cars pass on streets that remember nothing and everything.

The anniversary moves toward midnight.

Soon the calendar will change.

The date will pass.

But passing is not erasing.

Tomorrow will come, and people will call that mercy.

Maybe it is.

But tonight, no one has to call it anything.

Tonight, the day remains what it is.

A marker.

A witness.

A return.

A reminder that grief does not obey the calendar, even when the calendar calls it back.

Evan turns off the light.

Across town, others do the same.

The darkness comes quietly.

Not empty.

Not resolved.

Holding what time has kept.

Part IV—**What Still Might Be Repaired**

Chapter 23—**Naming What Happened**

Part I—Saying It Plain

There comes a point when silence is no longer neutral. Not because silence was wrong at the beginning, but because what it once protected begins to change shape. Sometimes silence gives space for what cannot yet be spoken. Sometimes it holds something safely until language is ready. But over time, silence can shift. It can move from protection to avoidance, from space to distortion, from care to something that keeps the truth from taking its full form.

Evan recognizes this before he knows what to do with it. It happens in a conversation that almost doesn't happen, in a question that seems simple on the surface but opens something larger beneath it.

"What do you call what happened?"

The person asking does not mean harm. They are trying to understand, trying to find the right words, trying to locate the event inside a language that makes sense to them. Evan opens his mouth to answer and then stops, because the answer is not simple.

There are words people use. Words that sound right in certain settings. Words that help organize what happened into something that can be discussed without overwhelming the conversation.

Incident.

Event.

Tragedy.

Each word holds something. Each word leaves something out.

He feels that as he considers them. "Incident" sounds contained, controlled, something that occurred and then ended. But it did not feel contained, and it did not end when the moment passed. "Event" sounds neutral, almost observational, as if it could be described without entering it. But nothing about it was neutral. "Tragedy" comes closer. It acknowledges loss, weight, irreversibility. But even that word can soften the edges, because it does not name what caused it.

Evan closes his mouth, not because he does not know, but because he does. The difficulty is not finding a word. The difficulty is choosing one that does not reduce what actually happened.

Across town, the mother encounters the same problem. Someone says, "I can't imagine what you've been through." She nods, because she understands what they mean, but the phrase feels incomplete. What she has been through is not abstract. It has a shape, a cause, a reality that resists being generalized. She wants to say it plainly, but she hesitates, because plain language can make people uncomfortable. She has learned how quickly people look away when the truth is not softened.

At the station, Reyes hears it too in different forms. "We lost people." "It was a bad situation." "It was one of those days." He understands why people speak this way. The job trains you to compress, to simplify, to keep moving. Language becomes functional, efficient, designed to carry information quickly rather than hold meaning fully.

But something in him pushes back. Because compression can become minimization, and minimization changes how the truth is carried. It turns something specific into something vague. It allows people to move forward without fully acknowledging what happened.

Keisha feels it in reports. Official language, precise, careful, structured to document without inflaming, to record without overwhelming. Terms that describe without fully naming. "Active situation." "Threat neutralized." "Casualties reported." Each phrase is technically accurate. None of them fully capture what it was like to stand there, to hear what was happening, to see what could not be unseen, to know what those words are trying to contain.

Marcus refuses most of the language entirely. He hears people speak and feels the distance immediately. "That's not what it was," he says once, in a room that goes quiet. He does not offer a replacement. He only rejects what feels insufficient. That refusal is its own kind of truth, even if it leaves the conversation suspended.

That is the problem. Naming what happened requires precision, but precision is not only about facts. It is about truth, and truth is not always comfortable. It does not always fit into the language people prefer. It does not always allow for distance.

Evan sits with it longer than he expects. The question does not leave him.

What do you call it?

He tries the words again.

Incident.

Event.

Tragedy.

Each one feels like a step away from something more direct, something harder, something that does not allow the speaker or the listener to remain at a distance.

Finally, he says it, not to anyone else at first, but to himself.

"It was violence."

The word lands differently. It does not soften. It does not generalize. It names what was done, not just what was experienced. It carries cause, not only consequence.

He feels the shift immediately. Not relief. Clarity.

Because the word does not carry only loss. It carries responsibility. And responsibility matters. Without it, what happened becomes something else over time, something easier to speak about, but less true.

Across town, the mother reaches a similar place. Someone says, "I'm so sorry for your loss." She nods, then, without planning to, says, "My child was killed." The room stills. The sentence does not allow for abstraction. It is direct, unavoidable, and for a moment, no one knows what to say.

But something has changed. The truth has taken shape. Not softened. Not hidden. Named.

That is the importance of language. Not to make things easier, but to make them clearer. To prevent what happened from becoming something else over time. Because time does not only mark. It also reshapes how things are remembered. And without careful naming, truth can erode.

Reyes says it to a new responder days later. "Don't rush to make it sound better."

The responder looks at him. "What do you mean?"

Reyes pauses. "Call it what it was."

Simple.

But not easy.

Evan understands that now. Naming what happened is not about accuracy alone. It is about integrity, about refusing to let language reduce what should not be reduced, about refusing to let distance replace reality.

He exhales slowly, because this is another step, not leaving, not returning, something else entirely. Saying it plainly. Holding it without disguise. Allowing the truth to remain what it is, even when it is hard to hear.

Part II—When Words Fail and Matter

Language does not arrive ready. It is not waiting somewhere, complete and intact, for the right moment to be spoken. It is shaped in real time, tested in conversation, adjusted in response to how others react, sometimes avoided entirely when the cost of saying something plainly feels too high. That is what they begin to understand. Words are not neutral containers. They do something. They move people closer or push them further away. They reveal or they protect. They clarify or they soften.

Evan notices this the first time he says it out loud to someone else. They are sitting across from each other, coffee between them, the conversation moving through ordinary topics before shifting, as it often does, toward what happened. The question comes in a familiar form.

"So what was it like?"

The question is not careless. It is not intrusive. But it carries an assumption that experience can be translated into description, that what happened can be summarized in a way that fits inside a conversation. Evan pauses, not because he does not know, but because he does. He feels the weight of choosing how to answer, the difference between saying something that will be received easily and something that will be received truthfully.

"It was violent," he says.

The word lands differently than the others have. The person across from him nods at first, as if the answer has been given, then hesitates. Something in the word requires more attention than expected. It does not allow the conversation to move forward as easily. It does not provide distance. It does not soften what happened into something that can be held without discomfort.

"What do you mean?" the person asks.

The question is genuine, but it reveals something important. People are not always prepared for words that do not soften. They expect language to create a buffer, to provide a way of engaging without being drawn too close. When that buffer is removed, the conversation changes.

Evan notices the shift. The space feels different now, less fluid, more deliberate. Each word carries more weight. Each sentence has to be chosen more carefully. He could step back, soften it, make it easier. He could say something that would allow the conversation to return to a more comfortable rhythm.

But he does not.

Across town, the mother experiences the same shift. A neighbor stops by, kind and well-meaning, trying to offer support.

"I heard the service was beautiful," they say.

She nods. "It was."

The word "beautiful" hangs in the air, and she feels the distance it creates. It describes something real, the care that went into the service, the way people gathered, the intention behind it. But it does not hold what the day means.

"My child was killed," she says.

The sentence changes everything. The neighbor's expression shifts, not away, but deeper. The word does not allow for abstraction. It names action, not just outcome. It brings the reality of what happened into the room in a way that cannot be redirected.

This is what language does when it is not minimized. It moves people closer to the truth, whether they are ready or not.

Keisha encounters it in a different setting. She is reviewing a report that has already been written. Every line is accurate. Every detail is accounted for. The structure is correct. And still, something is missing. Not fact. Truth. The language is precise, but it distances the reader from what actually occurred.

"Subject engaged."

"Threat neutralized."

"Casualties confirmed."

Each phrase is technically correct. Each one does its job. But none of them say what it was like to stand there, to hear what was happening, to see what could not be unseen, to understand in real time what those words are trying to contain.

She picks up a pen and pauses, not to change the facts, but to reconsider the language. Not to make it harsher, but to make it clearer. Because clarity is not cruelty. It is respect for what happened.

Marcus resists the process entirely. He has heard too many versions, too many attempts to describe it in ways that feel manageable.

"They keep changing it," he says. "Making it sound like something else."

Evan listens.

"Like what?"

Marcus shakes his head. "Like it was just bad luck. Or something that happened without anyone doing anything."

The frustration is steady, not explosive, but persistent. What he is resisting is not language itself, but what happens when language removes responsibility. When words soften too much, they do not only comfort. They distort. They create distance between cause and consequence, between action and impact.

Reyes addresses it directly in a training session. A room full of new responders, people who are learning how to speak about what they will encounter.

"Be careful how you describe things," he says.

They look at him, expecting instruction, a guideline, a rule.

"Not because you need to make it sound better," he continues. "Because you need to keep it true."

A hand raises.

"What if the truth is too much?"

Reyes nods. "It usually is."

There is a pause, then he adds, "That doesn't make it optional."

Evan understands that now in a way he did not before. Naming what happened is not about reliving it. It is about refusing to let it become something it was not. He sits with that after the conversation ends, the word still present.

Violent.

It does not resolve anything. It does not make sense of what happened. But it keeps the truth intact. And that matters.

Because without language that holds the truth, memory begins to shift. Not intentionally. Gradually. Edges soften. Details blur. Responsibility disperses. What remains becomes easier to carry, but harder to recognize.

Evan exhales slowly, because this part is not about healing. It is about honesty. And honesty requires words that do not always fit comfortably in conversation.

He looks up. The room is quiet again, ordinary, unchanged on the surface. And yet something has shifted. Because now, the language is different. Clearer. More precise. Less willing to become something else.

That is the work of naming. Not to solve. Not to fix. To tell the truth in a way that does not disappear over time.

Part III—The Cost of Telling It True

Telling the truth has a cost. Not always immediately. Not always in ways that are obvious. But over time, it becomes clear that language does not only describe reality, it shapes how people are able to stay in relationship with it. When the language changes, the relationships around it change too.

Evan begins to notice this the more he refuses to soften what happened. At first, it seems simple. Use clearer words. Say it plainly. Avoid language that creates distance. But clarity does something he did not expect. It alters how people respond to him.

Some lean in.

Others step back.

Not because they do not care. Not because they disagree. Because truth, when it is not minimized, removes the space people often rely on to protect themselves. It asks more of them than they anticipated giving.

He sees it in small conversations. Someone asks, "How are you doing with everything?" The question is familiar, almost automatic, part of the way people check in without necessarily expecting a complicated answer.

"It hasn't really gone away," Evan says.

The person nods, then quickly adds, "Well, at least time helps, right?"

There is the shift again, the instinct to move the conversation toward something more manageable, something that can be resolved or at least softened. Evan feels the choice in front of him. He could agree. He could say, "Yeah, it does," and allow the conversation to continue comfortably.

Instead, he says, "Not in the way people mean."

The silence that follows is not hostile. It is uncertain. The conversation no longer has an easy path forward. The usual phrases do not apply. The other person does not know what to say next, and Evan does not offer a way out.

Across town, the mother feels the same cost. People visit less often now. Not because they have stopped caring, but because they do not know how to remain in conversations that do not resolve. She has stopped softening it for them. When someone says, "I can't imagine," she no longer redirects the statement into something lighter. She says, "You shouldn't have to." When someone offers, "At least you have memories," she responds, "I wanted more than memories."

Her responses are not unkind. They are precise. But precision removes the comfort of familiar phrases. Without those phrases, people hesitate. They stay for shorter periods of time. They speak more carefully, or not at all.

Lila notices the change without understanding it. Fewer visitors. Quieter rooms. Conversations that stop when she enters, or shift in tone when she lingers nearby. She does not know that the language has changed. She only knows that something about the way people move through the house feels different.

Marcus moves in the opposite direction. He becomes sharper with his words, less willing to tolerate anything that feels like avoidance. "It wasn't an accident," he says when someone uses that word. "It wasn't random." The correction is immediate, direct, and sometimes it creates tension. People respond not to the content of what he is saying, but to how it is being said. Truth, delivered without a buffer, can feel like confrontation, even when it is not intended that way.

Keisha encounters the cost in more formal settings. Meetings, reports, briefings. She chooses her words more carefully now, not to soften them, but to resist the pressure to do so. When someone says, "It was handled," she pauses, then replies, "It happened." The difference is subtle, but significant. "Handled" suggests closure, containment, something resolved. "Happened" keeps the reality open, present, unresolved.

Reyes names the cost directly. "You'll lose people when you stop making it easier for them," he tells Evan.

"Lose them how?" Evan asks.

"They won't know what to say," Reyes replies. "So they'll say less. Or nothing."

There is a pause before he adds, "That's not always a bad thing."

Evan considers that. Silence has changed meaning for him. Not all silence is avoidance. Some silence is honest. Some silence is what remains when there are no words left that can hold the truth without distorting it.

Still, the cost remains. Conversations become fewer. Shorter. More deliberate. There is a sense of standing in truth without as many people standing beside you. It is not quite loneliness, but something close to it, the feeling of occupying a space that others are unsure how to enter.

But something else happens too.

Not everyone leaves.

Some people stay.

And those who stay listen differently. They do not rush to respond. They do not redirect. They do not try to resolve the conversation or move it toward something more comfortable. They allow it to remain open, unfinished, real.

Evan notices this with Reyes, with Keisha, even with Marcus in his own way. The conversations are fewer, but they carry more weight. They are less about resolution and more about recognition, about allowing the truth to exist without trying to reshape it.

He sits with that one evening, alone, the quiet familiar now. The word is still there.

Violence.

It has not changed. It has not softened. But his relationship to it has shifted. Not easier. Clearer.

And clarity has its own weight.

He exhales slowly, recognizing that naming something truthfully is not about controlling how others respond. It is not about ensuring understanding or agreement. It is about refusing distortion, about allowing the truth to stand even when it narrows the space around you.

The cost is real.

But so is the alternative.

A language that erases.

A memory that shifts into something easier to carry but less true.

Evan knows which one he cannot accept.

So he stays with the harder words, the ones that do not resolve, the ones that hold what happened without changing it.

And in that, there is something steady.

Not comfort.

Not closure.

But integrity.

And for now, that is enough.

Chapter 24—The Danger of Moving On Too Quickly

Part I—The Pressure to Be Okay

The pressure does not arrive loudly. It does not announce itself as force. It comes dressed as care, shaped in questions that sound kind, concerned, even hopeful. "How are you doing now?" "Are things getting better?" "You seem stronger." The words themselves are not harmful. They are familiar. They are the language people use when they want to check in, when they want to show that they have not forgotten.

But beneath them is something else.

An expectation.

A direction.

A timeline that no one has formally agreed to, but that everyone seems to feel.

Evan notices it first in tone, not in what people say, but in how they say it. The way "now" is emphasized, as if time itself should have produced change. The way "better" is assumed to be the goal, not one possibility among many, but the outcome toward which everything should be moving. The way "stronger" is offered as both observation and encouragement, something he is expected to become whether he feels it or not.

He answers carefully. "I'm . . . still in it."

The phrase is honest, but it does not land the way he expects. There is a pause, then a nod. "Oh. Well . . . that makes sense." The response is not dismissive. It is not unkind. But the tone shifts, subtly, almost imperceptibly, as if staying "in it" is understandable, but not ideal, as if it is something temporary that should eventually give way to something more resolved.

Across town, the mother hears it more directly. "At some point, you have to move forward." The sentence is offered gently, as encouragement, as a kind of wisdom drawn from experience or belief. But it lands as instruction. Move forward. As if forward is the only acceptable direction. As if staying is failure.

She nods, because arguing would take more energy than she has. But inside, something resists. Moving forward suggests leaving something behind, and there are things she will not leave. Not because she is unwilling, but because they are not disposable. They are not phases to be passed through. They are part of what remains.

Lila feels the pressure without understanding it. People say, "You're so brave." "You're doing so well." "You're such a strong girl." She does not know what those words mean in this context. She only knows they come when she is quiet, when she does not cry, when she answers politely and does not disrupt what is happening around her.

So she learns something without being taught.

Quiet equals strong.

Not talking equals doing well.

Stillness equals healing.

Something in her begins to shape itself around that, not because it is true, but because it is reinforced.

Marcus rejects the pressure outright. "I'm not over it," he says when someone suggests that time should have changed things. "I don't think I'm supposed to be." The statement creates tension, because it refuses the expected arc, the movement from pain to resolution, from disruption to closure, from grief to something that can be set aside.

That is the cultural expectation.

Not always spoken.

But deeply present.

That pain should move.

That grief should progress.

That healing should look like distance.

And that distance should arrive on a timeline that feels reasonable to others.

Evan begins to see how strong that pressure is, not because people intend harm, but because people need resolution. They need to believe that what happened can be contained, that it can be processed, that it can be moved past. Because if it cannot, then what does that mean for everything else?

He hears it in conversations that shift too quickly. "That was such a hard time . . . but look at how far everyone has come." The sentence moves from acknowledgment to conclusion in a single breath. Too fast. Before the weight has been fully held. Before the truth has had time to remain present.

Reyes names it in a way the others do not. "They want a story with an ending," he says.

Evan looks at him. "What if there isn't one?"

Reyes nods. "That's what makes people uneasy."

Spiritual language enters here too, not always helpfully. "Everything happens for a reason." "God has a plan." "You'll find meaning in this." The words are meant to comfort, to offer a framework, to place suffering inside something larger and more understandable. But sometimes they do something else.

They bypass the reality that has not yet been named.

They move too quickly to interpretation before acknowledgment is complete.

The mother hears it and feels the dissonance. "God needed another angel." She closes her eyes, not in agreement, but in restraint. The statement does not meet what she is holding. It moves past it too quickly, offering explanation where presence is needed.

Evan encounters it in a different form. "You're stronger because of this." He considers the sentence. It may be true in some ways. But the timing matters. Saying it now feels like closing something that is still open, like drawing a conclusion before the experience has settled into anything that can honestly be called growth.

Spiritual bypassing does not always deny pain. It relocates it. It moves it into meaning before it has been fully experienced. In doing so, it risks disconnecting people from what they are actually carrying, replacing presence with explanation.

Marcus refuses those statements entirely. "Don't tell me there's a reason," he says. "Not yet." The "not yet" matters, because it leaves space for something later, but refuses premature closure. It protects the integrity of the present moment, the reality that meaning cannot be forced without distorting what is still unfolding.

Evan begins to understand the danger, not of healing, but of rushing it. Of forcing movement before something has been fully held. Of replacing truth with conclusions that arrive too soon.

He sits with that longer now, noticing when language shifts, when conversations move toward resolution before he is ready. He notices where he feels it, in the tightening in his chest that signals something is being skipped, something important being moved past too quickly.

He exhales slowly, because this is another kind of awareness, not just of what happened, but of how people try to move beyond it. The danger is not moving on. It is moving on too quickly, before truth has been fully named, before grief has been fully held, before the weight has been allowed to exist without being redirected.

Evan looks around the room. It is quiet again, ordinary, unchanged. And yet something is clearer. Healing is not the same as closing. Movement is not the same as resolution. Staying with what is real, even when it is uncomfortable, may be the most honest thing he can do.

For now, that is enough.

Part II—When Meaning Comes Too Soon

Meaning arrives quickly. Too quickly. That is what they begin to notice, not because meaning itself is wrong, but because of when it shows up and how it is used. It appears in conversation, in reflection, in well-intentioned attempts to make sense of what has happened before the experience has been fully lived through. Meaning, offered too soon, can feel less like understanding and more like pressure.

Evan hears it in the way people respond after the initial shock has passed. At first, the questions were about survival. "What happened?" "Is everyone okay?" "What do you need?" The focus was immediate, grounded in the present, oriented toward what was necessary. But now the questions have shifted.

"What do you think this means?"

"How has this changed you?"

"What have you learned from it?"

The shift is subtle, but it carries an assumption. It assumes that meaning is already available, that something coherent has already been formed out of what happened, that the experience has moved far enough along to be interpreted.

Evan does not know how to answer, not because there is no meaning, but because it is not settled. It is not something he can name clearly or consistently. It changes depending on the moment, depending on what surfaces, depending on what he is able to hold at any given time.

"It's still happening," he says once.

The person nods, but there is confusion in the response. "Still happening" does not fit the expectation that the event has already become something else, something completed, something that can now be reflected on from a distance.

Across town, the mother hears it in quieter forms. "I know this must have changed your perspective." She nods, because of course it has. Everything has shifted. But the statement moves too quickly to the result. It skips over the ongoing nature of that change, the reality that perspective is not something she has chosen or completed, but something she is still learning to live within.

The change is not finished.

It may never be.

Lila hears it in language she does not fully understand. "You're going to grow from this." She looks at the person speaking and says nothing, because the word "grow" does not match what she feels. Growth suggests expansion, development, something becoming more than it was before. But she does not feel larger. She does not feel stronger. She feels altered, and she does not yet have the language to describe that alteration.

Marcus reacts with resistance. "I don't need a lesson out of this," he says. The sentence comes quickly, sharply, not because he rejects the possibility of meaning entirely, but because he resists the pressure to produce it. The suggestion that something good or instructive must emerge feels like an imposition, a demand to conclude something that is still unresolved.

That is the danger of meaning arriving too soon. It replaces presence with interpretation. It asks for understanding before experience has been fully acknowledged. It turns something ongoing into something that appears finished.

Reyes names it carefully. "Meaning takes time," he says. "Not because it's complicated, but because it has to be honest."

Evan looks at him. "What if it never comes?"

Reyes shrugs slightly. "Then we don't force it."

The answer removes an expectation Evan had not fully recognized. The idea that meaning must be found, that something must be made out of what happened, that suffering must lead somewhere specific. Without that expectation, something shifts. The pressure eases, even if only slightly.

Spiritual language often intensifies this pressure. "God will bring something good out of this." The statement is offered with sincerity, with hope, with a desire to place suffering inside a larger framework. But it carries an assumption, that good must be found, that meaning must be extracted, and that this process should happen soon enough to provide comfort.

Keisha hears it in conversations that move from reality to reassurance too quickly. "This will make the community stronger." She understands the intention, but she also knows what is being skipped. The fracture, the loss, the damage that does not contribute to strength but simply remains as evidence of what happened.

"Maybe," she says once. "But not yet."

The phrase creates space. Not for denial, but for timing. It acknowledges the possibility of something later without forcing it into the present. It allows the truth to unfold without being reshaped prematurely.

Evan begins to recognize how often language moves ahead of experience. How quickly people reach for conclusions, how naturally they try to place suffering into a framework that makes it easier to hold. And how that framework can become a kind of pressure, an expectation to arrive somewhere he has not yet reached.

He sits with that one evening, the quiet familiar now, the absence of immediate demands allowing space for reflection. He thinks about the questions.

"What have you learned?"

"What does this mean?"

He tries to answer, not for anyone else, but for himself. But the answers do not settle. They shift. They remain incomplete.

And for the first time, he allows that.

Maybe the goal is not to arrive at meaning. Maybe the goal is to remain honest about where he is. And where he is is still inside it.

He exhales slowly, recognizing that this is another kind of resistance, not rejecting meaning, but refusing to manufacture it before it is real. The danger is not meaning itself. It is timing. When meaning comes too soon, it can distort what is still unfolding. It can replace truth with interpretation. It can create closure where none exists.

Evan looks around the room. Nothing has changed on the surface. The space is the same. The objects are the same. But something inside him has shifted. He does not need to have an answer. He does not need to make sense of what cannot yet be made sense of. He does not need to move forward in the way others expect.

For now, it is enough to remain where he is, to let meaning arrive in its own time, or not at all, and to resist the pressure to turn something real into something resolved before it is ready.

Part III—Staying When Others Leave

Eventually, people leave. Not all at once, not in a way that feels abrupt or intentional, but steadily, almost imperceptibly at first. The calls stop coming as often. The messages become less frequent. Invitations shift in tone, less about support, more about returning to something that resembles normal life. It is not abandonment. It is movement. But movement, when it happens at a different pace than one's own, can feel like distance.

Evan notices it gradually. At first, he interprets it as a good sign. Things are settling. People are returning to their routines. The intensity of the immediate aftermath has passed. That is what is supposed to happen. But something in him does not return at the same pace. The external world moves forward. Internally, he remains in a space that does not match that movement.

The result is a gap.

The world moves.

He stays.

It shows up in small moments. Someone says, "We should get together—like old times." The phrase is meant to reconnect, to bridge the distance that has formed. Evan nods, because he understands the intention, but the words carry a quiet tension. Like old times. As if the past is accessible in the same way it was before. As if nothing essential has changed.

But something has.

Not because he refuses to return, but because he cannot return to a version of himself that no longer exists in the same way.

Across town, the mother feels it differently. The house grows quieter. Not suddenly, not dramatically, but over time. Fewer visits. Fewer people stopping by. Fewer moments where others sit with her in the weight of what has happened. The assumption, unspoken but present, is that she needs less now. That the hardest part has passed because time has passed.

But grief does not follow that assumption. In some ways, it deepens. Not louder, not more visible, but more defined. More present in the spaces where others are no longer looking. The absence of constant attention does not mean the absence of pain. It means the pain is carried more privately.

Lila notices it in absence. Fewer adults speaking softly in the kitchen. Fewer hands resting on her shoulder. More ordinary days. The routines of life returning. She senses the difference, even if she cannot explain it. Something in her wonders whether the change in others means she should feel differently too. She does not. But she recognizes the expectation.

Marcus reacts by pulling back. "If they're done with it, fine," he says. The words sound dismissive, but they carry something more complicated. He is not done with it. The distance between his experience and the way others are moving on feels sharper now. What was once shared begins to feel individual again.

That is the second layer of pressure. Not just to move on, but to keep pace with others who have already begun to do so. To match a timeline that is not your own. To arrive somewhere because others appear to have arrived there.

Evan feels it most clearly in conversation. "What have you been up to?" The question is normal, expected, part of the rhythm of everyday interaction. But it assumes continuity, a sense that life has resumed in a recognizable way. Evan answers simply. "Just . . . figuring things out."

The response does not invite further discussion. It does not fit easily into the flow of casual exchange. The conversation moves on, not because the other person does not care, but because they do not know how to stay in a space that does not offer clear direction.

Reyes names it when Evan brings it up. "They're not wrong for moving forward," he says.

Evan nods. "I know."

"But you're not wrong for not being there yet," Reyes adds.

The distinction matters. It removes comparison. It separates individual experience from collective expectation. It allows for the possibility that healing does not follow a single path or timeline.

Spiritual language appears here as well, often reinforcing the idea of forward movement. "God is doing a new thing." "Leave the past behind." "Step into what's next." The phrases are oriented toward progress, toward change, toward something beyond what has already happened. But they carry an assumption, that the past can be left, that it should be left, that staying connected to it is a form of resistance rather than a form of honesty.

The mother hears it and feels the tension. She believes in moving forward in some sense, in continuing to live, to function, to engage with what remains. But not in leaving behind. What was lost is not something to move past. It is something to carry. Not in the same way as before, not with the same intensity in every moment, but still present.

Keisha encounters it in policy language. "Return to normal operations." The phrase appears in reports, in meetings, in planning documents. It is necessary. Systems need to function. Communities need to stabilize. But the word "normal" feels misplaced. Because normal no longer exists in the same way.

There is before.

And there is after.

And after does not become before again.

Evan sits with that one evening, the quiet now familiar, the absence of urgency allowing space for reflection. He thinks about what it means to stay, not physically, but internally. To remain with something that others have begun to set down.

At first, it feels like isolation, like being left behind while others move forward. But as he sits with it, something shifts. Staying is not failure. It is attention. It is refusing to move past something that still needs to be held.

He exhales slowly, recognizing this as another kind of truth. Healing does not always look like movement. Sometimes it looks like remaining, like allowing something to exist without forcing it to change.

The danger of moving on too quickly is not only what is left behind. It is what is never fully seen, never fully named, never fully held. When movement happens too soon, parts of the experience are skipped, compressed, or lost.

Evan looks around the room. It is unchanged, ordinary, familiar. But his understanding is different. He does not need to match anyone else's pace. He does not need to arrive where others have already gone. For now, it is enough to stay, to remain with what is real, and to trust that not moving too quickly is its own form of care.

Chapter 25—**Listening Without Fixing**

Part I—The Work of Staying Present

The instinct to fix is immediate. It rises almost without thought, appearing in the space between hearing something difficult and responding to it. Someone speaks, and the response forms quickly—advice, reassurance, perspective, anything that might ease what is being said. The intention is rarely harmful. In many cases, it is rooted in care. But care, when expressed too quickly, can shift into something else.

Evan recognizes it in himself first. Not in the obvious moments, but in the small ones. A conversation with someone new to the work. They are describing their first difficult call, the hesitation they felt, the second-guessing that followed, the questions that stayed with them long after the moment had passed.

Evan listens and feels the urge to respond.

"You did what you could."

"That's part of the job."

"It gets easier."

All of it is true. All of it comes easily. And all of it, in that moment, feels incomplete. Not wrong, but insufficient.

He pauses.

Because something in him has begun to understand that fixing is not the same as listening. The difference is subtle but significant. Fixing moves toward an outcome. Listening stays with the experience itself.

Across the room, Reyes notices the pause. He does not interrupt or correct. He simply observes. Later, when the conversation has ended, he says quietly, "You don't have to tie it up."

Evan looks at him. "What do you mean?"

Reyes shrugs slightly. "Not everything needs a conclusion."

The sentence stays with him, not because it is complex, but because it names something he has been feeling without fully recognizing. The pressure to resolve, to offer something that makes the conversation feel complete, is not always helpful. In fact, it can interrupt something more important.

Help is not always resolution.

Sometimes it is presence.

The difference is not always obvious. Fixing closes space. Listening holds it open. Fixing moves the conversation forward. Listening allows it to deepen. Fixing offers direction. Listening offers attention.

The mother experiences this difference immediately when someone gets it right. A friend sits with her, not speaking right away, not filling the silence with words meant to comfort or explain. They simply sit.

After a while, the mother begins to speak. Not in a structured way, not with a clear beginning or end, but in fragments. Thoughts that come as they arise. Memories that do not follow order. Questions that do not have answers.

The friend listens. They nod. They do not interrupt. They do not redirect. They do not say, "At least . . . " or "Everything happens . . . " or anything that would move the conversation away from what is being said.

And something shifts.

Not in the grief itself, but in the space around it. It becomes more bearable, not because it has been solved, but because it has been shared without being altered.

Lila notices this too, though she would not describe it in the same way. An adult sits beside her and says, "You don't have to talk if you don't want to." The sentence removes pressure. It gives her a sense of control in a situation where much has been taken from her.

After a while, she speaks. Not everything. Not in order. But something. And the adult listens. They do not correct her. They do not interpret what she says. They do not turn her words into something else. They simply receive them.

That is enough.

Marcus struggles with this. Silence feels insufficient to him, like a failure to respond, a missed opportunity to say something that might help. Someone tells him what they are feeling—anger, confusion, guilt—and he responds quickly.

"That's not your fault."

"You shouldn't feel that way."

The words are meant to reassure. But something in the response creates distance. The person stops speaking. Not because they disagree, but because being corrected is not the same as being heard.

Later, Reyes says to him, "Let them have it."

Marcus looks at him. "What?"

"The feeling," Reyes replies. "Even if it's messy. Even if it doesn't make sense."

Marcus shakes his head. "But what if it's not true?"

Reyes nods. "It doesn't have to be true to be real."

That distinction is difficult. It asks for restraint, for presence without control, for listening without correcting. It challenges the assumption that accuracy is always the goal. Sometimes the goal is simply to allow something to be expressed.

Keisha practices this in her work. In interviews, in conversations, in moments where people are trying to make sense of what they experienced, she asks open questions.

"What stands out to you?"

"What do you remember most?"

Then she waits. She does not fill the silence. She does not guide the response. She allows what emerges to come on its own. Often, what comes after the pause is more honest, more precise, more reflective of the person's actual experience than anything that could have been prompted.

Listening without fixing is not passive. It requires attention, restraint, and an awareness of one's own impulse to intervene. It requires recognizing when the urge to help is actually an urge to resolve discomfort, one's own as much as the other person's.

Evan begins to practice it intentionally. In small conversations. In moments where the urge to respond is immediate. He notices what rises first—advice, reassurance, interpretation—and then he lets it pass. Not suppressing it, not acting on it, but choosing something else.

Presence.

Someone speaks. He listens. He does not interrupt. He does not finish their sentence. He does not move toward a conclusion. When he responds, it is simple.

"That sounds heavy."

"That stayed with you."

The words are not complex. They do not direct or correct. They acknowledge.

The effect is subtle but real. People continue. They go deeper. They say things they might not have said if the space had been closed too quickly.

That is the practice. For caregivers. For communities. For responders. Not to remove pain. Not to resolve experience. But to create space where truth can exist without being reshaped.

Evan exhales slowly. This kind of listening is harder than fixing. It requires less control, more patience, a willingness to stay with what is unfinished.

He looks around the room. It is quiet. The conversation is still open. And for the first time, he understands that not fixing is not failure.

It is care of a different kind.

One that does not rush toward resolution, but stays long enough for something real to be heard.

Part II—Practices That Hold

Listening without fixing is not instinctive. It runs against the way most people are trained to respond to difficulty. From an early age, people learn to solve problems, offer answers, and move situations toward resolution. When something painful is shared, the reflex is to do something about it. That reflex does not disappear simply because the problem cannot be solved. It has to be recognized and, at times, deliberately set aside.

Evan begins to understand that listening without fixing is not about having the right personality. It is a practice. It requires intention. It requires choosing, in each moment, not to move too quickly toward resolution. The question shifts from "What can I say to make this better?" to "What is being said, and can I stay with it without changing it?"

That shift alters everything.

He notices it in a conversation with someone new to the field. The person describes a call that has stayed with them, not because it was the most dramatic, but because something about it unsettled them in a way they cannot fully explain. They speak in fragments, circling around the experience rather than moving directly through it.

Evan listens. He feels the familiar urge to respond with reassurance, to normalize what they are feeling, to offer perspective that might reduce the weight of what they are carrying. Instead, he waits.

When the person finishes speaking, he says, "That sounds like it stayed with you."

The response is simple. It does not explain. It does not interpret. It reflects.

The person nods and continues. They go further than they did before, not because Evan guided them there, but because the space remained open long enough for more to emerge.

This becomes one of the practices.

Reflect, don't redirect.

For communities, the practice takes a broader form. It requires a shared willingness to resist the urge to organize grief too quickly into something manageable. It means creating spaces where people can speak without being immediately reassured, where silence is not treated as a problem to solve, and where conversation is allowed to unfold without a predetermined outcome.

The mother experiences this in a small gathering. There is no formal structure, no agenda, no expectation that anyone will say the "right" thing. People sit together. Someone eventually speaks. "I've been thinking about you."

The sentence is simple. It is not followed by advice or explanation. It is allowed to stand.

Others speak in turn. Not in full stories, not in polished reflections, but in pieces. A memory. A question. A moment that has stayed with them. Each offering is received without being reshaped. No one rushes to interpret. No one redirects toward resolution.

The conversation is slower than most. Less efficient. But more real.

This becomes another practice.

Allow incomplete expression.

Lila encounters a version of this that fits her experience. An adult offers her something to draw with, not as a distraction, but as an invitation. “You can show me if you want,” they say.

There is no expectation attached to the offer. No requirement that what she creates will be explained or understood. She draws. Not everything. Not clearly. But enough to express something she cannot put into words.

When she is finished, the adult does not ask, “What does this mean?” They say, “Thank you for showing me.”

The drawing is not analyzed. It is received.

This becomes another practice.

Honor expression without interpretation.

Marcus finds this more difficult. He is used to responding directly, to challenging statements that do not seem accurate, to correcting what he perceives as misinterpretation. He begins to see how that instinct, while understandable, can close conversations rather than open them.

Someone says, “I feel like I should have done more.”

Marcus feels the immediate urge to respond, “You couldn’t have.” Instead, he tries something different.

“What makes you feel that way?” he asks.

The question shifts the conversation. It invites exploration rather than correction. The person continues, explaining the thought process behind the feeling, the moments they replay, the decisions they question. The conversation becomes deeper, not because the feeling was resolved, but because it was allowed to exist without being dismissed.

This becomes another practice.

Ask, don’t answer.

Keisha integrates these practices into her work with intention. In interviews, she avoids leading questions. She resists the urge to summarize too quickly. She allows pauses to extend, even when they feel uncomfortable. She understands that what emerges after a pause is often more accurate than what comes immediately.

She also pays attention to language. She mirrors the words people use rather than replacing them with more technical or socially acceptable terms. If someone says, "I was scared," she stays with that word. She does not translate it into something else. She trusts that the person's language is the most accurate representation of their experience.

This becomes another practice.

Use the speaker's language.

Reyes models something different. He listens without urgency. He does not lean forward in anticipation of responding. He does not interrupt, even when he recognizes where the conversation is going. He allows people to arrive at their own conclusions, or to remain without one.

When he does speak, his responses are brief. "I hear you." "That makes sense." "That's a lot." Statements that acknowledge without closing.

This becomes another practice.

Keep responses minimal and grounded.

Evan begins to integrate these practices in his own way. He notices when the urge to fix rises and names it internally. He allows it to pass. He returns his attention to the person speaking. He learns to tolerate silence, not as something to endure, but as something to trust.

Silence is not empty.

It is where people gather what they are about to say next.

He resists the need for resolution. Not every conversation needs to end with clarity. Not every experience needs to be summarized. Some things remain ongoing, and the conversation can reflect that.

Listening without fixing becomes a shared discipline for caregivers, communities, and responders. It requires awareness, patience, and a willingness to let go of the idea that help always looks like answers.

Evan reflects on this one evening. Conversations that are not shaped toward resolution feel different. Slower. Less predictable. But more honest. People say things they might not have said otherwise. They remain longer in the space of what is real.

He realizes that listening without fixing does not remove pain. It does not change what happened. But it changes how that pain is held, how it is shared, how it is allowed to exist without being immediately altered.

That is the practice.

Not to solve.

Not to fix.

But to stay long enough for something real to be heard.

Part III—The Courage to Stay

There is a moment in almost every conversation where the instinct returns. It is quick, almost automatic, rising in the space between what is heard and what is about to be said.

Fix it.

Say something helpful.

Move it forward.

Relieve the tension.

The impulse feels like care. It feels responsible. It feels like what a good listener should do. But more often than not, it interrupts something that has not yet fully surfaced.

Evan notices it now as it happens, not afterward, not in reflection, but in real time. Someone is speaking, describing something they cannot quite name. Their words come slowly, unevenly, pausing in places where something deeper is trying to form.

The silence stretches.

It feels long.

Longer than is comfortable.

He feels the urge to fill it. He notices it physically, in the way his breath shifts, in the slight forward movement of his body, in the forming of a sentence that is ready to close the gap.

This time, he does something different.

He stays.

Not withdrawn.

Not disengaged.

Present.

The silence continues, but it changes. It is no longer empty. It becomes a space where something is gathering.

Then the person speaks again.

They say something they had not said before. Something more direct. Something closer to what they are actually trying to express.

Evan recognizes what would have been lost if he had spoken too soon.

This is the shift.

Listening without fixing requires courage, but not the kind that is visible or dramatic. It is quiet courage, the kind that resists interruption, that tolerates uncertainty, that remains in a space where nothing is resolved.

Across town, the mother experiences it in a different form. Someone sits with her, someone who is not practiced, not trained in how to respond. They begin awkwardly.

"I don't know what to say."

The statement is simple, unpolished, and entirely honest. It does not attempt to fix anything. It does not try to shape the moment into something more manageable.

The mother nods. "Okay."

Something settles.

Not knowing is not the problem. Pretending to know is.

The person stays. They do not try to correct themselves or replace the statement with something more comforting. They allow the moment to remain as it is.

And because of that, the conversation continues.

Not because it was guided.

Because it was allowed.

Lila encounters this kind of presence in a quieter way. An adult sits beside her while she works, not asking questions, not offering help unless she asks for it. Just present.

At first, it feels unnecessary. Then it becomes something else.

Comforting.

Because presence without pressure is rare.

After a while, she speaks. Not about what she is working on, but about something else, something that has been on her mind. A memory. A question. A moment she has not shared before.

The adult listens. They do not shift the topic. They do not redirect her back to what she was doing. They allow the conversation to become what it is becoming.

Marcus learns this in a more difficult way, through a conversation that ends too quickly. Someone shares something vulnerable, something they have carried alone. Marcus responds immediately, trying to fix it, trying to correct what feels inaccurate or misplaced.

The conversation stops.

Later, he replays it. What he said. How quickly he said it. What might have happened if he had waited.

The realization is uncomfortable. Not because he intended harm, but because he moved too quickly.

The next time, he waits.

Not perfectly.

Not easily.

But intentionally.

And the conversation lasts longer. It moves further. Not because he did more, but because he did less.

Keisha names this in training. "Your presence is not a tool to get somewhere," she says. "It is the space where something can happen."

The room is quiet. The statement is simple, but it challenges the assumption that listening is a means to an end. It reframes presence as the work itself.

Reyes demonstrates it without explanation. Someone speaks. He listens fully, not preparing a response, not anticipating the conclusion. When they finish, he nods.

"I'm glad you told me."

That is all.

And it is enough.

Evan begins to practice this more deliberately. He notices the moments where he wants to move the conversation toward clarity, toward resolution, toward something that feels complete. He recognizes the impulse and lets it pass.

He listens with his full attention, not dividing it between what is being said and what he will say next. He allows pauses. He lets silence do its work.

When he responds, it is minimal.

"That sounds heavy."

"I hear you."

"That matters."

The words are simple, but they do not close the conversation. They leave it open, allowing the other person to continue if they choose.

The effect is not immediate or dramatic, but it accumulates. People stay longer in those conversations. They return to them. They share more, not because they are being guided, but because they are being heard.

That is the difference.

Fixing ends something.

Listening allows it to continue.

Not endlessly, not without movement, but honestly, without forcing it toward a conclusion it is not ready to reach.

Evan exhales slowly, recognizing that this kind of presence requires something different from him. It requires letting go of control, accepting that he cannot change what is being said, only how he receives it.

He looks around the room. It is quiet. The conversation is still open, unresolved.

And for the first time, he does not feel the need to change that.

Because staying is not failure.

It is care.

The kind of care that does not rush, does not close, does not fix, but remains long enough for something true to be spoken and heard.

Chapter 26—**Accountability and Repair**

Part I—What We Do With What Happened

At some point, the questions change. Not what happened, but what do we do with it now. The shift is subtle, but it matters because it moves from description to response, from memory to responsibility. Evan feels it in a conversation that no longer stays theoretical. Someone says, "Someone should be held accountable." The sentence lands with weight. There are quiet nods, a shared recognition that something must be named. But then comes uncertainty, because accountability is not as simple as it first appears.

It requires language that is often confused or used interchangeably without care. Blame. Responsibility. Repair. They are connected, but they are not the same.

Marcus speaks first. "It's someone's fault." His words are direct, unfiltered. Blame feels clear. It assigns cause. It points. It identifies who or what is responsible for what happened. There is power in that clarity because it resists erasure. It refuses to let the event become abstract or generalized into something that no longer has edges.

But blame also narrows. It can stop at identification. It can become an endpoint rather than a beginning, a place where anger settles but does not move. Evan hears that and understands. Blame names something real, but by itself, it does not change anything.

Keisha shifts the conversation. "We have to look at what systems failed," she says. Her language moves the focus from individual to structure, from a single action to a broader pattern. This is responsibility. Not a denial of fault, but an expansion of it. Responsibility asks different questions. What contributed? What allowed this to happen? What conditions made this possible?

It widens the frame, but it carries its own risk. When responsibility is spread too broadly, it can become diffuse. It can be shared in a way that no one feels it directly. In trying to include everything, it can lose its weight.

The mother listens to both. Blame and responsibility. Neither feels sufficient on its own. Each names something true, but something is still missing. Something forward-facing. Something that moves beyond explanation.

"Then what?" she asks.

The question shifts the room. It moves the conversation beyond identifying cause and contribution into the territory of response. It asks not only what happened or why, but what comes next.

Reyes answers quietly. "Repair."

The word lands differently. It is not backward-looking. It does not center on who caused the harm. It turns toward what is done in response. Repair does not erase what happened. It does not pretend that anything can be undone. But it refuses to leave the harm untouched.

Evan sits with that. Blame names cause. Responsibility names contribution. Repair names response. They are connected, but they are not interchangeable. Each carries a different function, a different direction, a different kind of weight.

Marcus resists at first. "Repair doesn't fix it," he says.

"No," Reyes replies. "It doesn't."

There is a pause. "But doing nothing doesn't either."

The distinction matters. Repair is not resolution. It is movement. Not toward undoing, but toward acknowledging and addressing what remains. It accepts that the past cannot be changed, but insists that the present and future are still open.

Keisha speaks again. "In our world, repair looks like change." Policies are adjusted. Procedures are revised. Training is expanded. These are tangible expressions of response. They can be measured, documented, evaluated.

But even as she says it, she knows it is not enough. Because repair is not only systemic. It is relational. It is lived out in how people show up with one another after the event itself has passed.

The mother feels that difference. For her, repair is not a policy change. It is how people speak. How they remember. Whether they avoid what happened or allow it to remain present. Whether they minimize it over time or continue to acknowledge its weight.

When someone says her child's name without hesitation, it matters. When someone remembers a detail, a story, a specific piece of who that person was, it matters. It does not fix anything. It does not lessen the loss. But it resists erasure, and that is part of repair.

Lila experiences it in smaller ways. When someone continues to show up, not just in the immediate aftermath, but later. When they remember what she said. When they allow the story to remain part of conversation instead of something that is quietly avoided. Repair, for her, is not a concept. It is presence that does not disappear.

Evan begins to see how these layers interact. Blame can identify harm, but it cannot carry the full weight of response. Responsibility can expand understanding, but it can lose clarity if it is not grounded. Repair requires both, and something more. It requires a willingness to act without the illusion that action will solve everything.

He starts to consider his own role. Not in terms of fault, but in terms of response. He was not the cause, but he was present. He carries something from what happened, and now he has to decide what to do with it.

That is the part no one explains clearly. Accountability is not only external. It is internal. It becomes a question of how he lives with what he knows. How he speaks about it. How he listens to others. How he resists the tendency to minimize or move on too quickly.

Repair does not begin with systems or statements. It begins with attention. With the refusal to look away. With a commitment to let what happened matter in what happens next.

Evan exhales slowly as the conversation settles. Nothing has been resolved. The tension between blame, responsibility, and repair remains. But something is clearer. These are not interchangeable ideas. They are part of the same work, each pointing in a different direction.

Blame looks back and names cause.

Responsibility widens the frame and names contribution.

Repair turns forward and asks what will be done now.

And the work is not finished.

Part II—When Responsibility Becomes Personal

Responsibility becomes more difficult when it is no longer abstract. It is easier to talk about systems, to name failures in policy, gaps in training, breakdowns in communication. Those things can be mapped, analyzed, discussed at a distance. They belong to structures, to organizations, to something larger than any one person. But eventually, responsibility moves closer. It becomes personal.

Evan feels that shift before he can fully articulate it. It does not arrive as accusation. It arrives as awareness, a quiet recognition that being present carries its own form of responsibility, even when he was not the cause of what happened. He finds himself replaying moments, not the obvious ones everyone talks about, but the smaller ones. The decisions made quickly. The assumptions made without noticing. The things that were said. The things that were left unsaid.

There is no single point where everything changes. No clear line where responsibility begins or ends. But there is a growing sense that it is not limited to blame. It is broader, something that includes participation, presence, and response over time.

Across town, Keisha encounters this shift directly. A review is underway. Reports are examined, timelines reconstructed, decisions revisited. The goal is not to assign fault in a simplistic way, but to understand how things unfolded. Still, the question lingers beneath the process.

Could something have been different?

It is not a comfortable question. It does not allow for easy answers. It requires looking closely at moments shaped by uncertainty, incomplete information, and pressure. Keisha answers carefully, not defensively, not definitively. "There were things we didn't see," she says.

The statement is honest, but it does not close the question. Because seeing something is not always the same as understanding it, and understanding is not always the same as acting. Responsibility, in this sense, is not about perfection. It is about acknowledging limits without using them as a shield.

Marcus struggles with this distinction. To him, responsibility feels too close to blame. "You're just spreading it around," he says. "Making it so no one is actually accountable."

The frustration is understandable. When responsibility expands without clarity, it can feel diluted. It can sound like a way of avoiding the harder truth that some actions are more directly connected to harm than others.

Reyes responds without dismissing the concern. "Blame and responsibility aren't the same," he says. "Blame points to who caused it. Responsibility asks what we do with it now."

Marcus shakes his head. "That sounds like letting people off the hook."

"Not if it leads to change," Reyes replies.

That is the difference. Responsibility is not meant to dilute accountability. It is meant to extend it beyond a single moment, to consider what continues after the event itself.

The mother experiences responsibility in a more personal way. People come to her with apologies, with statements meant to acknowledge what happened, with words that express regret. Some of them matter. Some of them feel incomplete.

"I'm sorry for your loss," someone says.

She nods, but the phrase sits at the surface. It does not reach what she is carrying. It does not name the reality that her loss has a cause, that it was not simply something that occurred but something that was done.

Another person says, "We should have done more."

The sentence lands differently. Not because it fixes anything, but because it acknowledges something beyond sympathy. It recognizes that responsibility is not only about what happened in a single moment, but about what surrounded it, what led up to it, what might have been different.

She does not respond immediately. She lets the words remain as they are. Responsibility, when it is real, does not need to be filled with explanation.

Lila encounters responsibility in smaller, quieter ways. An adult tells her, "If you ever want to talk, I'm here." The sentence is simple, but it carries a commitment. It is not a one-time offer. It is an ongoing posture.

Later, when she does speak, the adult listens. They remember what she said. They return to it in later conversations. They do not treat her words as something that needed to be addressed once and then set aside.

That is another form of responsibility.

Not to solve.

To stay.

Evan begins to understand that responsibility is not a single act. It is a pattern. It shows up in how people respond over time, not just in the moment when something is first named. It is visible in consistency, in attention, in the willingness to remain engaged even when the intensity of the moment has passed.

He considers his own role again, not in terms of fault, but in terms of response. What does it mean to carry responsibility for something he did not cause but was part of?

The question does not produce a clear answer. But it changes how he moves. He listens more carefully. He speaks more deliberately. He resists the urge to minimize or move past something too quickly. He stays in conversations longer than he might have before.

These are small actions, but they accumulate. They shape the way he participates in what comes next.

Keisha sees this in institutional terms as well. Responsibility is not only about acknowledging what went wrong. It is about committing to what changes as a result. Training is adjusted. Procedures are reviewed. Communication is reevaluated.

But she knows that structural change, while necessary, is not sufficient. Responsibility also requires a cultural shift, a willingness to remain aware of what happened rather than allowing it to fade into the background.

That is harder to measure. Harder to enforce. But no less essential.

Reyes puts it simply. "Responsibility isn't a statement. It's a pattern."

The sentence stays with Evan because it reframes accountability as something ongoing. Not something completed once it is acknowledged, but something that continues in how people act moving forward.

Marcus begins to see this, even if he does not fully accept it. He notices how different it feels when someone takes responsibility without defensiveness, without explanation, without trying to balance it with something else.

"I should have listened more," someone says to him.

There is no justification attached. No attempt to explain why they didn't. Just the statement.

Marcus does not respond right away. There is nothing to argue with. The responsibility is owned.

That is what makes it real.

Evan exhales slowly as he sits with all of this. Responsibility is not as clear as blame. It does not provide the same sense of resolution. But it opens something else.

Possibility.

Not the possibility of undoing what happened. That is not available. But the possibility of responding differently, of allowing what happened to shape what comes next without being reduced to a single moment or a single cause.

The room is quiet again. The conversation has not produced a conclusion. It has not resolved the tension between blame and responsibility. But something has shifted.

Responsibility is no longer abstract.

It is personal.

It is ongoing.

And it is something that must be lived, not just named.

Part III—What Repair Actually Requires

Repair sounds clearer than it is. It feels actionable, concrete, like something that can be done once the right steps are identified. Do something. Change something. Make it better. The language suggests movement, and movement suggests progress. But when Evan begins to look at it more closely, repair becomes harder to define. It cannot undo what happened. It cannot restore what was lost. It cannot return anyone to where they were before.

So what is it?

What does repair actually mean when nothing can be made whole again?

The question does not stay abstract for long. It moves into conversation, into expectation, into tension between what people hope for and what is actually possible. Marcus names the frustration directly. "People keep talking about repair," he says, "but what does that even look like?"

The question is not dismissive. It is a demand for clarity. Without clarity, repair risks becoming a placeholder, a word people use to suggest movement without specifying what that movement requires.

Keisha answers from where she stands. "In my world, it looks like change." Policies are adjusted. Protocols are rewritten. Training is expanded. These are necessary actions. They are visible, measurable, and accountable. They create the sense that something has shifted in response to what happened.

But even as she says it, she recognizes the limitation. Structural change is necessary, but it is not sufficient. Repair cannot stop at systems. It has to move into relationships, into memory, into the ways people continue to live with what has happened.

The mother understands this without needing it explained. Repair, for her, is not something that can be completed. It is something she watches for over time. It appears in how people speak, in what they remember, in whether the story is told truthfully or softened into something easier to hold.

Someone says her child's name without hesitation. They do not avoid it or lower their voice as if it is something too fragile to carry. That matters. It does not fix anything. It does not reduce the loss. But it resists erasure, and resisting erasure is part of repair.

Lila experiences repair in ways that are smaller but no less significant. For her, it is consistency. The same people showing up. Not just in the immediate aftermath, when attention is focused and support is visible, but later, when the urgency has passed and others have returned to their routines.

Those who remain become part of repair, even if they never use that word. Their presence communicates something steady, something that does not disappear when it becomes less convenient to stay.

Reyes reframes the conversation in a way that brings it into focus. "Repair isn't about fixing," he says. "It's about responding."

The distinction matters. Fixing implies completion. It suggests that something can be resolved and then set aside. Repair acknowledges that what happened remains. It is ongoing. It requires attention over time.

Evan sits with that. Repair is not a single act. It is a pattern. It is sustained, repeated, chosen again and again. It is not a moment of response, but a posture.

Marcus pushes back. "So what, we just keep trying forever?"

Reyes nods. "In some ways, yeah."

Marcus exhales. "That's not an answer."

"No," Reyes says. "It's reality."

The room goes quiet. Because this is the part that is difficult to accept. Repair does not end, not because people fail, but because what was broken does not disappear. It remains part of what has to be carried.

Keisha adds something that shifts the tension slightly. "It changes over time," she says. "What repair looks like now won't be what it looks like later."

That creates space. It allows for movement without demanding completion. It recognizes that response evolves, that what is needed immediately after an event is not the same as what is needed months or years later.

Evan begins to consider what repair looks like in his own life. Not in systems, but in relationships. In how he shows up in conversations. In whether he listens without minimizing. In whether he names things truthfully. In whether he stays when it would be easier to move on.

These actions are small. They are not dramatic. They are not easily recognized as repair. But they accumulate. They shape how the past continues to exist in the present.

The mother sees this in what is not said. When someone does not change the subject. When someone does not rush past a difficult moment. When someone allows reality to remain present without trying to soften it into something more acceptable.

That is repair.

Not because it fixes.

Because it honors.

Lila experiences it as reliability. Knowing who will still be there. Knowing that what matters will not be forgotten. Knowing that she does not have to remind people of what has already been lived.

Marcus begins to recognize it reluctantly. Not in large gestures, but in smaller ones. Someone follows up on something he said days later. They remember. They return to it. They do not treat it as something that was addressed once and then completed.

He notices, even if he does not name it.

Evan exhales slowly. This is a different kind of work. Less visible. Less defined. But no less real. Repair is not a solution. It is a commitment. To remain engaged with what happened. To refuse to let it fade into abstraction. To allow it to shape what comes next without pretending it can be undone.

He looks around the room. The conversation is still open. Still unresolved. But something has shifted. Repair is no longer a vague idea. It is something they are already participating in, whether they realize it or not.

In how they speak.

In how they listen.

In how they remember.

In whether they stay.

That is what repair actually requires. Not perfection. Not completion. But presence, consistency, and a willingness to keep responding to what happened, even when it would be easier to move on.

Chapter 27—**Caring for Children Honestly**

Part I—Telling the Truth Without Breaking It

Adults hesitate with children, not because they do not care, but because they do. The instinct to protect is immediate. To soften what feels too heavy. To shield what seems too complex or painful to carry. That instinct shapes how adults respond in the aftermath of something difficult. They say less. They change the subject. They offer something gentler.

"It's going to be okay."

"They're in a better place."

"You don't need to worry about that."

The words are not careless. They are protective. But protection, when it replaces truth, can create something else. Confusion. Distance. Silence.

Evan sees it in the way adults speak around children after what has happened. Voices lower. Conversations pause. Details disappear. Children are present, but not included, as if the absence of information will create safety.

But children notice. More than adults expect. They see the looks exchanged between people. They hear the tone of voices even when they cannot hear the words. They feel the shift in the room when something is being avoided. When the truth is not spoken, they begin to fill in the gaps.

And what they imagine is often more frightening than reality.

Lila experiences this directly. She hears whispers. She sees adults glance at her and then look away. She feels conversations stop when she enters the room. No one tells her what is happening fully, clearly, or in a way she can understand.

So she begins to guess.

Maybe it was her fault.

Maybe something she did.

Maybe something that could happen again.

The silence does not protect her. It leaves her alone with questions no one has answered.

The mother sees this before it is named. She recognizes the gap between what has happened and what is being said. She understands that saying nothing is not neutral. It communicates something, even if it is unintended.

She sits with Lila. Not prepared. Not certain of the right words. But aware that avoiding the conversation will not make it safer.

"There was a man," she begins. "He hurt people."

The sentence is simple. Direct. It does not include unnecessary detail. It does not overwhelm. But it is true.

Lila looks at her. "Why?"

The question comes immediately, because children do not remain at the surface. They move toward meaning, toward cause, toward understanding what does not make sense.

The mother pauses. "I don't know," she says.

The answer is honest. It does not provide closure. It does not resolve the question. But it does not replace it with something untrue.

That is the tension. Children ask questions that adults cannot fully answer. The instinct is to fill the space with something more certain, something that feels safer to say. But certainty, when it is not real, creates another kind of harm. It teaches children that answers matter more than truth.

Evan listens to this later, when the mother tells him how the conversation unfolded. "I didn't want to say too much," she says. "But I didn't want to lie."

He understands. That is the line. Not full explanation. Not full silence. Something in between.

Age-appropriate truth.

Reyes names it simply. "They don't need everything," he says. "But they need something that's real."

Age-appropriate truth does not mean less truth. It means right-sized truth. Language that matches what a child can hold without distorting what actually happened. It requires attention to what is necessary and what is not, to what will help a child understand and what will overwhelm them.

Keisha applies this in her own way. When children are present, she does not avoid the topic. She adjusts the language. "There was danger," she might say. "People worked to keep others safe. The danger is over now."

Each sentence is grounded in reality. Not vague. Not dismissive. Clear enough to answer questions without introducing new fear.

Marcus struggles with this approach. He prefers directness, full truth without adjustment. "They should know what happened," he says.

Reyes shakes his head. "They should know what they can carry."

The distinction matters. Too much information can overwhelm. Too little creates confusion. The balance is not exact. It requires attention, listening as much as speaking, adjusting based on what the child is asking and how they are responding.

Lila asks another question later. "Is it going to happen again?"

The room stills. Because this is the question beneath all the others. Safety. Predictability. The future.

The mother answers slowly. “I don’t think so,” she says. “But if anything ever felt unsafe, there are people who will help.”

The answer does not promise what cannot be guaranteed. It offers reassurance without false certainty. It acknowledges uncertainty while still providing a sense of support.

That is the second tension. Avoiding false reassurance. Not saying everything will be okay when that cannot be known. But also not leaving a child without any sense of safety.

Evan begins to understand this in a deeper way. Children do not need perfect answers. They need honest ones. Answers that acknowledge what is real and what is not known. Answers that do not contradict what they will later learn or feel.

Silence creates stories.

False reassurance creates confusion.

Honest presence creates trust.

The mother sees this in Lila after the conversation. She is quieter, but not withdrawn. Thoughtful. Engaged. The questions do not disappear, but they are no longer carried alone.

Evan exhales slowly as he reflects on this. This kind of care is different. It is not protection through avoidance. It is protection through truth. Care that does not hide, but also does not overwhelm.

He looks around the room. It is the same as before, unchanged in its physical form. But his understanding has shifted. Children are not outside the story. They are inside it.

And how the story is told matters.

Not only for what they know.

But for how they learn to trust what is real.

Part II—Listening to What Children Actually Ask

Adults often prepare for the wrong questions. They anticipate needing to explain what happened, rehearsing how to describe events in ways that feel manageable and safe. They think about details, about wording, about how much is appropriate to say. They prepare answers. But when children begin to ask questions, those questions rarely stay focused on the event itself. They move quickly to meaning, to safety, to what happens next.

Evan notices this when he sits with Lila after her first conversation with her mother. He expects her to ask again about what happened, to return to the event in concrete terms. Instead, she asks something else.

"Why didn't anyone stop him?"

The question is quiet, but it carries weight. It is not simply curiosity. It is a question about trust, about the reliability of the world, about whether the people who are supposed to keep others safe can always do so.

Evan pauses. This is where adults often shift too quickly into reassurance. They reach for statements that protect the idea of control. "They tried." "It happened fast." "People did everything they could." These responses may be true, but they move quickly toward defending the system rather than staying with the question.

Why didn't anyone stop him?

What Lila is asking is whether safety is guaranteed.

Whether danger can always be prevented.

Whether she can trust that someone will intervene.

Evan answers slowly. "Sometimes people try to stop something," he says, "and it still happens."

The sentence is simple. It does not explain everything. It does not provide certainty. But it stays with the truth.

Lila looks at him. "That's scary," she says.

He nods. "Yeah," he replies. "It can feel that way."

He does not move past it. He does not correct the fear. He does not immediately reassure. He allows the feeling to exist without trying to resolve it.

That is part of listening honestly. Not just answering the question, but hearing what is underneath it.

Across town, the mother encounters a similar moment. Lila asks her, "Did it hurt?"

The question is unexpected. It is not one the mother has prepared for. The instinct is to protect, to soften, to give an answer that reduces the image forming in Lila's mind. But she pauses.

"What do you think?" she asks.

Lila shrugs. "I don't know."

The mother nods. "I think it probably did," she says carefully. "But I also think it was quick."

The answer is not certain. It does not go into detail. But it is honest enough to acknowledge reality without expanding it unnecessarily. Children do not need full sensory explanations, but they do need answers that do not contradict what they may later imagine or learn.

Keisha approaches these moments by focusing on the question behind the question. When a child asks something difficult, she does not always respond immediately. Sometimes she reflects the question back.

"That's an important question," she might say. "What made you think of that?"

The goal is not to avoid answering, but to understand the context. Sometimes children are asking about something specific. Other times, they are testing whether it is safe to ask at all. Listening becomes more than hearing words. It becomes recognizing tone, timing, and patterns.

Marcus struggles with this approach. He prefers directness. When a child asks a question, he wants to answer it clearly and completely. The idea of slowing down, of reflecting instead of responding, feels unnecessary to him.

"They asked a question," he says. "Just answer it."

Reyes shakes his head. "They're not always asking what you think they're asking."

Marcus frowns. "Then what are they asking?"

Reyes pauses. "Sometimes they're asking if you can handle the question."

The statement shifts the understanding. Children are not only seeking information. They are assessing whether the adult can stay present with the topic. If a question creates discomfort, if it is deflected or avoided, they learn something.

Not just about the answer.

About whether it is safe to ask.

Lila tests this quietly. She asks a question, then watches closely. Does the adult hesitate? Do they change the subject? Do they seem uncomfortable? Each response teaches her what is allowed.

When someone stays, when they answer without rushing or deflecting, she asks another question. The conversation builds not because she has more questions, but because she feels safe enough to continue.

Evan begins to understand that listening to children requires a different kind of attention. It is not about delivering information. It is about staying present long enough to hear what is actually being asked.

Children often ask in layers. A surface question. A deeper concern. An unspoken fear.

"Is it going to happen again?"

The words are simple. But they hold something more.

Will I be safe?

Can this be prevented?

Is the world predictable?

The answer cannot be absolute. It cannot promise what cannot be guaranteed. But it also cannot leave the question unanswered.

Evan responds carefully. "I don't think it will," he says. "But if something ever feels wrong, there are people who will help."

The answer does not remove uncertainty. But it does not abandon reassurance either. It stays grounded in what can be said honestly.

The mother sees the effect over time. Lila continues to ask questions, but they change. They become less urgent, less driven by immediate fear, more reflective. Not because everything has been explained, but because nothing has been shut down.

Keisha names this clearly. "Listening is how you teach them what's safe to say," she explains. If children learn that difficult questions are met with presence, they continue to ask. If they learn that those questions create discomfort or silence, they stop.

And when they stop asking, they do not stop wondering. They simply wonder alone.

Evan exhales slowly as he reflects on this. Caring for children honestly is not about having perfect answers. It is about creating space where questions can exist without being dismissed or redirected too quickly.

It requires patience.

Restraint.

A willingness to remain in uncertainty.

It also requires trust. Trust that children can hold more than adults often assume. Not everything, but more than silence allows.

He looks at Lila as she sits nearby, drawing, the conversation still present but not overwhelming. The questions are not gone. They may never be.

But they are shared now.

And that changes something.

Listening to children honestly does not remove fear.

It removes isolation.

And that, for now, is enough.

Part III—Trust Is Built in What We Don't Avoid

Children remember what adults avoid. Not always immediately, and not always in ways they can explain, but over time the patterns become clear. What is talked about. What is redirected. What is left unsaid. These patterns teach as much as any direct answer.

Evan begins to notice this in the spaces between conversations. It is not only what adults say to children that shapes them, but what they consistently move around. Avoidance creates its own kind of message. It signals that something is too much, too dangerous, or too complicated to face directly.

Lila feels this before she can name it. A name that is not spoken. A question that is answered too quickly. A conversation that shifts just as she begins to understand what is being discussed. She does not always ask again. She does not always challenge it. But she notices.

Children notice patterns long before they can explain them.

When something is avoided repeatedly, it begins to feel unsafe. Not necessarily because of what it is, but because of how people respond to it. Silence does not neutralize the subject. It marks it.

The mother becomes aware of this gradually. At first, she tells herself she is protecting Lila by changing the subject, by redirecting, by keeping certain things out of reach. Each time, it feels justified. Each time, it feels like care.

But over time, she notices the distance it creates. The way Lila watches her more closely. The way questions become less direct. The way conversation narrows instead of opening.

Protection through avoidance creates distance.

Not safety.

She sits with Lila again. Not because she has better answers, but because she understands that the conversation itself matters more than the completeness of what she can say.

"You can ask me anything," she says.

The sentence is simple, but it carries weight. It is not about having all the answers. It is about not turning away.

Lila looks at her carefully. "Anything?" she asks.

The mother nods. "Anything."

The promise is not about certainty. It is about presence.

That is where trust begins.

Not in perfect responses, but in consistent availability.

Keisha sees the same pattern in her work. Children who are spoken to honestly continue to engage. They ask more questions. They revisit topics. They test boundaries, not because they are trying to challenge authority, but because they are trying to understand what is safe to explore.

Children who encounter avoidance behave differently. They stop asking directly. Their questions become indirect. They observe more than they speak. They begin to construct their own understanding without guidance.

Avoidance does not stop curiosity.

It redirects it inward.

Reyes names this in a way that reframes the issue. "They don't need you to have all the answers," he says. "They need to know you won't leave the conversation."

That distinction is critical. Leaving the conversation does not always look like physically walking away. It can look like changing the subject, offering a quick reassurance, or giving an answer that closes the discussion instead of allowing it to continue.

Marcus begins to see this, though it challenges his instincts. He values clarity, directness, and resolution. The idea of staying in a conversation without bringing it to a conclusion feels incomplete.

But he notices something.

When he answers quickly, the conversation ends.

When he pauses, when he allows the question to remain open, when he says, "I don't know, but we can think about it," the conversation continues.

That continuation is what builds trust.

Lila tests this again. "Are you scared?" she asks him.

The question is unexpected. It is not about the event itself. It is about him.

Marcus hesitates. His instinct is to reassure, to present stability, to say that everything is under control. But he stops.

"Sometimes," he says.

The honesty shifts something. Lila nods. "Me too," she says.

The moment is small, but it connects. Children are not only looking for information. They are looking for alignment. They are trying to understand whether their own feelings fit within what adults are willing to acknowledge.

When adults present only certainty, children learn to hide uncertainty.

When adults allow complexity, children learn that their own experience has space.

Evan reflects on this as he watches the interactions unfold. Caring for children honestly is not about managing their experience. It is about meeting it without distortion. It requires a willingness to remain in discomfort, to allow questions that do not have clear answers, to admit what is not known.

It also requires consistency. Not a single conversation, but a pattern of response over time.

The mother continues to show up. She answers when she can. She says "I don't know" when she cannot. She does not promise what she cannot guarantee. She does not avoid what is difficult.

Over time, Lila's questions change. They become less urgent, less driven by fear. Not because everything has been resolved, but because the space around the questions has become stable.

Stability does not come from certainty.

It comes from reliability.

Keisha articulates this in a way that stays with Evan. "Trust isn't built on what you say once," she explains. "It's built on what you don't avoid over time."

The phrasing shifts the focus. Not only on speaking truth, but on refusing to move away from it.

Evan considers how often adults believe they are protecting children by avoiding certain topics. The intention is understandable. The desire to shield is strong.

But shielding without honesty creates confusion.

Children sense the gap between what is felt and what is said.

They live inside that gap.

He exhales slowly. This kind of care requires more than good intentions. It requires attention, discipline, and a willingness to stay.

Lila looks up from what she is doing. "Can we talk about it again later?" she asks.

The question is quiet, but it carries something important.

"Yes," the mother says. "Anytime."

The answer is not final. It is ongoing.

And that is what makes it trustworthy.

Caring for children honestly does not remove fear. It does not provide complete understanding. It does not resolve what cannot be resolved.

But it builds something else.

A place where questions can return.

Where truth does not disappear.

Where presence remains.

And in that place, children learn not only what happened, but how to live with what is real without being left alone inside it.

Chapter 28—**Staying Human**

Part I—What Remains

The question beneath everything is not only what happened. It is what remains. Not the event itself, not the moment of rupture, but what continues after. Evan feels this more clearly now than at any point before. The urgency of the immediate aftermath has passed. The conversations have shifted. The language has deepened. But something has not disappeared.

The weight remains.

Not constant.

Not always visible.

But present.

Moral injury does not announce itself in every moment. It does not demand attention the way crisis does. It settles into the background, into memory, into the way a person sees the world and themselves within it. That is what makes it difficult. It is not gone, but it is not always named.

Evan notices it in small ways. In the pause before answering certain questions. In the hesitation before trusting a simple explanation. In the way certain memories return without warning, not as images but as questions.

What should have happened?

What could have been different?

What does this mean about who we are?

These questions do not resolve easily. They do not disappear with time. They remain.

Across town, the mother feels it differently. For her, moral injury is not only a question. It is a presence. It appears in ordinary moments, in the space where something is missing, in the absence that cannot be filled. She moves through her day. She functions. She speaks. She participates. But underneath it, something has shifted.

The world is no longer as it was.

Not because everything is broken.

But because something essential has been changed.

Lila carries it in ways that are harder to see. It appears in how she asks questions, in how she watches adults, in how she measures what is safe to say and what is not. She has learned something, not in words, but in experience.

That the world can change without warning.

That safety is not absolute.

That adults do not always have answers.

These are not lessons she was taught. They are lessons she absorbed.

Marcus experiences moral injury as tension. It does not settle easily. It resists resolution. It shows up as anger, as frustration, as a refusal to accept explanations that feel too clean.

"People keep trying to make sense of it," he says. "But it doesn't make sense."

The statement is not a rejection of understanding. It is a rejection of simplification. Because moral injury disrupts the frameworks people use to interpret the world. It challenges assumptions about justice, about protection, about what should happen and what actually does.

Reyes names it differently. "It changes the questions," he says.

Not the answers.

The questions.

Evan hears that and understands. Before, the questions were about what happened. Now, they are about what it means to live with what happened. That is the shift, from event to existence.

Moral injury does not have the final word, but it is never erased.

That is the tension at the center of everything.

It does not disappear.

But it does not define everything.

It remains, but it does not stand alone.

Evan begins to see this in the way people continue. Not by resolving what cannot be resolved, but by integrating it into something larger. Not moving past it, but moving with it.

The mother lives this daily. She does not get over what has happened. She does not return to who she was before. But she continues. She remembers. She speaks. She allows the presence of what was lost to remain part of her life without allowing it to consume everything.

That is not resolution.

It is endurance.

Lila carries it forward differently. Her understanding will continue to develop. The questions she asks now will change. The meaning she makes will evolve. But the experience will not disappear. It will become part of how she understands the world, part of how she understands herself.

Marcus resists the idea that anything good can come from it. "I don't see how this leads to anything better," he says.

Reyes does not argue. "Maybe it doesn't," he replies.

The honesty matters. Because it removes the pressure to produce meaning. Not everything has to become something else. Some things remain as they are.

And yet, people continue.

That is where the central question returns.

What does it mean to stay human after this?

Evan sits with that. Because staying human is not automatic. It requires something. Attention. Choice. Practice. To remain open in a world that has shown its capacity for harm. To remain present when it would be easier to withdraw. To remain connected when trust has been disrupted.

These are not small things.

They are daily decisions.

Keisha lives this in her work. She continues to show up, to engage, to respond, even knowing that systems fail, that outcomes are not always what they should be. She does not ignore those realities. She works within them.

That is part of staying human.

Not denying what has happened.

Not being defined only by it.

Evan exhales slowly. This is not a conclusion. It is an orientation.

Moral injury does not disappear.

But neither does everything else.

Care remains.

Connection remains.

Presence remains.

The world is not reduced to a single event, even one that changes everything.

He looks around. The room is quiet. Ordinary.

And yet, not the same.

Because the people in it are not the same.

And still, they are here.

Still speaking.

Still listening.

Still choosing to remain.

That is what remains.

Not resolution.

Not erasure.

But humanity.

And the decision, again and again, to stay within it.

Part II—Living With What Does Not Leave

What does not leave has to be lived with. That is the reality few people name at the beginning, not because it is hidden, but because it is not yet understood. In the early moments, everything is immediate. The focus is on response, on survival, on what must be done right now. There is urgency, movement, direction. But over time, that movement slows. The urgency fades. What remains is quieter, less visible, but more enduring.

Evan notices it in the way certain thoughts return. Not constantly, not in a way that overtakes everything, but consistently enough to be recognized. A phrase surfaces. A memory reappears. A question returns without resolution. These things come and go, but they do not disappear.

He used to think that meant something was wrong.

Now he understands it differently.

Some things return because they belong.

Not as problems to be solved.

As realities to be carried.

Moral injury does not remain fixed in one form. It shifts over time. It changes depending on context, on what is happening in the present, on what is being remembered. There are moments when it feels distant, almost like something that has already been processed. Then something small brings it back into focus.

A conversation.

A headline.

A passing remark.

The return is not failure.

It is continuity.

Across town, the mother experiences this as rhythm. There are days that feel manageable, days when the weight is present but not overwhelming. Then something interrupts that balance. A memory surfaces. A detail returns. The absence becomes sharper.

She no longer interprets this as regression.

She recognizes it as part of what remains.

Living with what does not leave requires a different expectation. Not that things will return to how they were, but that they will continue in a different form. That there will be fluctuation. That some days will feel steady and others will not.

This is not instability.

It is reality.

Lila experiences this without naming it. It shows up in how she responds to situations, in how she asks questions, in how she notices shifts in others. She pays attention to tone, to changes in behavior, to moments when something feels different.

These are not conscious strategies.

They are adaptations.

Marcus experiences it as resistance. Not only to what happened, but to how others try to move past it. He hears language that feels too resolved, too certain, too quick to conclude, and something in him pushes back.

"That's not how it works," he says more than once.

The statement is not always welcomed.

But it is honest.

Because part of living with what does not leave is refusing to pretend that it has.

Reyes approaches it differently. He does not resist openly, but he does not rush either. He allows the presence of what remains without needing to define it constantly.

"It's still part of it," he says.

Not as explanation.

As acknowledgment.

Evan begins to see that staying human is not about eliminating what remains. It is about integrating it without allowing it to take over everything else. This is where the tension becomes most apparent.

Moral injury is not erased.

But it is not the only thing that exists.

There are still moments of connection.

Still moments of care.

Still moments that are not defined by what happened.

The challenge is holding both.

Not replacing one with the other.

Not forcing resolution.

Holding.

Keisha lives this in her work. She continues to respond to new situations, to make decisions, to show up. She does not forget what has happened. It informs how she prepares, how she leads, how she thinks.

But it does not paralyze her.

It informs her.

This is what living with what does not leave looks like in practice. Not avoidance. Not constant focus. But integration. Allowing past experience to shape present action without collapsing everything into that experience.

Evan reflects on this in quieter moments. There are stretches of time when he is not thinking about it, when his attention is on something immediate, something ordinary. Then it returns.

And when it does, he responds differently.

He does not push it away.

He does not assume it should be gone.

He acknowledges it.

Then continues.

That is a form of staying human.

Not because it resolves anything.

Because it allows continuation.

The mother experiences something similar. She does not expect the absence to disappear. She does not expect the questions to resolve. But she continues to engage with what is in front of her.

She participates.

She listens.

She responds.

Not as someone who has moved past.

As someone who is still present.

Lila continues to grow within this reality. Her understanding changes over time. What she holds now will not be what she holds later. But the presence of what happened will remain part of that understanding.

It will not define everything.

But it will not disappear.

Marcus begins to recognize that his resistance is part of this process. It is not only reaction. It is a way of maintaining honesty, of refusing to allow what happened to be simplified or reduced.

Even when it creates tension.

Even when it complicates conversations.

Evan exhales slowly. Living with what does not leave is not something that can be mastered. It is something that must be practiced.

Daily.

In small ways.

In choices that often go unnoticed.

How to respond.

How to speak.

How to remain present.

There is no final point where it is completed.

No moment where it is finished.

But there is movement.

Not away from what happened.

With it.

The room is quiet again. Not empty, but settled. Conversations continue without urgency, without the need to resolve everything at once.

Evan looks around.

The people are still here.

Still engaged.

Still responding.

That is what it means to stay human.

Not to erase what remains.

Not to be defined only by it.

But to continue living with what does not leave, and still choose to remain present in what is here.

Part III—What Has the Final Word

There is a question that does not go away. It is not always spoken, not always named directly, but it is present beneath everything.

What has the final word?

Moral injury introduces this question in a way that cannot be avoided. It disrupts assumptions people rely on, that the world is predictable, that justice holds, that harm is prevented or corrected in ways that make sense. When those assumptions break, the question emerges, not as theory, but as lived reality.

Evan feels it most clearly in moments that should feel ordinary. A conversation that moves too quickly to resolution. A statement that suggests everything is now understood. A reassurance that feels disconnected from what has been experienced.

He notices the gap.

The space between what is said and what is true.

That gap is where the question lives.

What has the final word?

Marcus answers it in one way. "Sometimes the worst thing does," he says.

The statement is not exaggerated. It is grounded in what he has seen. If the worst thing does not have the final word, then why did it happen? Why was it not stopped? Why does it remain?

These are not abstract questions.

They are rooted in experience.

Reyes does not dismiss this. He does not respond with immediate correction or alternative. He allows the statement to stand, because answering it too quickly would create something false.

Across town, the mother holds the question differently. She does not phrase it in those exact terms, but it shapes how she remembers, how she speaks, how she refuses to let what happened be reduced or minimized.

If the worst thing has the final word, then everything else becomes secondary. Everything else becomes smaller.

She resists that.

Not by denying what happened.

By refusing to let it stand alone.

She remembers who her child was, not only how they died. She speaks their name, not only the event. She holds the fullness of what was, not only the rupture that ended it.

This is not erasure of moral injury.

It is resistance to its total dominance.

Lila encounters this question in quieter ways. She does not ask it directly, but it shapes how she understands the world. She holds two realities at once. That harm can happen. That safety is not guaranteed. And also, that people remain. That questions can be asked. That presence continues.

These realities do not resolve into one.

They exist together.

Marcus struggles with that tension. He wants clarity, a definitive answer that determines what ultimately matters. But that clarity does not come in the way he expects. The question resists a single conclusion.

Keisha approaches it through action rather than abstraction. She does not attempt to resolve the question in words. She responds through what she does next, through how she prepares, how she leads, how she refuses to ignore what has been revealed.

In her work, the final word is not a statement.

It is a pattern.

What continues.

What changes.

What is carried forward.

Evan begins to understand this more personally. The question of what has the final word is not answered once. It is answered repeatedly, through choices, through attention, through what is allowed to remain central.

Moral injury speaks.

It names rupture.

It names failure.

It names what should not have happened and did.

But it is not the only voice.

There is also care.

Connection.

Presence.

Memory.

These do not erase moral injury.

But they exist alongside it.

The question is not which one exists.

It is which one is given the final word.

Reyes says it simply. “You don’t get to choose what happened. But you get to choose what you return to.”

The statement does not resolve the tension. It reframes it. The final word is not a single moment. It is a direction.

What is returned to.

What is reinforced.

What is lived out over time.

The mother returns to memory, to the fullness of what was.

Lila returns to presence, to the consistency of those who remain.

Marcus returns to truth, even when it is uncomfortable.

Keisha returns to action, to the work that continues.

Evan sits with this. It does not remove what has been seen. It does not make the world simpler. But it prevents the question from collapsing into a single answer that would distort reality.

Moral injury does not have the final word.

But it is never erased.

That is not a contradiction.

It is a tension that must be held.

The room is quiet.

Not empty.

Not resolved.

But steady.

People are still here.

Still speaking.

Still listening.

Still choosing what to return to.

That is what shapes the final word.

Not only what happened.

But what continues after.

And what continues is not only rupture.

It is also what remains human.

Care.

Connection.

Presence.

The decision, again and again, to stay.

Conclusion—What Remains in the Silence

In the beginning, there was a moment. A sound. A rupture. Something that could not be taken back. It arrived suddenly, without warning, and everything after was shaped by it.

Now, at the end, there is something else. Not resolution. Not clarity. Silence.

Not empty silence. Not absence. But the kind that follows when everything that can be said has already been spoken, and still something remains.

Evan sits in it. The room is familiar. The space is unchanged. But it is not the same. He remembers the beginning, not in detail, not in sequence, but in feeling. The disorientation. The urgency. The sense that something had broken that should not have been able to break.

That has not been undone.

It has been carried.

Across time. Across conversations. Across every attempt to understand what cannot be fully understood.

The silence now is not the absence of that moment. It is what holds it.

Memory does not disappear. It changes. It settles. It returns. Not always when expected. Not always in ways that can be easily named. The mother knows this. She does not move through her days without remembering. She moves through them with it.

Memory is not only what is recalled. It is what shapes how the present is lived. A name spoken. A detail held. A refusal to let what was be reduced to how it ended. This is not closure. It is continuation.

Lila carries memory differently. It grows with her. It changes as she changes. What she understands now is not what she will understand later. But the presence remains, not as a single story, but as part of many.

Memory does not ask to be resolved.

It asks to be held.

Witness becomes part of that holding. To witness is not only to see. It is to remain. To refuse to look away. To allow what happened to matter beyond the moment it occurred.

Evan understands this now in a way he did not before. Witness is not passive. It is a form of participation. To say, this happened, and to continue saying it, not loudly, not constantly, but faithfully. Without distortion. Without reduction. Without allowing time to erase what should not be erased.

Marcus embodies this in his own way. His resistance. His refusal to accept explanations that feel too simple. He does not allow the story to be smoothed over, even when it would be easier. That is witness. Not agreement. Not resolution. Attention that does not turn away.

Keisha carries witness into action, into systems, into decisions, into the way what has been learned is not forgotten. Witness does not remain only in memory. It moves into responsibility.

And responsibility does not end.

It continues.

Not as burden alone, but as commitment. What is known changes what is required. Evan feels this most clearly, not as obligation imposed from outside, but as something internal. He cannot unknow what he has seen. He cannot return to a version of himself untouched by it.

So the question becomes not how to move on, but how to live with what remains.

Responsibility is not a single act.

It is a way of being.

How he listens. How he speaks. How he refuses to minimize what has been carried through every chapter of this story.

There is no neat ending. No point where everything resolves into something clean. That is not failure.

It is honesty.

Moral injury does not conclude.

It continues.

But so does everything else.

Care continues.

Connection continues.

Presence continues.

The silence holds all of it, not choosing one over the other, not reducing the tension, but holding both.

Evan looks around one last time. The room is quiet. The people are still here. Changed, but present. Still listening. Still speaking. Still choosing to remain.

This is what remains in the silence.

Not answers.

Not resolution.

But memory.

Witness.

Responsibility.

And the quiet, ongoing decision to stay human in the presence of what cannot be undone.

Acknowledgements

This book was not written alone.

It may have been shaped in quiet hours, in long stretches of reflection and revision, but the voices within it are not mine alone. They belong to people who have trusted me with their stories, their questions, their grief, and their honesty. Some are named in these pages. Many are not. All of them have shaped what this book has become.

To those who have lived through what should never have happened and found the courage to speak about it—thank you. Your willingness to tell the truth, even when that truth is unfinished, is the foundation of this work. I have learned more from listening to you than I could ever express here.

To those who carry moral injury quietly, without language for it, without recognition, without resolution—you are not unseen. If this book names even a small part of what you have been holding, then it has done something worthwhile.

To my colleagues in disaster response, spiritual care, and community leadership, especially those who continue to show up in the aftermath of loss and disruption—your work matters. Not because it fixes what cannot be fixed, but because you remain present in places where presence is the only honest offering. You have taught me what it means to stay human in environments that make that difficult.

To those who have challenged me, disagreed with me, and pushed back against easy answers—thank you. This book resists simplification because of you. You have reminded me that truth is rarely clean, and that integrity requires staying with what is complicated.

To the communities I have served, learned from, and been shaped by—you have shown me that healing is not linear, that repair is ongoing, and that witness is a form of care. Your resilience is not something I admire from a distance. It is something I have been humbled to stand alongside.

To my family, who have lived with the weight of this work in ways that are not always visible—thank you for your patience, your support, and your willingness to hold space for the parts of this work that do not end when the writing does. You have reminded me, again and again, what it means to remain connected.

To mentors and companions along the way, those who have guided, encouraged, and corrected me—your influence is present in every chapter. You have shaped not only what I write, but how I listen.

And finally, to the reader:

Thank you for staying.

This is not an easy subject. It does not resolve cleanly. It does not offer simple conclusions. But your willingness to engage, to sit with what is difficult, to resist the urge to move on too quickly—this is part of the work.

If there is anything this book hopes to do, it is not to provide answers, but to name what is real, to hold space for what remains, and to remind us that even in the presence of moral rupture, we are still capable of care, of witness, and of staying human.

That is not a small thing.

It is everything.

About the Author

Rev. Gregory C. Smith, PhD is a pastor, author, and disaster spiritual care leader whose work focuses on moral injury, faith, and the human experience in the aftermath of crisis. With three decades of ministry experience, he has served in congregational leadership while accompanying individuals and communities through moments of profound disruption, loss, and ethical complexity.

Since 2011, he has been an active volunteer with the American Red Cross, serving as a disaster spiritual care specialist and contributing to local and national responses. He has also been a long-standing member of Presbyterian Disaster Assistance, where he has supported deployments, shelter operations, and care for responders. In addition, he serves as a board member of the Iowa Disaster Human Resources Council, working to strengthen collaborative response efforts across sectors.

Dr. Smith is the founder of The Moral Injury Project, a body of writing, teaching, and training dedicated to naming, understanding, and responding to the moral weight carried by survivors, responders, and communities. His books explore the intersection of theology, ethics, and lived experience, offering language for what is often difficult to articulate and space for what cannot be easily resolved.

Across his work, he is committed to helping people remain present to what is real—without rushing to closure, without minimizing harm, and without losing sight of what it means to stay human.

He lives in Iowa with his family and continues to write, teach, and serve at the intersection of faith and disaster response.

Appendix A—**Recognizing Moral Injury After Human-Caused Disaster**

Moral injury is not always immediately visible. It does not always present as crisis. It often emerges gradually, across time, through patterns of thought, emotion, behavior, and relationship. Recognizing it requires attention—not only to what people say, but to how they carry what has happened.

The signs below are not diagnostic. They are indicators—ways of noticing when something deeper than stress or trauma may be present. They are offered across four groups represented throughout this book: survivors, family members, children, and responders. Many experiences overlap. Moral injury is not contained neatly within categories.

---

1. Survivors (Directly Exposed to the Event)

Internal Experience:

- Persistent questioning of meaning: Why did this happen?
  Why here? Why us?
- Sense that the world is no longer morally coherent or predictable
- Feelings of betrayal (by systems, institutions, or others present)
- Guilt about survival or perceived inaction
  (I should have done more)

- Loss of trust in previously held beliefs (including faith or moral frameworks)

Emotional Patterns:

- Anger that feels unresolved or without a clear outlet
- Numbness or emotional disconnection from others
- Shame that is not tied to a specific action but to identity (Something is wrong with me)
- Oscillation between intensity and withdrawal

Relational Signs:

- Difficulty engaging in conversations that feel "too resolved" or simplistic
- Withdrawal from community, especially where experiences feel minimized
- Increased sensitivity to language that bypasses or reframes the event too quickly

Behavioral Indicators:

- Replaying moments of decision or non-decision
- Avoidance of places, people, or conversations that trigger moral reflection
- Increased vigilance or need to monitor surroundings and others' actions

---

2. Family Members (Secondary Impact and Ongoing Loss)

Internal Experience:

- Persistent sense that what happened should not have been allowed
- Questions of accountability that remain unresolved

- Tension between grief and anger, often held simultaneously
- Desire for acknowledgment that extends beyond sympathy

Emotional Patterns:

- Grief that evolves but does not diminish in significance
- Anger toward individuals, systems, or broader societal failures
- Fatigue from repeated explanations or from feeling unheard

Relational Signs:

- Sensitivity to how the story is told—or not told—by others
- Withdrawal from conversations that minimize or generalize the loss
- Deep value placed on those who remember and name what happened accurately

Behavioral Indicators:

- Advocacy or pursuit of accountability (formal or informal)
- Maintaining memory through storytelling, naming, or ritual
- Continued monitoring of how others respond to the event over time

---

3. Children (Developing Understanding in Real Time)

Internal Experience:

- Emerging awareness that the world is not always safe or predictable
- Confusion when adult responses do not match what is sensed or observed
- Questions that return repeatedly, often in different forms

Emotional Patterns:

- Anxiety expressed indirectly (through behavior rather than words)
- Fear of recurrence (Will it happen again?)
- Increased need for reassurance, paired with skepticism of overly certain answers

Relational Signs:

- Careful observation of adult reactions before asking questions
- Withdrawal or silence when topics feel avoided or unsafe
- Increased attachment to consistent, trustworthy adults

Behavioral Indicators:

- Changes in play (themes of danger, rescue, control)
- Repetitive questioning about specific aspects of the event
- Difficulty concentrating or changes in sleep patterns
- Testing boundaries of what can be asked or expressed

---

4. Responders (Professional and Volunteer Caregivers)

Internal Experience:

- Accumulation of unresolved moments (the decision that stayed)
- Questions about adequacy of response (Was it enough?)
- Awareness of systemic limitations that could not be overcome
- Tension between role expectations and lived reality

Emotional Patterns:

- Functional engagement paired with internal fatigue
- Irritability or frustration with systems or leadership

- Emotional compartmentalization that becomes harder to maintain over time
- Delayed emotional response after the immediate work is completed

Relational Signs:

- Difficulty explaining experiences to those outside the field
- Withdrawal from conversations that simplify or romanticize the work
- Strong connection with peers who share similar experiences

Behavioral Indicators:

- Continued work without pause or reflection
- Avoidance of debriefing or reluctance to revisit certain moments
- Increased reliance on routine or structure to maintain stability
- Considering leaving the field without clear articulation of why

---

Across All Groups: Shared Indicators

While each group experiences moral injury differently, several patterns appear across all:

- A persistent sense that something morally significant has been disrupted
- Difficulty accepting explanations that feel too simple or too resolved
- Ongoing questions that do not have clear or satisfying answers
- Tension between what is known and what can be said
- A need for honest acknowledgment more than reassurance

A Final Note

Recognizing moral injury is not about labeling people. It is about noticing when something deeper is being carried—something that cannot be addressed through surface-level responses.

The goal is not immediate resolution.

It is attention.

To listen more carefully.

To respond more honestly.

To recognize that what is present may not be visible at first—but is real nonetheless.

And to remain willing to stay with it.

Appendix B—**Questions for Reflection and Processing**

These questions are offered as invitations, not requirements. Moral injury does not unfold in a linear way, and neither does reflection. Some questions may resonate immediately. Others may not feel accessible right now. That is not failure—it is pacing.

These can be used for individual reflection, small groups, care teams, or facilitated settings. There is no expectation to answer every question. The goal is not completion. It is attention.

Guidelines for Use

- Move slowly. Do not rush through questions.
- Silence is part of the process, not something to avoid.
- Share only what feels appropriate. Listening is participation.
- There is no "right" answer.
- If a question feels overwhelming, pause and return later.

Section 1—Naming What Happened

These questions help ground reflection in reality without minimizing or distorting the event.

- What happened, in your own words?
- What part of the experience stays with you most clearly?
- What feels unfinished or unresolved when you think about it?
- What do you find yourself returning to, even when you try not to?
- What do you wish others understood about what happened?

Group Variation:

- What differences do you notice in how each person tells the story?
- Where do your experiences overlap? Where do they differ?

Section 2—Moral Impact

These questions explore the ethical and moral disruption that may not be immediately visible.

- What about this experience feels morally significant to you?
- Did anything happen that felt like a violation of what should have been?
- Where do you feel tension between what happened and what you believe should happen?
- Do you experience anger, guilt, or betrayal connected to this event? How?
- What questions about fairness, justice, or responsibility remain for you?

Group Variation:

- How do different people name or describe what "should have happened"?
- What tensions exist between individual and shared interpretations?

Section 3—Internal Experience

These questions invite awareness of what is happening internally—emotionally, cognitively, and spiritually.

- What thoughts return to you repeatedly?
- What emotions feel most present? Which feel hardest to access?
- Do you notice any shifts in how you see yourself?
- Has this experience changed how you see others or the world?
- What feels hardest to put into words?

Group Variation:

- What similarities do you notice in internal responses?
- What differences stand out, and how are they held within the group?

Section 4—Relationships and Community

These questions explore how moral injury affects connection and communication.

- How has this experience affected your relationships?
- Are there conversations that feel difficult or impossible to have?
- When do you feel most understood? Least understood?
- Who has been able to stay with you in this experience?
- Where do you find yourself withdrawing, and why?

Group Variation:

- What helps people feel safe to speak honestly?
- What makes it harder to stay in conversation?

Section 5—Faith, Belief, and Meaning

For those engaging spiritual or existential frameworks, these questions invite reflection without forcing resolution.

- Has this experience affected your beliefs about God, justice, or meaning?
- Are there beliefs that feel harder to hold now?
- Do you find yourself asking different questions than before?
- What feels disrupted? What, if anything, still feels steady?
- What does faith (or doubt) look like in this moment?

Group Variation:

- How do different people hold belief and uncertainty together?
- What language feels honest? What feels forced?

Section 6—Responsibility and Response

These questions move toward what follows the experience without rushing to closure.

- What do you feel responsible for, if anything?
- How do you understand the difference between blame and responsibility in this situation?
- What does accountability look like to you?
- What would meaningful repair involve, even if incomplete?
- What feels possible now that did not feel possible before?

Group Variation:

- How do different people define responsibility and repair?
- Where is there agreement? Where is there tension?

Section 7—Staying Human

These questions return to the central theme of the book.

- What helps you remain present to what is real?
- When do you feel most disconnected? Most grounded?
- What does it mean, for you, to "stay human" after this?
- What practices, relationships, or rhythms support that?
- What feels worth holding onto, even now?

Group Variation:

- What does "staying human" look like in community?
- How can people support one another without trying to fix or resolve everything?

Closing Reflection

- What are you taking with you from this reflection?
- What remains unanswered—and is it okay for it to remain that way for now?
- What would it mean to return to these questions again later?

A Final Word

These questions are not a pathway to resolution.

They are a way of staying in conversation with what remains.

Used individually, they can help name what is often difficult to articulate.

Used in groups, they can create shared space where honesty is possible.

The goal is not to arrive somewhere new.

It is to remain present to what is already here—

with attention,

with care,

and without rushing past what matters.

Appendix C—**Supporting Children After Violence**

Practices for Honest, Grounded, and Ongoing Care

Children do not experience violence as an abstract event. They experience it through disruption—of safety, of trust, of what they believed the world to be. Supporting children after violence is not a one-time conversation. It is an ongoing posture of presence, honesty, and attention over time.

This appendix offers specific, practical guidance for caregivers, responders, educators, clergy, and communities. It is grounded in one central principle:

Children need truth they can carry, and people who will stay with them while they carry it.

---

1. Start With What the Child Already Knows

Before explaining, ask.

Children often know more than adults assume, but not in a complete or accurate way. Begin by understanding their current picture.

Try:

- "What have you heard about what happened?"
- "What do you think is going on?"

Why it matters:

- Prevents overwhelming the child with unnecessary detail
- Reveals misunderstandings (including self-blame)
- Builds trust by centering their perspective

Avoid:

- Launching into explanations without checking their understanding
- Assuming silence means lack of awareness

---

2. Offer Age-Appropriate Truth (Not Silence, Not Overexposure)

Children do not need full detail.

They do need honesty.

Guideline:

- Use clear, simple language
- Name what happened without graphic detail
- Avoid euphemisms that distort reality

Examples:

- Younger child: "Someone hurt people, and it wasn't supposed to happen."
- Older child: "A person made a choice that caused harm, and people are trying to understand and respond to it."

Why it matters:

- Silence creates confusion and imagination-based fear
- Overexposure overwhelms and destabilizes
- Honest simplicity builds trust

---

3. Answer the Question Beneath the Question

Children's questions are often layered.

"Will it happen again?" may really mean: Am I safe?

"Why didn't someone stop it?" may mean: Can adults protect me?

Practice:

- Listen for emotion and meaning, not just content
- Respond to both the surface question and the deeper concern

Example:

- Child: "Will it happen again?"
- Response: "I don't think so. And there are people working to keep everyone safe. If something ever feels wrong, you can tell me."

Why it matters:

- Addresses fear without false certainty
- Helps children feel seen, not just answered

---

4. Avoid False Reassurance

Statements like "Everything will be okay" can feel comforting—but may not be true.

Children recognize inconsistency.

Instead:

- Offer grounded reassurance
- Acknowledge uncertainty while naming support

Examples:

- "I can't promise that nothing bad will ever happen, but I will always be here to help you."
- "There are people who work very hard to keep others safe."

Why it matters:

- Builds long-term trust
- Prevents future confusion when reality contradicts reassurance

---

5. Normalize Emotional Responses Without Directing Them

Children may express fear, anger, confusion, or nothing at all.

All responses are valid.

Practice:

- Name emotions without assigning them
- Allow expression without forcing it

Examples:

- "Some kids feel scared after something like this.
  Some feel confused."
- "It's okay if you don't know how you feel yet."

Avoid:

- "You must feel scared."
- "Don't worry about it."

Why it matters:

- Reduces pressure to perform a "correct" emotional response
- Keeps communication open

---

6. Expect Questions to Return

Children do not process in a single conversation.

They revisit.

They ask again.

They ask differently.

Practice:

- Welcome repeated questions
- Respond consistently over time
- Do not treat repetition as a problem

Why it matters:

- Reflects developmental processing
- Reinforces that the topic is safe to revisit

---

7. Watch Behavior as Communication

Children often express what they cannot verbalize.

Common indicators:

- Changes in sleep or appetite
- Repetitive play themes (danger, rescue, control)
- Increased clinginess or withdrawal
- Difficulty concentrating

Response:

- Stay curious, not corrective
- Gently name what you observe

Example:

- "I notice you've been thinking about this a lot.
  Do you want to talk about it?"

Why it matters:

- Behavior often precedes language
- Early attention prevents isolation

---

8. Maintain Predictable Routines

Routine communicates safety.

Even when the world feels uncertain, predictable patterns create stability.

Focus on:

- Regular meals and sleep
- Familiar activities
- Consistent caregivers

Why it matters:

- Grounds children in what remains stable
- Reduces anxiety without needing explanation

---

9. Model Honest, Regulated Presence

Children watch adults closely.

Not just what is said—but how it is said.

Practice:

- Be honest about your own feelings in measured ways
- Demonstrate calm, not perfection

Example:

- "Sometimes I feel sad about what happened,
  but I'm here with you."

Avoid:

- Hiding all emotion (creates distance)
- Over-sharing (creates burden)

Why it matters:

- Teaches emotional regulation
- Builds relational trust

---

10. Do Not Avoid the Topic Over Time

Avoidance teaches children that something is unsafe to discuss.

Practice:

- Bring it up occasionally, especially if it has not been mentioned
- Keep the invitation open

Example:

- "I've been thinking about what happened. Have you thought about it too?"

Why it matters:

- Prevents silent isolation
- Reinforces ongoing availability

---

11. Support Through Community, Not Just Individually

Children are shaped by the environments around them.

Encourage:

- School-based support (when appropriate)
- Faith or community rituals that acknowledge loss honestly
- Safe group conversations with peers

Why it matters:

- Expands support beyond one adult
- Reinforces that the experience is shared, not isolated

---

12. Know When Additional Support Is Needed

Some responses require more than informal care.

Consider referral when:

- Symptoms persist or intensify over time
- The child is unable to engage in daily activities
- There is ongoing distress without relief

Important:

Seeking additional support is not failure.

It is care.

A Final Word

Supporting children after violence is not about finding the right script.

It is about developing a consistent way of being.

- Honest without overwhelming
- Present without forcing
- Steady without pretending certainty

Children do not need perfect answers.

They need adults who will not leave the conversation.

Who will tell the truth in ways they can carry.

Who will remain when the questions return.

Because they will return.

And each time they do, the response matters.

Not as a single moment—

but as part of a pattern

that teaches the child something enduring:

That what is real can be spoken,

and they will not have to hold it alone.

Appendix D—Facilitating Listening Circles Safely

Creating Space for Honest Speech Without Harm

Listening circles are not conversations in the usual sense. They are structured spaces where people speak from lived experience and are heard without interruption, correction, or immediate response. When used in the context of moral injury, they can become places of truth-telling, witness, and shared presence.

But without care, they can also become overwhelming, unsafe, or unintentionally harmful.

This appendix offers practical guidance for facilitating listening circles safely, drawn from field experience in disaster response, congregational settings, and community-based care.

---

1. Purpose of a Listening Circle

A listening circle is not:

- A debate
- A problem-solving session
- A place to reach consensus
- A setting for advice-giving

A listening circle is:

- A space for truth-telling
- A practice of witness
- An environment for non-interruptive listening
- A way of staying present without fixing

Core aim:

To allow what has been carried—often silently—to be spoken and heard without being reshaped or resolved too quickly.

---

2. Preparing the Space

Safety begins before anyone speaks.

Physical Environment:

- Quiet, private, and free from interruptions
- Chairs arranged in a circle (no hierarchy)
- Clear entry and exit access

Emotional Environment:

- Clear expectations communicated in advance
- Voluntary participation (no one is required to speak)
- Acknowledgment that difficult emotions may arise

Time Structure:

- Defined start and end time
- Built-in pauses or breaks if needed

---

3. Establishing Shared Agreements

Before beginning, facilitators should name and gain agreement on core practices.

Essential Agreements:

- Speak from personal experience ("I" statements)
- No interrupting
- No fixing, advising, or correcting
- Confidentiality (what is shared stays within the group)
- Permission to pass (silence is participation)
- Respect for differences in experience and perspective

Facilitator Language Example:

"This is a space to speak and to listen. We are not here to respond to each other's stories, but to witness them."

---

4. Role of the Facilitator

The facilitator is not the center of the circle.

Their role is to hold the space, not control the content.

Primary Responsibilities:

- Maintain structure and pacing
- Reinforce agreements gently when needed
- Monitor emotional safety
- Intervene if harm is occurring
- Model presence and restraint

What the Facilitator Does Not Do:

- Interpret or analyze participants' stories
- Offer solutions
- Redirect content unless necessary for safety

Key Skill:

Comfort with silence.

---

5. Structuring the Circle

A simple, repeatable structure supports safety.

Opening (5–10 minutes)

- Welcome participants
- State purpose and agreements
- Offer a grounding moment (breathing, silence, brief reflection)

First Round (Optional Prompt)

Invite each participant to respond briefly to a shared prompt.

Examples:

- "What brings you here today?"
- "What has stayed with you since the event?"

Participants may pass.

Open Sharing

- Participants speak as they feel ready
- No cross-talk or response during sharing
- Facilitator ensures one person speaks at a time

Closing Round

- Optional brief reflection from each participant
- "What are you taking with you from this time?"

Closing Grounding

- A moment of silence or a simple statement of acknowledgment

---

6. Managing Emotional Intensity

Strong emotions are not a problem.

But they must be held carefully.

When Emotion Rises:

- Allow expression (tears, pauses, silence)
- Do not rush to stop or redirect
- Maintain calm presence

If Someone Becomes Overwhelmed:

- Gently check in: "Would you like to pause or step outside?"
- Offer a support person if available
- Normalize stepping out as a form of care

Group Impact:

- Acknowledge shared weight without analyzing it
- "There is a lot being carried here."

---

7. Responding to Harm in the Circle

Even with preparation, harm can occur.

Examples:

- Dismissive language
- Attempts to correct another's story
- Statements that generalize or minimize

Facilitator Response:

- Intervene calmly and directly
- Restate agreements

Example:

"I want to pause us. In this space, we listen without responding or correcting. Let's return to that."

If harm continues:

- Redirect or pause the session
- Speak privately with the individual if necessary

---

8. Inclusion and Power Awareness

Not all participants enter the circle with equal comfort or power.

Facilitators should be aware of:

- Cultural differences in communication
- Hierarchies (professional, social, relational)
- Who speaks easily and who does not

Practices:

- Encourage space for quieter voices
- Avoid forcing participation
- Be attentive to patterns of dominance

---

9. Closing the Circle Well

Ending matters.

Participants should not leave abruptly from intense sharing.

Closing Practices:

- Acknowledge what was shared without summarizing
- Offer a brief grounding moment
- Remind participants of available support

Example:

"Thank you for the honesty in this space. What was shared here matters. As we leave, take a moment to notice where you are and what you need."

---

10. Aftercare and Follow-Up

Listening circles do not end when the session ends.

Facilitator Responsibilities:

- Remain available briefly after the session
- Provide resources for additional support if needed
- Check in with participants when appropriate

Important:

Do not assume closure has occurred.

---

11. When Not to Use a Listening Circle

Listening circles are not appropriate in every situation.

Avoid when:

- Immediate crisis intervention is needed
- Participants are unwilling or unable to follow agreements
- There is active conflict requiring mediation
- Safety (emotional or physical) cannot be reasonably maintained

---

A Final Word

Listening circles are simple in structure, but not easy in practice.

They require restraint in a culture that values response.

They require presence in a context that often rushes to resolution.

They require trust in the belief that being heard matters—even when nothing is fixed.

When facilitated with care, listening circles become something rare:

A place where people can speak what is real,

be met without correction,

and leave knowing

they were not alone

in what they carry.

www.ingramcontent.com/pod-product-compliance
Lightning Source LLC
LaVergne TN
LVHW052214200926
848481LV00001B/107